THOMSON FONTAINE

The Maroons of Dominica 1764 - 1818

Resistance Rebellion and Freedom From Slavery

Cover Photo depicting Maroons blowing the conch shell courtesy of Giftus John

BALA PRESS

BALA PRESS

BALA PRESS is a subsidiary of THE BALA GROUP and is committed to literary excellence and improved education by making available its publications across the globe.

Published in the United States of America
by the BALA Press
9615 Kings Grant Road, Laurel MD 20723

Thomson Fontaine
The Maroons of Dominica 1764 - 1818: Resistance
Rebellion and Freedom From Slavery
ISBN:978-1-7370081-0-1

Dedicated to my mother, father and our ancestors who embodied the spirit of resistance, rebellion and eventual freedom from the clutches of slavery; and left us the legacy

Contents

Author's Note

I was born and grew up in the village of Grand Fond just two miles from the Rosalie Estate on the South Eastern coast of Dominica, and in the vicinity of Balla's camp. During my early childhood, every Sunday I would make the 30 minute walk with my mother, siblings and other villagers to the Roman Catholic Church situated on the estate. Years before, both my parents, born roughly 100 years after the abolition of slavery, attended school on the estate. During the period of slavery, my ancestors worked there as slaves but were eventually forced out after abolition and settled in the village where I was born.

Surrounded by cavernous valleys and towering mountains, Grand Fond, during the period of slavery, was a perfect hiding place for the Maroons (Neg Mawon) and their Chief Balla, arguably the most feared and highly esteemed leader of the movement. The village was also at the centre of the Chemin L'Etang (Lake Road), which linked the South Eastern Coast of Dominica to the capital city Roseau on the West Coast. On 6 December 1784, Balla and more than 100 of his fellow Neg Mawon launched an unprecedented and audacious attack on the Rosalie Estate. In all, four white men, including the estate manager were killed, the plantation set on fire and destroyed, and more than 150 slaves were liberated.

As a child, I heard the story of Balla and the Maroons, and over the years, as my interest in the unique history of Dominica, its people, and my ancestors grew, I vowed to someday retell the story of the men, women and children, who simply refused to be enslaved. When, in 1813, Governor Ainslie imposed Martial Law and issued a proclamation to put to death men, women and children, who refused to return to the estates, this simply inspired more of the enslaved to break loose from the oppression of slavery and to bravely risk the ultimate punishment of death.

Rather than submit to slavery, the Maroons of Dominica instead chose a path of resistance, rebellion and freedom, deep within the mountains, valleys and forests of Dominica. The retelling in this book is their story, found buried in the British archives and several newspapers of the day from Dominica, the United States and Great Britain.

So dramatic were their exploits, unparalleled bravery and sacrifice, that it stirred the consciences of the British public, including William Wilberforce and Granville Sharp, and helped focus attention on slave conditions in the West Indies. Ultimately, the mistreatment and suffering of the Maroons and those enslaved in Dominica, would ignite the debate in Great Britain and prove pivotal in putting an end to the slave trade and the abolition of slavery in the British West Indies.

In June 1815, at a British Parliamentary debate, Robert Heron MP, observed that 'the Maroons of Dominica were not like those in Jamaica; the Jamaica Maroons…were acknowledged by repeated treaties, and obtained a political existence. The Dominica Maroons, on the contrary, more numerous and far more savage, consisted entirely of runaway slaves, never acknowledged by any treaty or truce whatever….but their chief dependence was on plunder, robbery their subsistence, their occupation murder.'

The book succeeds in painting a holistic struggle for freedom from slavery in Dominica, and its impact on the rest of the British West Indies. Carefully woven into the narrative is the influence of the French Revolution, free people of colour, and the fight for Independence in Haiti; on the ultimate success of the Maroon movement.

My hope is that the history recounted within these pages will reignite our own desire to fight injustice while we wholeheartedly embrace the deep ideals and singular premise of our ancestors, to die free rather than live as slaves. This is an inspiring tale, which needs to be told and will undoubtedly live on for generations to come. I'm pleased that I can add to the record. May the ancestors be proud.

Foreword: The Princes of Calabar

Old Calabar or Duke Town is located along the Lower Guinea Coast in the Bight of Biafra[1], on the continent of Africa, separated from the Bight of Benin by the Niger River Delta, which extends all the way from Southern Nigeria to the North of Gabon. Long before the arrival of Europeans in the sixteenth century, the area known as Akwa Akpa, was a well-developed and trafficked trade route. Calabar was founded by the Efik, a branch of the Ibibio-speaking people, who moved to the Cross River estuary in the early sixteenth century and lived primarily as fishermen and traders.[2] Their earliest encounters with Europeans were with Portuguese traders followed by the British.

With the sighting of the West Indian territories by Columbus in the late fifteenth century and subsequent entry of Europeans eager to exploit the islands for the growing of crops, the Bight of Biafra became an entry route for the seizure of slaves, ultimately resulting in the forced capture of over three million Africans. The main ethnic groups captured during the period of the slave trade, came from the Igbo and Ibibio people who today can be found in South Central and South Eastern Nigeria as well as Equatorial Guinea.[3]

Over time, the British slave merchants formed partnerships with African traders who would use canoes to travel the Niger River Delta in search of slaves to be sold. 'The canoes were manned by a crew of forty to fifty enslaved "canoe-boys" who paddled the twenty to thirty traders, and other armed men. In addition, each had a three or four pound cannon lashed to the bow and another on the stern. These expeditions lasted from ten days to three weeks. Using the extensive Cross River network as their highway, the traders sought out slaves; they sometimes acquired slaves who had been captured in war; but also launched surprise raids on villages.'[4]

A British Newspaper *The Derby Mercury* reported that 'the great droves (called Caffellas or Caravans) of slaves brought from inland, by way of Galam, to Senegal and Gambia, were prisoners of war. Others were procured either by pillage or by robbery of individuals. The smaller parties generally lie in wait about the villages, and take off all they can surprise; which is also done by individuals, who do not belong to the king, but are private robbers. These sell their prey on the coast, and it is well known that no question as to the means of obtaining it are asked. Children are torn from their parents, parents bereaved of their offspring; wives from their husbands; and husbands from wives in a manner the most diabolical.'[5]

Once captured, the slaves had their arms tied behind their backs with twigs and grass ropes and thrown into the bottom of the canoes, where they remained until arrival at Old Calabar. On landing, they were taken to the traders' houses, fed and their skin oiled before the Europeans were summoned to inspect them. They were then transported to the ships anchored in the port, and unceremoniously packed in groups of forty to fifty men, women and children, below deck, usually in irons, for the duration of the dangerous several weeks long trans-Atlantic crossings. The majority of these slaves, more than 85 percent, were ultimately transported on British slave ships owned by merchants in Bristol and Liverpool, over what became known as the Middle Passage to the new world. This trade in slaves from the Bight of Biafra would last for more than 140 years, only coming to an end in 1807, after an abolition act was passed in the British Parliament.

The newly acquired slaves did not always accept their fate quietly. Many would rebel while on the ships making their way across the Atlantic. One such account is given in *The Derby Mercury*: 'a few days ago the Ship Brothers, Captain Glinn, belonging to Liverpool arrived here [Dominica] from the coast of Africa, with 212 slaves, soon after they sailed the negroes rose but the sailors soon overpowered them, when nine of the slaves were killed, and sixteen wounded; the white people came off pretty well as five only of them were wounded.'[6] This spirit of resistance would characterise the attitude of a large number of the slaves making their way to the West Indies.

Sometime in 1767, a Prince by the name of Balla, who hailed from Equatorial Guinea was captured and sold into slavery in Dominica. That same year, two princes of a ruling family in Old Calabar brothers Little Ephraim Robin John and Ancona Robin John, were also captured and sold into slavery. The two brothers were among 336 men, women and children from Old Calabar, who in July 1767 were tricked by the British to come on board their six vessels under the guise of negotiating a truce with rival families. They were subsequently captured and along with 270 survivors, sold into captivity in Dominica. A year later, another Prince by the name of Jacko would suffer a similar fate.

The two Princes of Calabar, Ephraim and Ancona, upon arrival in Dominica, were sold together to a French physician residing in Roseau. Although they were fairly well treated, this did not stop their yearning for freedom. Just seven months after their arrival, they made their way to a slave ship, *Peggy* captained by William Sharp. The slave captain had made several voyages to Dominica carrying slaves from the coast of Africa. He was apparently familiar with the brothers and their yearning to return to Africa. Sharp got word to them that he would transport the two back to Africa. Unfortunately, after boarding the ship, it became obvious that they were tricked by Sharp, who took them to Virginia and resold them into slavery.[7]

Ultimately, the two princes would succeed in going to Britain where they secured their freedom and eventually returned to Old Calabar as free men in 1774. 'The Robin Johns made the most of their skills and accomplished what very few African slaves did in the eighteenth century--they escaped slavery, freed themselves, and returned to their 'Deserved Country'.'[8] Meanwhile, the other two princes, Balla and Jacko had strikingly different experiences, with both remaining in Dominica as free men, at the head of the group of Maroons, collectively spanning a period of almost fifty years. The two princes became legendary and were among the most feared leaders of the resistance to slavery on the slave plantations of Dominica.

The term Maroon was originally a derivative from the word Marrano, a hog of one year old, and was the name given by Spaniards to hunters of wild hogs. In its more familiar form Maroon was a designation given to the negro and coloured race made free by convention with the British government, in Jamaica, beginning in 1739. In Dominica, the Maroons were referred to as *Neg Mawon*[9], where although no treaty was ever signed between the escaped slaves and the British government, they were however deemed of a similar description as those of Jamaica.

The excellent leadership of Balla and Jacko to the Maroon movement would exemplify the spirit of resistance, rebellion and eventual freedom from slavery in the island of Dominica. The two would greatly influence other leaders like Pharcelle, Congo Ray, Pangloss, Mabuyah, Quashey, and Elephant. It would also echo in the actions of the many women like Rachel, Geneviève, Francoise and Adelaide, who paid the ultimate price of death in their yearning for freedom. More importantly, their actions struck fear in the hearts of the white planters, and their bold affront to slavery helped fuel first, the abolition of the slave trade debate, and later that of an end to slavery itself. It was that shared longing and yearning for freedom by the princes of Calabar, which beat prominently within the breast of every African slave who survived the trans-Atlantic crossing, and that would never be extinguished.

1

Europeans and Early Settlement

Europeans reportedly first set eyes on Dominica on 3 November 1493 with the arrival of Cristopher Columbus on his second sponsored voyage to what was then referred to as the New World. Columbus left Cadiz, Spain on 25 September 1493 with seventeen vessels and about twelve hundred men. After a voyage of roughly thirty-nine days, early on Sunday morning of 3 November, as the outline of a ruggedly mountainous Island came into view, Columbus summoned his men to the deck, where they sang hymns and gave thanks to God for the relatively short journey. He then called the island Dominica, due to the fact that it was a Sunday. For more than thirty minutes Columbus and his men sailed up the Eastern side of the Island searching in vain for a suitable place to make anchor.

Unable to find a landing place, the fleet moved further North to the small island of Marie Galant while one vessel was left behind to continue the search. Several hours later, the lone vessel re-joined the group in Marie Gallant and the men reported that they had successfully gone around the Northern tip of the island. As they left the rough waters of the Atlantic behind, they came upon a body of calm and pristine waters, and saw, much to their surprise, dwellings and people.

The people spotted on that Sunday morning were residing in modern day Portsmouth, and would come to be known as the Kalinago, remnants of whom remain in Dominica to this day. Columbus himself referred to them as Caraibes[1], and was told on his first voyage while in Hispaniola that there were 'savages' living on the island. Believed to be descendants of a tribe to have migrated from the Orinoco River area in South America, the Kalinagos had made their way to Dominica and other islands in the archipelago dating back to 1200 A.D. By the time Columbus arrived, the Kalinagos had already displaced the more peaceful

Arawaks, who had occupied the islands since 3 000 B.C., by warfare, extermination, and assimilation.

Situated at the center of the arc of islands forming the Lesser Antilles, Dominica is twenty-nine miles long and fifteen miles across. This pristine land consists of sixteen active volcanos, numerous mountain peaks, hot Sulphur springs and verdant forests. Guillermo Coma, one of the sailors accompanying Columbus on his second voyage in 1493, was stunned by the beauty of the island.

In a letter written to the Duke of Millan in 1494 he remarked: "Dominica is notable for the beauty of its mountains and the charm of its verdure."[2] Another companion of Columbus on that voyage, Dr. Diego Alvarez Chanca, in a letter to the city of Seville, commented: "As much of the island as was in sight was very beautiful, and very green mountains, right down to the water, which was a delight to see.'[3]Following the initial sighting by Columbus, and during the sixteenth and early part of the seventeenth centuries, Dominica would remain a largely neutral territory.

However, France and Britain eventually began to challenge Spain's dominance on this and other West Indian islands. For the scores of explorers, adventure seekers, pirates, traders, and others seeking access to the New World, Dominica was often the first landfall after the exhausting trans-Atlantic excursion. There they would stock up on fresh water, engage the Kalinagos in small trade, and enjoy the country's weather and other natural pleasures.

Among these adventurers were John Hawkins, Francis Drake, and George Clifford, Earl of Cumberland[4]. All were famed British privateers and Hawkins and Drake featured among the early British slave traders; George Clifford would later go on to capture Puerto Rico from the Spanish. Dominica, meanwhile, became a regular stop on their journeys, where they would stock up on clean water and fruits to refresh their cargo of slaves, and otherwise enjoy the beauty of the island.

Clifford's Chaplain, Dr Layfield would later write an account of one such voyage: 'wee were met with many canoes, manned with men wholly naked…the cause of their coming was to exchange their tobacco, pinos, plantins, potatoes and pepper with any triffle if they were gawdie....There his Lordship found the hote bathe fast by the side of a river...here our sick men specially found good refreshing.'[5]

Another adventurer was René Laudonnière, who was selected by the French to establish a strategic base in the Caribbean region. He later described his voyage to Dominica in April of 1564 as follows: 'Dominica is one of the fairest Islands of the West Indies, full of hills, and of every good smell. Whose singularities desiring to know as we passed, and seeking also to refresh ourselves with fresh water, I made the mariners cast anker, after wee had sayled about half along the coast thereof. As soon as we had cast anker, two Indians (inhabitants of that place) sayled towards us in two canoas full of a fruite of great excellencie which they call Ananas... The Place where we went on shore was hard by a very high Rocke, out of which there ran a little river of sweet and excellent good water: by which river we stayed certaine days to discover the things which were worthy to be seene, and traffiqued daily with the Indians.'[6]

Hawkins on his second voyage between 1585-86, during which he spent time in Dominica wrote: 'wee were not above eighteene days in passage between the sight of Saint Iago aforesaid, and the island of Dominica, being the first island of the West Indies that we fell withal, the same being inhabited with savage people, which goe all naked, their skinne coloured with some painting of a reddish tawney, very personable and handsome strong men, who doe admite little conversation with the Spanyards.....albeit they used us very kindly for those few hours of time which wee spent with them, helping our folks to fill and carry on their bare shoulders fresh water from the river to our ships boates, and fetching from their houses great store of tobacco, as also a kind of bread which they fed on, called cassava, very white and savourie..'[7]

The state of affairs continued until 2 July 1627, when Dominica along with the other British possessions were granted to the Earl of Carlisle by King Charles, this being a confirmation of a former concession given by King James I to Lord Carlisle. However, in a move that would signal English and French rivalry over Dominica for the next two hundred years, starting in 1632, the French Compagnie des Îles de l'Amérique claimed Dominica along with all the other 'Petite Antilles' but no settlement was attempted at that time.

The Compagnie des Îles de l'Amérique (The Company of the American Islands) was a French chartered company that in 1635 took over the administration of the French portion of Saint-Christophe island from Compagnie de Saint-Christophe, which was the only French settlement in the Caribbean at that time. It was mandated to actively colonise other islands, starting with Dominica in 1632 (formerly as Compagnie de Saint-Christophe). The company then moved on to the following islands before it was dissolved in 1651: Guadeloupe (28 June 1635 to 1649); Martinique (15 September 1635 to 27 Sept. 1650); St. Lucia (1643 to 27 Sept 1650); St. Martin (23 March 1648); St. Barts (1648); Grenada (17 March 1649 to 27 Sep 1650); and St. Croix (1650).

Between 1642 and 1650 a French missionary Raymond Breton became the first regular European visitor to Dominica. Then on 30 March 1660, while on his death bed, Phillipe de Lonvilliers de Poincy, governor general of the Compagnie de St Christophe, in the presence of some Kalinagos and French and English settlers signed an agreement, stipulating that both Dominica and St. Vincent should not be settled, but instead, left to the Kalinagos as neutral territories.

Again on 3 January 1668, this time on a ship in the Nevis harbour, and overseen by Lord Francis Willoughby, governor of the English Caribbees, and Joseph de Labarre, governor of the French Isles of the Americas, along with Kalinagos from Dominica and St Vincent; the earlier agreement of 1660 was reconfirmed. Consequently, at least officially, the two countries remained neutral territories, a situation, which would persist for more than half of the eighteenth century.

It was therefore within this unique island of Dominica that the Kalinagos successfully resisted early attempts at colonization and survives even to this day. Using their superior knowledge of the island they remained largely hidden from the Europeans, at least for most of the fifteenth, sixteenth and seventeenth centuries. During that period of neutrality, Dominica, like St Vincent, became increasingly attractive to former slaves brought in from Africa, and fleeing from sugar plantations elsewhere in the Caribbean. They were drawn from as far away as Jamaica and Santo Domingo to the North. For the most part, these newcomers were welcomed by the Kalinagos and quietly assimilated on the island.

Another interesting phenomenon played out during the years of Dominica serving as a neutral country. It became increasingly frequented by rival expeditions of English and French foresters, harvesting its timber, and other intrepid travellers attracted by its abundant water and other resources. The French came mainly from Martinique and Guadeloupe, where they required an increasing amount of wood to be used as fuel for their sugar boiling houses on the large estates, and timber for building. These lumberjacks would often negotiate with the Kalinagos for the rights to exploit and export the timber in exchange for rum, tools, and other necessities.

In their efforts to extract the timber from Dominica, the French planters and lumberjacks would often use African slaves to do the work. Many of these slaves would however escape into the forests of Dominica, and in the process, being numbered together with those fleeing from the other islands, among the first Maroons or 'Neg Mawon', as they later became more affectionately known. These Maroons would sometimes live in the Kalinago villages, but for the most part preferred the relative safety of the forests in the interior of Dominica, far out of reach of the French planters. Overtime, some of the same French planters and lumberjacks, notwithstanding the country's neutrality, established estates on the island to cultivate crops, and began bringing African slaves to do the work. By the end of 1730 there were an estimated 425 slaves on the island.

Lord Rollo in 1760

The town of Roseau in 1760 showing Lord Rollo's fleet.

2

Slave Trade Begins

On 18 October 1748, the *Treaty of Aix La Chapelle* was signed by Britain, France and the Dutch Republic, in which the neutrality of the islands of Dominica and St Vincent was reaffirmed. The country's neutrality was however shattered on 6 June 1761, during the Seven Years War (1756-1763)[1], when a British amphibious force captured and occupied Dominica, wrestling control from the mainly French settlers. The British land forces were commanded by Lord Andrew Rollo and included the 22nd and the 94th Regiments of Foot, while Sir James Douglas led the Royal Navy squadron[2]. A month earlier on 3 May 1761, Lord Rollo, Commander of the 22nd Regiment of Foot had sailed with his regiment of 2500 men from New York to launch an attack on the French settlement of Roseau.

Following the successful capture of Dominica, Lord Rollo was made Commander-in-Chief of the Island,[3] until France formally ceded possession of Dominica to the British, under Article IX of the Treaty of Paris, on 10 February 1763. St Vincent also lost its neutral status acquired under the Treaty of Aix-La Chapelle, and Grenada and Tobago, also reverted to Great Britain. Dominica's ownership was widely discussed during the negotiations at the Treaty of Paris. France for its part, made a very strong case for it to revert back to their possession. The Earl of Bute who led the negotiations for Great Britain on the other hand, countered the French claim, calling it his peace, and made Dominica one of the principal articles of the treaty. [4]

A few months later on 7 October 1763, a proclamation was issued by King George III, restating his claims agreed to under the Treaty of Paris and further outlining authorities extended to Governors to take charge of his possessions. The Proclamation read in part:

> *WHEREAS we have taken into our Royal consideration, the extensive and valuable acquisitions in America, secured to our Crown, by the late definitive treaty of Peace, concluded at Paris the 10th of February last; And being desirous that all our loving subjects, as well of our Kingdoms as of our colonies in America, may avail themselves with all convenient speed of the great benefits and advantages which must accrue therefrom to their commerce, manufactures , and navigation; We have thought fit, with the advice of our Privy Council, to issue this our Royal Proclamation, hereby to publish and declare to all our loving subjects, that we have with the advice of our said Privy Council, granted our letters patent under our great seal of Great Britain, to erect within the countries and islands ceded and confirmed to us by the said treaty, four distinct and separate Governments, stilled and called by the names Quebec, East Florida, West Florida, and GRENADA.*
>
> *1st.-Boundaries of Quebec described. 2d. Do. do. East Florida, do.* 3d.--*Do. do. West Florida, do. 4th.-the government of Grenada comprehending the island of that name, together with the Grenadines, and the islands of Dominica, St Vincent and Tobago. For the enjoyment of the benefit of the laws of our realm of England; for which purposes we have given power, under our great seal, to the Governors of our said colonies respectively, to erect and constitute, with the advice of our said Councils respectively, Courts of Judicature and Public Justice, within our said colonies, for the hearing and determining all causes as well criminal as civil, according to law and equity, and as near as may be agreeable to the laws of England.*[5]

And so it was by the close of 1763, the Legislative authority in Dominica was vested in the Commander-in-Chief, who was the military and civil governor, together with a Council of twelve gentlemen and a House of Assembly or Legislative of

Commons comprised of nineteen members.[6] Robert Melville Esq. became the first representative of the King of England, of the Ceded islands of Dominica, Grenada, St Vincent and Tobago; a position he held until 1771.[7] In Dominica, every indulgence was given to the French inhabitants including the planters, and they intermixed with the British settlers under a form of government similar to the one in existence in Jamaica.

Within months of the British taking firm control of the island, Commissioners were appointed under the seal of the British Crown to sell and dispose of the lands by public sale,[8] to English subjects, in allotments 'of not more than one hundred acres of such land as was cleared; and not exceeding three hundred acres in woods, to any one person, who should be the best bidder for the same.'[9] The Commissioners used to sell the land argued that it was best to retain the French planters rather than have them leave. However, most of the lots sold around that time consisted of estates abandoned by the French in different parts of the island including in Roseau, Layou, Portsmouth and Grand Bay.[10]

The sale of land was best achieved by posing as few restrictions as possible. Although they were not to be granted absolute freehold of their cleared land, the buyers would however be granted lands upon lease for various periods of 14, 21, 32 or 42 years, on condition that they declared themselves loyal to the British crown. In addition, they were obliged to bind themselves not to dispose of the acquired lands to anyone, under any pretence, without first receiving the permission of the governor. Unappropriated lands became the property of the crown, which amounted to ninety-four thousand three hundred and forty-six acres, or roughly one half of the island.

Under this very unusual arrangement, in just ten short years, the sugar industry was established in Dominica. Later Thomas Coke, a Methodist Bishop and author[11] would note that "the free enjoyment and full security which were given to private property, now placed under the mild and equitable laws of the British government, introduced among all ranks a spirit of enterprise which was before unknown.[12] Early reports out of the island also pointed to the suitability of the land for agriculture. "The settlement of that island increases with the greatest rapidity, the soil is found to be a rich, strong mould, very durable and fertile. The planters from the old islands migrate hither continually and say that it is equally calculated for the growth of coffee and sugar."[13]

By the time Dominica was ceded in 1763, and after more than a hundred years of being a neutral island, there were an estimated 1 718 Frenchmen and 5 872 slaves cultivating coffee, cocoa, and spices, as well as some 50 families of free Kalinagos, numbering several hundred. There were also a well-established but undetermined number of Maroons roaming free in the mountains and forests of Dominica. Already, Britain had a large footprint in the West Indies, where to Dominica's North, in Jamaica, and to its South in Barbados, it was firmly in control and was already importing slaves from Africa to work on the many plantations.

In the case of Jamaica the trade in African slaves went back as far as 1513, while that of Barbados had been in existence since 1627. It was therefore not surprising that within a short time of gaining control of Dominica, the trans-Atlantic import trade in slaves started, with the first British ship arriving on the island in May 1764.

In an effort to further cement the Treaty of Paris and to deescalate hostilities between the French and the English, King Louis XV of France wrote a letter to le Count d'Ennery and le President de Peinier of Martinique on 16 December 1764. In the letter the King retracted a 1727 order, which had ordained that 'no foreigners should touch, with their ships or vessels, at the ports, roads or creeks of my islands and colonies, nor navigate a league around the same, upon pain of confiscation of their ships or vessels, together with their cargoes, and a fine of one thousand livres to be paid by each captain and his crew.' [14]

The King noted the close proximity of the Ceded islands to his French possessions and allowed that it was almost impossible for vessels to move within the islands without them coming to within one league distance. Consequently, while maintaining that 'no foreign vessels touch at the ports,' he decreed that the 'Captains of English ships and other vessels, be not arrested or anywise detained, if they should even navigate within a league of my said islands until further orders from me.'[15]

Meanwhile, on 26 January 1765, the Legislative Assembly of the Ceded islands passed its first bit of legislation regarding the slaves.[16] The act was for '*the regulation and trial of the slaves in all criminal matters in the islands of Grenada, the Grenadines, Dominica, St Vincent and Tobago*.'[17] This was quickly followed up on 9 March 1765 with an act '*for the more effectual suppression of the runaway slaves*.' Passage of this act was the first sign of the pending problems that the white planter class would encounter with the slaves, who were desirous of maintaining their freedom in the face of slavery.

In an effort to further facilitate the trade in slaves, the British Parliament passed the Free Port Act of Jamaica and Dominica in 1766.[18] The Act enabled British merchants to legally trade with the neighbouring Danish, Dutch, French, and Spanish Caribbean colonies. In Dominica in particular, the Act facilitated a booming trade in slaves with the neighbouring French territories of Martinique, St Lucia, and Guadeloupe, to where the majority number of slaves were shipped. The slaves were first imported into Portsmouth in the North of Dominica, which at the time served as the country's capital, and later moved to Roseau, the replacement capital. By the end of the decade in 1770 at least 10, 551 slaves had landed, significantly boosting the slave population on the island.[19]

Thomas Atwood[20] who served as Chief Justice of Dominica, between 1766 to 1773, observed that by 1773, of the 15 000 to 16 000 thousand slaves on the island, only about half of that number belonged to the British inhabitants. This he attributed to: 'the rather imprudent conduct of some of the first British settlers, after the cessation to Great Britain under the Treaty of Paris.' [21] He notes that many of the blacks who were on Dominica, when the British arrived, were in the capacity as domestics. Others were banished from neighbouring islands for their crimes, and yet others were newly arrived slaves from Africa.

'In addition, on assuming the territory in 1763, the Jesuits handed over the sugar plantations to the British planters along with the many negros. However, the newly designated slaves, were immediately put to work by the English settlers to: cut down massy, hard wood trees, to lop and burn the branches, clear the ground of the roots, and to labour at difficult, though necessary business, for which they were by no means qualified.'[22] By 1774, the white population had risen to 3 850, along with 15 753 slaves.

William Young Bart became governor of Dominica in April 1771 replacing governor Melville, after having served as his deputy since 1768. Upon his appointment, Dominica was separated from the ceded islands and now had its own governor working in concert with the Council and the House of Assembly. Born in Antigua, Young was responsible for building the main military stronghold of Dominica in Roseau, Fort Young in 1770 and also the Government House, which became his residence near the fort. He left Dominica suddenly in 1772, to travel to St Vincent to participate in the Carib War on that island, and to protect his estates there. On his departure, Lieutenant Governor William Stuart acted as governor until November 1774 when he was replaced by Governor Thomas Shirley.

As early as 1771, when Young became governor, there were rumours that the French were preparing for war against the British interest. In November, a British planter wrote that 'the prospect of war we find confirmed from all the French isles. Our engineer is now beginning a battery of 18 guns to defend the town. Count Dennevie, the governor of Martinico is exceeding busy at present, with a vast number of hands, in fortifying Martinico and St Lucia…the merchants at Martinico and Guadeloupe are buying up all the Bermuda sloops and schooners they can lay their hands on…if we have not some sloops of war to protect our trade, and defend the new ceded islands, we shall not be able to keep a slave upon our estates.'[23] That same month the British Parliament ordered three regiments of foot to

Dominica, St. Vincent and Tobago.[24]Ultimately, most of the troops were diverted to St. Vincent to fight against the Black Caribs.

In late May 1774, a dispute arose that pitied the Dominica Council against the House of Assembly. It turned out that the House had proposed a duty of four and a half percent be imposed on the produce from the island. The Council took exception from the proposed measure and sent a message to the Assembly that they had 'unanimously come to a resolution to do no further business with their House; in consequence of which the Assembly addressed his Excellency Governor and Commander in Chief Thomas Shirley requesting him to suspend the Members of His Majesty's Council, dissolve the House of Assembly or adopt such other remedy for the evils explained of, as his Excellency should think meet.'[25]

Accordingly, on 15 June 1774, Governor Shirley summoned both Houses to a special session. He lamented that instead of putting an end to the session with a speech conveying such an applause as proceedings distinguished for wisdom and utility could merit, that 'such heats and animosities had been introduced as seemed to make a reconciliation between both Houses impracticable, and a dissolution of the Assembly unavoidably necessary.'[26] And so it was the Governor dissolved the House 'with great reluctance.'[27]

In 1775 with the outbreak of the American War of Independence, or the American Revolutionary War, Governor Thomas Shirley Esq. concerned about the island's security, had attempted to beef up the fortifications around Dominica.[28] This he did against instructions from the colonial authorities in London. In particular, he focused on Fort Cachacou situated at the Southern tip of the island. The Fort was set on a hill of about three hundred square feet, surrounded on three sides by the sea and joined to the rest of the island by a narrow strip of land less than three feet in width. Easy to defend, Governor Shirley shored up its fortifications and stationed a number of men to guard it. The Governor also began construction of a garrison in the North of the Island, overlooking Prince Rupert Bay, which was ultimately named after him, Fort Shirley.

On 10 June 1777, Stephen Sayre a British diplomat stationed in Berlin made a proposal to Prussian King, Frederick the Great, which envisaged Dominica becoming a Prussian protectorate guaranteed by the Americans in return for Prussian intervention in the American war of Independence. This would take the form of a corps of Prussian officers sent by Frederick to assist the rebel army.[29] The proposal entitled '*Ideas on the manner of establishing a colony in the Island of Dominica, in the event that it can be acquired from Great Britain by Your Majesty,*' states 'as the principal object that merits sustained attention is to allure rich and industrious settlers, and since it is to be supposed that the most able and steadfast planters will come from other British islands and from North America, it will be necessary to employ the greatest care to make the form of government for the Island of Dominica as good as, and even preferable to, those which the different settlers will leave.'[30]

Stephen Sayre, in his proposal suggested that planters from the United States could be enticed to move to Dominica with their slaves. 'The southernmost parts of America can furnish very valuable settlers, since their black slaves are experienced in the cultivation of tobacco and indigo. Here there will be three or four harvests a year, instead of only one, as in America, where they are in addition obliged to clothe their slaves during winter, an expense that can be saved in the West Indies.'[31] He suggested that the island be divided into parcels of between 10 and 100 acres, with a large area in the Bay of Prince Rupert set aside for the principal town.

The colonists would be required to pay annual rents either in cash or tobacco for acquiring the lands, further, '…the settlers will be given five acres of land for each able slave they bring. Each white man who presents himself in good faith as a planter will have 10 acres.'[32] By Stephen Sayre's estimation, Frederick the Great would be able to extract rents of over 1.6 million pounds a year. In his opinion, 'the Island of Dominica will therefore be an ornament of Your Majesty's crown, and though it would appear to belong to Him only as a protectorate, it would be established on a firmer base than all the other islands, being the asylum of the unfortunate, the refuge of the persecuted, the warehouse of all merchants, and the common market of all nations, in summary, a monument…'[33]

On the surface, Sayre's proposal appeared to be sufficiently enticing to the King. However, it was eventually rejected with some observers believing that the King was not willing to antagonise the British, in case they kept control of America. It was in his interest to protect trade between Prussia and Britain. In fact, at the start of the American war of Independence, 'the British turned to the Baltic for the products they had formerly imported from America, especially grain and lumber, and Prussia, more than any other country, benefited from this war boom… it was therefore definitely not in Prussia's interest to disrupt its secure and growing trade with England for the sake of risky relations yet to be established with a nation not yet independent.'[34]Just one year later, Dominica was firmly under the control of the French.

With 1777 coming to an end, the French were starting to openly challenge the British authority in Dominica. In October, American privateers captured the *Black Prince*, a British slaver traveling from Senegal to Dominica with 215 slaves on board and the *Darly*, also full of slaves, and took both ships to Martinique. Governor Shirley then sent an officer with a letter to the governor of Martinique, Marquis de Bouillé, demanding restitution for the lost ships.[35] His emissary however was summarily dismissed and was not able to get an audience with any authority of note in Martinique. From that time onwards relations between the French and English would steadily worsen culminating in the eventual invasion of Dominica by a superior French force in September 1778.

Slaves sold at a port in Africa.

3

French Conquest of Dominica

The American war of Independence was already being waged for about three years when France joined on the side of the thirteen colonies against Great Britain in 1778. What until that time was considered a civil war between the British empire, suddenly became an international one, with the involvement of the French, and later Spain. When France joined in early 1778, it was viewed as an opportunity for it to avenge the humiliating losses suffered in 1763, at the hand of Great Britain, including having to give up Dominica and several other West Indian colonies. With Great Britain occupied in prosecuting the war, the perfect opportunity was therefore presented for France to retake Dominica. As far as France was concerned, of the many West Indian colonies open to reconquest, Dominica was undoubtedly high on the list.

A thriving free port at the centre of the arc of the islands, Dominica was also strategically located in the middle of the two French colonies of Martinique and Guadeloupe. At least one French official, the Marquis Duchilleau, Colonel Commandant of the Viennois Regiment stationed in Martinique, had repeatedly noted its importance in promoting communication between the two French islands as well as for preventing privateers from having a serviceable base.[1] In the years of British rule since 1763, the French had actively supported their planters stationed on the island, encouraged trade with Dominica, and generally dreamed about repossessing it. Recapture of the island would help improve communication among the French islands, and importantly deny the use of Dominican ports to privateers who preyed on French shipping.

On 28 July 1778, Governor Shirley oblivious of the pending French attack set sail for Britain on a leave of absence, leaving Lieutenant Governor William Stuart to act in his place. Before his departure, Governor Shirley had started to erect defences on the island against the prospect of a naval invasion. He however, was not fully supported by the colonial administration or the local assembly. Lord George Germain, the British colonial secretary, I775-82, was at odds with Shirley, choosing instead to place his confidence on English sea power, which was traditionally the case. On hearing of Governor Shirley's efforts, Lord Germain lashed out at him publicly. 'The defence of such island colonies, depended not on regular troops… but on a superior fleet in the surrounding waters. Any works beyond the reach of the shipping, would only serve to make the recovery of the Islands more difficult if an enemy should, in the absence of the ships, find means of getting possession of them,'[2] Germain stated.

Less than a month after Governor Shirley's departure, on 17 August 1778, a French frigate *Concorde* arrived in Martinique with news of the French involvement in the United States hostilities, and a letter from Marquis de Sartine, Minister of Marine, to Governor General François Claude Amour, Marquis de Bouillé. The message in the letter was clear, the Governor should make immediate plans to capture Dominica.[3] The Marquis de Bouillé was already fairly well prepared and awaiting just such an opportunity. He knew from Thomas Chabaud Arnault, a French planter residing in Roseau that the British were in the process of erecting new artillery batteries at Fort Cachacou, Charlottesville (Newtown), and Roseau. He also knew that those at Roseau and Newtown were not yet completed, and that there were only about 'fifty men fit for duty' on the island.

Arnault was a prominent Frenchman in Dominica having being appointed in 1763 by the British as a trustee of French church lands in Roseau. *The Newcastle Weekly Courant*, reports that 'after regaining the Island in 1783, the Grand Jury presented to the Court of the Kings Bench and Grand Sessions that Thomas Chabaud Arnault, a Planter, as having contrary to his oath of allegiance, on the 7th September 1778 invited the French troops coming then to attack that island, to land at Mahaut, with offers to assist them with guides to conduct them to Roseau. It was requested that the proper officers of the Crown investigate the same, to prevent further crimes in the future.' [4]

The Marquis de Bouillé was also keenly aware that Rear Admiral Barrington of the British navy was stationed for the past two months in Barbados, with three ships of the line and twelve frigates, vastly superior to what he had at his disposal. He needed to act quickly. On 3 September he sent an officer, Gabrouse[5] to Dominica to investigate the presence of one of Barrington's ships at Prince Rupert's Bay. Lieutenant Governor Stuart got suspicious of the sudden presence of French personnel in Dominica, and ordered him to be arrested as a spy. However, after questioning he was released.

In the meantime, as the plans for the French attack moved ahead, the Marquis de Bouillé attempted to act like everything was normal, even meeting and signing an agreement with Lieutenant Governor Stuart, to formally prohibit plundering by the crews of privateers. On 5 September de Bouillé received the news that the British frigate had left Prince Rupert Bay. He was now ready to act. On the evening of 6 September 1778, 1800 soldiers and 1,000 creole volunteers, under his command, sailed out of Martinique on 18 ships headed for Dominica. At the head of the convoy were the King's Frigates *la Tourterelle* commanded by the Chevalier de la Laurencie; *la Diligente*, by the Viscount du Chilleau, *l'Amphitrite*, by the Sieur de Jassaud, and the *Corvette l' Eteourdie*, by the Marquis de Montbas; all four lieutenants in the navy.

The Marquis de Bouillé intended to execute the attack at day break in order to avoid the fire of Forte de Cachacou and that of Roseau, fortified with twenty-two pieces of cannon.[6] There were to be two principal attacks, with all the troops between the town of Roseau and Cachacou and a false attack was to be made on the North side of Roseau.[7] By the early morning of 7 September, Fort Cachacou was taken. The previous day, French sympathisers had provided alcohol to the men guarding the Fort and poured sand into the barrels of the canons, thus effectively demobilizing them. Some of the men guarding the garrison were killed and the rest made prisoners.

The French attackers would later encounter some resistance at Loubiere and Roseau, but eventually at around noon succeeded in securing both areas along with Morne Bruce, which overlooked the town of Roseau.

Completely overwhelmed, the British troops comprised of officers, ninety-four privates, and about one hundred twenty militia, capitulated. By five o'clock on 7 September the articles of capitulation were signed. At six the English troops numbering some 500 men including the militia laid down their arms and the French troops entered Fort Young in Roseau. Lieutenant Governor Stuart capitulated likewise, surrendering all the forts batteries and fortresses around the island. The officers, subalterns and soldiers of the regular troops were made prisoners. The militias were dismissed after having laid down their arms, thus completing the successful takeover of Dominica by the French from the British. Dominica was now firmly in French hands.

The Marquis de Bouillé moved quickly to appoint Marquis Duchilleau as governor of Dominica, the Baron du Fagan second in command, and the Sieur de Beaupuy as Kings Lieutenant of the town and Fort of Roseau. The loss of Dominica to the French was a bitter blow to the British, since they had now lost an excellent location, situated within sighting distances of two French colonies. Also, the British had just expended an enormous amount of money to fortify the island, complete with numerous pieces of artillery sent from England. However, when the island was captured, Britain was caught in the vortex of the American war, and could ill afford to spare men or materiel to protect the island. Inexplicably, Rear Admiral Barrington did not receive the intelligence, nor orders to set sail for Dominica on time. By the time he received orders to sail to Dominica, the French had already consolidated their defences on the Island.

The presence of Rear Admiral Barrington's fleet, however, served to deter the Marquis de Bouillé from furthering his conquest in the region, but the French were deeply pleased with their prized possession of Dominica. De Bouillé for his part was careful not to wreak havoc on Dominica, firmly believing that it would eventually be ceded to the French. He would also turn his efforts at transforming the country into an impregnable fortress, and extend pleasant courtesies to the British population on the island.[8]

What the English lacked in faithfully defending the island, they gained from the very moderate terms agreed on by the Marquis de Bouillé. He concurred without difficulty or reserve to practically every condition that was proposed in favour of the British inhabitants. This included the honours of war and the liberty of retaining their arms, with the fullest security to their estates, property of every sort, rights, privileges, and immunities. They were also allowed to retain their civil and religious governments in all their parts, with all their laws, customs, ordinances, courts, and ministers of justice and until the conclusion of a peace treaty. If the island would be formally ceded to France, they would have the choice of whether to adhere to their own political form of government or to adhere to that established in the French islands.[9]

Other favourable terms to the British inhabitants included the fact that they could sell their possessions and retire wherever they pleased, if they chose not to live under the French Governor. Finally, they were allowed to pay the same amount of duty to the French King as they would to their British Sovereign. In effect, the only change to the British inhabitants was in their sovereignty. More importantly, they were treated with utmost respect from the French troops, and there was no plundering nor disorder. To express his satisfaction to the troops for their bravery and good conduct, the Marquis de Bouillé rewarded the soldiers and volunteers with a gratuity of a considerable sum of money.

Duchilleau's instructions from the French hierarchy called on him, in addition to promoting general contentment, agriculture and commerce, to hasten the immediate fortification of the island, maintain a strong garrison, establish military hospitals, form a militia of French inhabitants, forbid the English to assemble, disarm those without real estate, require all not well-known to deposit their arms with leading residents of each parish in case of British attack, and prohibit any slave from carrying arms.[10] Within days of assuming control, Duchilleau addressed a joint gathering of the Council and Assembly, which was still largely controlled by the British. He requested them to disarm all Negro slaves, furnish cattle at a reasonable price for the occupying troops and draw up within five days a list of 'superior' persons to whom the English could give up their arms if and when required.

In the days ahead, Duchilleau, much to the surprise of the British planters, set up a militia of French inhabitants, comprised mainly of free negroes. He would also go on to keep close surveillance on the British subjects, and issued a proclamation, forbidding the assembling together of the English inhabitants of more than two in a place. 'That no lights were to be seen in their houses after nine o'clock at night; that no English person was to be out after that hour, in the streets, without a candle and lantern, or a lighted pipe in his mouth; and that no servant of theirs was to be seen at night, without a ticket from his master; under no less a penalty to white people, than being shot by the sentinel at the post they passed by, of being imprisoned, or sent out of the island; and the servants were to be whipped in the public market, besides a fine on their masters. Many of the English inhabitants were imprisoned by him on the slightest pretence; and one of them, Robert Thou, was actually shot, and later died.'[11]

The demands made on the British inhabitants did not sit well with them and only added to their distrust of Duchilleau, something which would ultimately define his reign. Thomas Coke would later write that 'the conduct of the subsequent governor toward the inhabitants, has sufficiently taught us, that agreement and signature, when compared with fidelity and honour, are words which convey very different ideas.[12] He went on to note that 'Bouillé was brave, generous, honourable and humane; Duchilleau was mean, dishonourable, vindictive, and suspicious. In the former character we find those dignified and manly actions which designate a nobleness of soul, but in the latter, those base ingredients which constitute the despot and display the coward.'[13] De Bouillé himself is said to have regretted making Duchilleau governor, after the Viscount de Damas turned down the offer to become governor.[14]

Not only did Duchilleau have to put up with a restive population, including the growing number of Maroons deserting the plantations, but his reign would be marred by several calamitous events. The first took place between 29 – 30 August 1779 when a major hurricane wreaked havoc on Dominica. Most of the country's canes, ground provisions, and coffee trees were completely wiped out, with damages estimated at over £100 000. Then on 30 September the sea suddenly rose 21 feet above its normal level, destroying several dwellings and ships at harbour. This was followed by a major hurricane making landfall on 11 October, believed to be the worst on record up to that time.[15] To compound matters, it was followed up by a tidal wave. Buildings that were left standing after the August hurricane were destroyed with many swept into the sea.[16]

Newspapers of the day reported widely on the destruction and devastation of the hurricane. *The Edinburgh Advertiser* reported that 'the loss sustained on the island is of such magnitude, that it cannot be as yet ascertained, and when the additional and peculiar distresses are considered in their present situation, under conquest, notwithstanding the humane and polite behaviour of the French commander, we tremble at the dreadful consequences of their calamity, the miserable sufferers being destitute of money, credit and resources of all kinds, and standing exposed not only to famine, but likewise to the rigour of that unhealthy climate, consequently must sink under their misfortunes, unless some relief be administered to them by this country.'[17]

By January 1780, many English residents both white and coloured had left Dominica, tired of Duchilleau's rule, and the growing number of calamities. 'Many of the planters were absolutely ruined. Some had abandoned cultivation of all articles, from a certainty that success would only be an aggravation of their misfortunes. Thirty sugar plantations were thrown up; and the works which had been erected at a vast expense, were permitted to yield to the corroding's of time and the injuries of the elements.'[18] Estates lay in ruin and several planters had lost everything so that by the middle of 1780, the population fell to 1066 whites, with the majority of them French, 543 free Negroes, 12,713 slaves, and some thirty Kalinago families.[19]

Duchilleau's rule also witnessed a huge fall in imports to and exports from the island. 'The island though conquered by France, was not visited by any ships of that nation during the period of five years and three months that it continued in their possession…with England they could hold no direct correspondence, …the circuitous course which their few articles of commerce were obliged to take to reach a market, so far reduced them in value, that their sale could hardly be considered as a benefit.'[20]

At one point, some commerce was conducted through St Eustatius, which was a neutral Dutch colony. From there the goods would be ferried to England. This was however short-lived as the country was captured by the British. Another part of the produce was sent via Dutch vessels to Rotterdam then re-exported to Britain. That route also closed when Holland joined the war. The fact that they were also unable to ship to France, since direct trade with Britain was forbidden, only added to the misery faced by the island inhabitants.

Calamity again struck Dominica when on 15 April 1781 (Easter Sunday), the town of Roseau erupted in flames. Between five and six hundred homes were consumed by the flames, including some of the main businesses and stores resulting in loses in excess of £200 000. Many of the British residents quickly put the blame on Duchilleau since he had threatened such an action in the past.[21]Others also accused him of only assisting French inhabitants during the fire, while he ignored the British inhabitants.

The Edinburgh Advertiser noted, 'we had the melancholy accounts of Roseau the principal town in Dominica being burnt; the fire began in the evening and by midnight most of the houses were destroyed. It is particularly hard upon the inhabitants, as they do not live very comfortably under the French government.'[22] A few months later Duchilleau suffering from ill health asked to be replaced as governor. In September 1781, the Marquis de Bouillé replaced him with the Count de Bourgon. However, his stint as governor was short lived and he was replaced by the Marquis de Beaupré shortly thereafter.

Between 9 - 12 April 1782, a British fleet under the command of Admiral George Rodney engaged a combined Spanish and French naval fleet in the Caribbean, commanded by François Joseph Paul, Comte de Grasse, Marquis de Grasse-Tilly. In what would later become known as the Battle of the Saints or to the French as *Bataille de la Dominique* (Battle of Dominica), the thirty-six ships of Admiral Rodney engaged the thirty vessels of de Grasse. The strategic objectives of the attack by the French and Spanish were to recapture St Lucia, Antigua and Barbados, conquer Jamaica and to aid the Americans by defeating the British naval force. The decisive battle took place on April 12 just a few miles North of Dominica, and in view of many on Dominica's East coast. The French fleet was roundly defeated and helped to put an end to the French designs on capturing Jamaica.

By the time of the French defeat at the *Bataille de la Dominique*, the English inhabitants were in almost daily despair. Thomas Coke observed that 'under the iron yoke of unfeeling despotism, and deprived of all internal and external resources, the suffering inhabitants felt all the horrors of their situation. The impenetrable doom that hovered over them had relaxed the springs of industry; their hopes were frozen, and their expectations had almost formed an alliance with despair.'[23]

French rule over Dominica in this instance would eventually stretch out over six years. Following the reign of the Marquis Duchilleau (1778 – 1781) was the Comte de Bourgon (1781- 82) and then the Marquis de Beaupré (1782 – 84). Much to the chagrin of Francois Claude Amour, and the Marquis de Bouillé, on 7 September 1784, British rule was once again restored over Dominica. Previously, under the terms of the 3 September 1783 Treaty of Paris, which brought an end to the American Revolutionary War, France had agreed to return all the territory it had captured from the British during the previous five years. Dominica was one of those countries that it was forced to grudgingly give up.

A joyous Coke triumphantly remarked that 'the gloom of melancholy was dispersed in an instant; joy sparkled in every countenance and gratitude broke forth from those lips which had almost forgotten how to smile. The night of affliction through which they had travelled between five and six years, disappeared in an instant, before those prospects with which the intelligence of their deliverance had filled their minds, and before those beams of future prosperity, at which they lighted up their departing hopes.'[24] The British could not have guessed at the time the extent to which the seeds of revolt and the yearning for freedom had already taken root among the Maroons of Dominica. This they would soon find out much to their dismay.

4

Revolts and the First Maroon War

Many of the former domestic slaves and new slave arrivals into Dominica were unaccustomed to the severe conditions, under which they were forced to work, and some simply refused to stay on the plantations. Unused to the climate and harsh work conditions, including inadequate shelter from the continuous rains many of them died, within a few months of their arrival. Others, rather than endure the hardships took off for the woods, where they hoped to fare better. Thomas Atwood notes that: 'many of the negros so purchased from the Jesuits, either from their attachment to them, or dislike to their new masters, soon after betook themselves to the woods with their wives and children, where they were joined, from time to time, by others from different estates.'[1]

Thomas Atwood observed further that: 'they secreted themselves for a number of years, formed companies under different chiefs, built good houses, and planted gardens in the woods, where they raised poultry, hogs, and other small stock, which, with what the sea, rivers, and woods afforded, and what they got from the negros they had intercourse with on the plantations, they lived very comfortably, and were seldom disturbed in their haunts.'[2]

Dominican historian Lennox Honychurch notes: 'like the Kalinagos before them, the enslaved Africans who had escaped to freedom in the mountains relied on natural materials to construct their huts and shelters and to produce utensils for their households. On the plantations, the cabins were thatched with sugarcane leaves while in the forest a wide variety of palm, heliconia, *woseau*, and *zel mouche* leaves were used for this purpose. The walls were made of woven gaulettes, which are thin saplings. The gaulettes were woven into panels which were held in place by wooden house frames made of round wood posts. In some cases the panels were plastered with clay and on plantations they were usually painted with white lime wash.'[3]

Honychurch further observes that calabashes and wooden forks were used for eating, and that small beds were planted with bush teas and herbs for medicines and food seasonings. Also, they planted fruit trees and banana and plantain plants. As for the camps they were 'military-style strongholds that took advantage of the steep topography of their location. Several were situated on top of plateaus surrounded on at least three sides by precipices.'[4]

These included Morne Negre Maroon, Colihaut Heights, Morne Rosalie, Grand Bay, Geneva, and other inaccessible parts of the mountainous interior of Dominica. It was in this kind of environment that the Maroon elders would raise their children, and keep away from the inhumane conditions on the plantations and the white planters. Indeed, much later when the colonists began to aggressively pursue and capture the Maroons some of the children would be seeing white men for the very first time.

The Maroons would also cling to their beliefs in Obeah, which they viewed as an essential part of their ability to resist the plantation system. Obeah was a kind of magic or black art, which had its roots in the occult practice of Obi, including the mystery of signs, spells and sorcery, dating back to the ancient Egyptians. 'Obi for the purposes of bewitching people, or consuming them by lingering illness, is made of grave dirt, hair, teeth of sharks, and other creatures, blood feathers, eggshells, images in wax, the hearts of birds, and some potent roots, weeds and bushes, of which Europeans are at this time ignorant, but which were known for the same purposes, to the ancients.'[5]

One observer of the practice in Africa, writing in *The Caledonian Mercury*, noted that 'they (Obi men and women) sell foul winds for inconstant mariners, dreams and fantasies for jealousy, vexation and pain in the heart for perfidious love, and for the perturbed, impatient and wretched, at the tardy acts of time, to turn in prophetic fury, to a future page in the book of fate, and amaze the ravished sense of the tempest tossed current.'[6]

All the Maroon leaders, held to those beliefs and used it effectively to create a mystic around them and more importantly to maintain effective control over their followers. Initially, the planters viewed the practice with bemused interest and allowed the slaves on the estate to practice their craft without interference. However, as the Maroon revolts built up over the years, and the white inhabitants began to appreciate the mystic around the practice of obeah, laws were passed to make it an offense punishable by death. One such law was passed by the Dominica Legislature in 1816 and read:

And whereas instances frequently occur of slaves assuming the art of witchcraft, or pretending to supernatural powers, or professing what is commonly called by them obeah, and dealing in spells, charms, and philtres, and thereby influencing the minds of weak and credulous slaves, and frequently stimulating them to actions of the highest atrocity against their masters, renters, managers, and overseers, by administering drugs, and potions of secret and generally of a poisonous nature, as well as to their fellow-slaves, or others to whom they bear evil intentions.

Be it, and it is hereby further enacted and ordained by the authority aforesaid, that any owner, renter, manager, or overseer of any plantation, or any person whatsoever, who shall discover any slave or slaves practising any of the above arts, or pretending to any supernatural powers, or in possession of any drugs or potions, he the said owner, manager, or overseer, shall cause the said slave or slaves, to be committed to the common goal of this island, to stand his, her, or their trial according to law, and on conviction of the said slave or slaves, of the aforesaid crimes, he, she, or they shall suffer death, or such other punishment at the discretion of the court, by banishment or flogging on the bare breech, as to the said court shall seem meet: Provided such flogging does not exceed thirty-nine lashes.[7]

Meanwhile, by 1764, a significant number of Maroons would establish a foothold in Dominica's mountainous interior thus setting the stage for a showdown with the white planter class. Word would also spread throughout the Caribbean of the growing resistance to slavery and many newly arrived slaves would seek for opportunity to escape.

In June 1764 one such newly arrived slave by the name of Balla, a Mandingo Prince from Guinea, successfully escaped his captors, without spending a single day on the estate and joined the growing ranks of the runaways. He quickly assumed the position of Chief of the runaways, establishing himself as the most powerful and feared leader of the emerging resistance to slavery. Twenty years later, his actions would help define the fighting spirit of the maroons and shake the colony to its very foundations.

Overtime, the runaways became better organized and actively sought new slaves to join them. This however, did not go unnoticed by the authorities who understood the growing threat posed by the increasing number of Maroons that had taken refuge in the mountainous interior of the island. While Dominica was still a ceded colony and just two short years after the signing of the Treaty of Paris, the Legislature on 23 April 1765 passed '*an act for the more effectual suppression of the runaway slaves*.'[8] Four years later, on 28 July 1769, and in an effort to curb the Maroon influence and control their burgeoning numbers, the Legislature passed '*an act to prevent the importation of slaves who have been convicted, or known to have been guilty of murder, or attempt to murder, or poison, insurrections, or other capital offences*.'[9]

The rationale given for the later legislation was as follows: 'whereas many evils have already happened and still continue to happen, to numbers of the inhabitants of this Island, by being put in great danger of their lives and properties from being attacked in their houses, as well as on the highways, by gangs of runaway negroes, headed, and encouraged by other slaves imported from neighbouring colonies, who were there convicted, or known to have been guilty of crimes which through lenity, or having been screened by their owners or others, have escaped punishment.-And whereas if an immediate stop be not put to such evils by preventing the importation of such offenders into the island, the inhabitants will still remain under great terror and apprehension, and may in the end be attended with fatal consequences to their lives and properties as well as the means of retarding the settlement of this infant colony.'[10]

This Act was quickly followed with another piece of legislation on 26 March 1770, this time '*an act to suppress runaways and for the better government of slaves, to prevent slaves being fraudulently carried off and to enable the commander in chief to send out detachments of free persons in pursuit of runaways*.'[11] Almost a year later, on 13 March 1771 another Act was passed 'to form a militia.'[12] who were issued caps fronted with silver, on which his Majesty's arms were set, and underneath was the label, '*Dominica Light Dragoons*.' The Legislature also offered cash rewards and the promise of liberty to the slaves who would help in spying on and apprehending the Maroons.

All the while the Maroon population continued to steadily increase as both newly arrived African slaves and those escaping from the horrors of plantation life, joined their erstwhile compatriots in the forests of freedom. For the most part, many slaves would voluntarily run away from the plantations to join the Maroons, however, others had to be persuaded to make that final decision. Maroon leaders like Jacko would therefore, embark on recruitment drives in which they would plead with the slaves from the estates to join them. Governor John Matson told the Legislative Assembly that the Maroons 'hold out enticing invitations to others to join them and render the parties formidable.'[13]

The Maroons justified their decisions to flee the estates by pointing to the cruel punishment meted out at the hands of the planters.[14] Juba, one of the Maroons who would later be captured and put on trial defended the actions of himself and thirteen other runaways as follows: 'because they were very hard worked and had nothing allowed them to eat.' Juba also talked of their initial survival in the forest before they could grow food in their own gardens. They would eat wild yams found growing in the interior as their ground vegetable-provision; for meat they would hunt agouties, and for salt boil [sea] water.[15]

Another slave Jacques complained bitterly of the inhumane treatment and fear of harsh punishment, which forced him and several others to seek refuge with other Maroons. Flora, after being raped and violated by her master sought the refuge of the forest after receiving encouragement from her husband, Joseph. In retaliation, he was severely punished and made to suffer, receiving 24 lashes in the marketplace and being asked to pay a fine.[16] Over time, punishment for those caught was swift and intended to deter others from running away. Several Maroons were consequently flogged publicly, others thrown into jail, where many wasted away and died. Joseph, a slave who had provided the Maroons with bananas, plantains, fowls and other provisions, was sentenced to be burnt alive at Colihaut on 11 March 1786, for 'harbouring and encouraging the Maroons.'[17]

Several slaves would use the pretext of spying on the Maroons to make their own escape and join them in the woods. Others would, however, accept money from the authorities as the cost of betrayal of the Maroons. In the 1770s, published reports from the Provost Marshal to the Legislative Assembly's Public Accounts Committee lists several payments made to slaves for assisting in the capture of Maroons. It also details payment for their placement in the public jail and for settling fees for doctors' bills, trials, burials, or advertisements for their capture.

On 23 August 1773, soon after Lieutenant Governor Stuart took over, the Legislature passed '*an act for suppressing runaways and for their better government*.'[18] Then after the appointment of Governor Gordon Shirley, another act was passed on 15 May 1778 '*to appoint a company of Rangers, for the suppression of runaway slaves*.' The Maroons, however, appeared largely untroubled by the British legislative action, and seemed content to go on with their existence in the forests of Dominica. All this would however change in dramatic fashion with the French conquest of Dominica on 7 September 1778. By that time, British animosity towards the French inhabitants had markedly increased, and was a far cry from the situation that existed in 1764, when offers of land were made to them. Some British inhabitants openly accused the French of favouring the Maroons and providing them with provisions, and worse, arms and ammunition.

Thomas Atwood observed that: 'the inferior French officers, and several of the French inhabitants of Dominica, encouraged thereto by the tyrannic behaviour of the Marquis Duchilleau, were not backward in their bad treatment of the English inhabitants: the officers usually insulting them as they walked the streets; throwing showers of stones on their houses in the night-time; saluting the English white women with indecent expressions as they passed by; taking the upper hand of the men in taverns, and other places of necessary resort, where they happened to be present, or indignantly driving them out; circumstances of such mean cruelty to a conquered people, that one should think, none but the dregs of mankind would ever be guilty of.'[19]

One irate planter remarked that: 'when the French gave up the island of Dominica, they left the English a legacy of 500 negroes in the woods, who had been armed, supported and protected by their governors, particularly by the Marquis Duchilleau.'[20] Thomas Atwood also claimed that Duchilleau provided the runaways with arms, encouraged their attacks on the British planters and even made 'a treaty of assistance' with them in helping to defend the island. 'For that purpose, they were given muskets and bayonets together with ammunition, which he took from the British planters.'[21] The notion that Duchilleau aided and abetted the Maroons was however disputed, not least by himself. In a message he sent to the legislature just one week after arrival in Dominica, on 14 September I778, Duchilleau had specifically stated: 'There are here, Gentlemen, armed negroes; I have myself seen them; it is necessary for your safety, that not one negro be allowed to bear arms.'

The behaviour of the French towards the British may very well have contributed to the disdain the Maroons felt towards the British planters in particular. Without weapons to defend themselves, the planters became easy prey for the Maroons, who by now were well armed. They began by robbing the English plantations of ground provisions, plantains, bananas, and small livestock. Later they took to shooting and killing cattle and carrying it away to their forest hideouts. For many years they carried out their raids on the plantations with seeming ease. They would descend suddenly from their hideouts, plunder the estates then disappear back into the woods with little fear of any effective chase from the planters or the militia.

The *Edinburgh Advertiser* observed that the hurricane of October 1780 had the effect of increasing the number of Maroons, which made them a greater threat to the planters. 'The town of Roseau is almost wholly destroyed, and from the general want of provisions, and other necessities, many slaves have deserted their owners, and being formed into bands in the woods, and from thence making frequent incursions on the estates, committing violent outrages and depredations, not even abstaining from murders.'[22]

By the year 1781 the Maroons began to escalate their attacks to include plundering of the estates, killing of white planters and overseers, and the burning of fields and buildings. By then they had radically altered their strategy of attack. The Maroons shifted from confronting the British slave masters in broad daylight, instead their surprise attacks were 'generally in the most secret manner, in the night-time, when they were under no dread of being apprehended.'[23]

The first reported attack on a British planter, which drew public outcry, and helped focus attention on the rebelliousness of the Maroons took place in 1781. Hugh Gould the manager of an estate resisted the attempts of some of the Maroons to steal provisions from him. Frustrated, a number of them later returned with the intention to kill him. On arrival, they found that he was absent on business, but instead found his companion Robert Grahame, a planter at the estate house. He was promptly murdered in his dwelling, as he pleaded with them on his knees to 'spare his life and take his possessions.'[24]

Outraged by the brazen attack on Grahame, the planters pleaded with Duchilleau to allow them access to arms, so that they could defend themselves. He however refused, instead dispatching some of his forces to search for those responsible for the attack. Several of the Maroons were caught and hastily executed. One newspaper lamented that 'the negroes have committed many depredations; they wantonly murdered one of the British overseers, yet the French would allow no redress nor suffer the negroes to be punished.'[25] The attack on Grahame would signal the start of a long battle between the Maroons and the authorities on the island, as each sought to dominate the other.

On 20 March 1782 while still under French rule, the British dominated Legislature in response to the outrageous attack on Grahame, passed 'an act to aid the act entitled '*an act for suppressing runaways called a Slave Act, and to alter and amend the same, and to provide a fund to defray expenses, and for encouraging a party of rangers for suppressing runaways, and to oblige the Planters to make returns of runaways, and for transportation of those taken or surrendered, and dangerous to the community*.' Those actions, however, proved futile even as the security situation rapidly deteriorated, and not withstanding that the English once again imposed their rule on the island.

Just two months after the arrival to Dominica of Governor John Orde, on 13 December 1784, two slaves on Jemmets estate seized their owner's gun and a quantity of ammunition, kidnapped the mill-wright, a white man by the name of John Sharpe, and made good their escape. Several hours later, the body of Sharpe was discovered, shot to death, between the Jemmets estate in Tarreau and Layou. The two had only recently arrived on the island and being unfamiliar with the surrounding forests, were caught six days later by a party of whites and negroes that were sent out in search of them. They however, did not surrender peacefully and fired at the search party when they were spotted. In the ensuing gun battle, a young negro boy was killed. The two were eventually arrested and put on trial the following day.

When questioned about the event, the one who had the gun revealed that he fired at the party because he took one of them for his master Jemmets, whom he was determined to kill, if ever he met him. After a trial lasting about twenty minutes, the Maroon who shot John Sharpe was sentenced to have his right hand cut off, and then to be burnt alive; the other to be hanged and his head to be afterwards cut off and exposed with the arm of the other maroon on a pole.[26] The sentences were carried out two days later.

During the first nine months of 1784, an uneasy calm prevailed between the Maroons and the white planters. The Maroons appeared content to do the occasional raid of the estate in their neighbourhood, to supply themselves with plantain and ground provisions, 'but rather in a pilfering manner than in bodies of armed men.'[27]All this would change in September 1784, when the Maroons fired on the negroes working on the Eden estate, just outside of Roseau, and drove them from there before carrying away almost all the plantains and ground provisions they found fit to gather. 'In October they murdered in a barbarous manner, Mr. Generand who interrupted them in a like attack, on the grand Marigot estate. The planters in the height of Colihaut, were in December attacked and kept in constant alarm by these savages, to such a degree, that some abandoned their estates.'[28]

With the violence escalating, the inhabitants started to apply pressure on Governor John Orde, headed by an increasingly vocal Legislative Assembly. *The Independent Gazetteer* reproduced a letter from one of the planters, in which it was observed: 'The dissentions between the Governor and the inhabitants of this island has arisen to an unhappy crisis. One Assembly is dissolved and another summoned. Yet, the same opposition headed by Governor Stewart constantly maintains it ground. Our ports are thin, the captains complain of the extraordinary charges, and the abandoned estates make the island a melancholy spectacle. Most of the troops from hence are sent up by order of General Matthews to St. Vincent to suppress the Caribs, who begin to be a formidable enemy numbering

1200. They are well supplied by the French who are very vigilant in each island. Straining every nerve to keep an interest, in case of another war, which in the West Indies is the constant discourse.'[29]

By now, it was becoming increasingly clear that the Maroons were very well organized, fully armed and prepared to go on the offensive. The authorities readily identified the key leaders to be Pharcelle, working around the estates to the West of the island, Balla operating out of a camp in the interior towards its South East, and Pangloss in the South. Determined to act, Governor John Orde pushed through legislation, in an effort to thwart their activities. On 17 December 1784, Dominica's Legislative Assembly passed '*an Act to regulate the sale of gunpowder and firearms, or provisions, salt, or other necessaries with runaway slaves, or having intercourse with them, directly or indirectly, and to authorize the governor, to issue proclamations and to grant more powers to magistrates, than heretofore, with respect to vessels at anchor, or hovering about the coast having arms or ammunition, or from onboard of which, slaves may have been landed.*'[30]

In the months that followed, several proclamations were issued by the Legislature, including one '*offering a pardon to all that would surrender themselves, except such as had been guilty of murder.*'[31]This were simply ignored by the Maroons confident in their ability to repel any attack launched against them by the authorities. So with the year 1784 drawing to a close the authorities were no closer to enticing the Maroons to return to the plantations. This would soon give way to an all-out war that pitied the might of the country's militia against hundreds of Maroons determined to cling to their newly found freedom.

With the numbers of Maroons increasing, the Legislature, in January 1785, passed '*an act for raising a fund to be applied for the purpose of forcing them into subjection.*'[32] Taxes were imposed by the authorities on the assessed value of rental property, vacant lots, various professions, male persons of colour, whites, house slaves, sugar, coffee and other items. The taxes would remain in place for a period of three years.

Following the passage of the legislation, the Assembly and planters continued to agitate for more to be done to hunt down and exterminate the Maroons, and in particular their leaders like Balla, Pangloss and Pharcelle. It would however take a further three months to 15 March 1785, before legislation authorizing the formation of a militia would be adopted by the Legislative Assembly. The militia formed was comprised of white men, free people of colour, and able negro men belonging to the different plantations, set up for the purpose of pursuing and capturing or killing the Maroons scattered in the woods of Dominica.

Then, eleven days later on 26 March another Act was passed, this time '*to make the testimony of negroes and persons of colour admissible in certain cases and under certain restrictions for a limited time, to forfeit runaway slaves who have been absent a certain time from their masters, and to oblige the inhabitants knowing situations of runaway slaves to communicate the same in manner described.*'[33] Then in that same month on 31 March, '*an act to encourage persons to go as commanders in the woods as leaders of parties or detachments in pursuit of runaways, was successfully enacted.*'[34]

The white planters no doubt hoped that the formation of the militia, along with the several pieces of legislation, would be enough to quell the attacks. For a while everything appeared to have gone quiet, until that day in July 1786, when the Colony erupted in a show of resistance, rebellion and mayhem, orchestrated by the Maroons of Dominica. It was the start of several months of discontent, later referred to as the Maroon War, which would forever change the course of the island, and sow the seeds for the eventual abolishment of the slave trade and ultimately slavery.

The story of what transpired on Cassada Garden Estate, owned by Thomas Osborne that fateful day in July is better told through an eyewitness account. 'We have been for some time past in the greatest dread of the runaway negroes. On Friday the 15th ultimo, a party of them came down to the plantain walk of Cassada Garden Estate (late Miller and Mc Allister's but now Millers) to plunder it. Most of the negro men belonging to the estate were at this bay. The women who were at home and saw them, gave an alarm and frightened the runaways away leaving their cowracous behind. The manager Mr. Mc Bean was also at the bay. When he returned home in the evening, he was informed of it, he then sent to Roseau for some cutlasses.

'The next Saturday he was obliged to be at the bay again, the runaways returned armed, and lay all day at a neighbouring abandoned estate, called Woodbridge. They were discovered by a negro in the afternoon who knew a great many and reckoned a great number of them. He informed the negroes of the Cassada Garden Estate of them. When the manager returned in the evening, he was told in a promiscuous manner that the runaways were nearby. He then enquired of the driver, if he had heard or knew anything of them, who denied it (but it has since been found that he did hear of them). On which the manager threatened to punish those who had told him the next morning, imagining it was to get him off the estate. He had three guns with him, but found only one to be in good order, which he loaded.

'In a short time after going to sleep, the watch came to alarm him that the runaways were come. He ran out only in his shirt with his gun. On seeing them he presented but they were quicker, but by the imposition of Providence, on seeing the flash he lowered his body, so that only one ball out of upwards of a dozen, took him in a superficial manner over the right shoulder. He took advantage of the smoke and made his escape. The ashpit of the stills offered itself an asylum for him, which he accepted.

'They now began to behave in a most outrageous and furious manner, plundered every article in the house, the boiling house of a large quantity of rum and sugar, set fire and burned down his house, kitchen, the hospital and a negro house. They kept up a constant firing huzzaing and hooping the whole time. The estate negroes could not come to his assistance, for they had the precaution to place three men to guard the road. After they had satiated themselves, they retired to the abandoned estate before mentioned and there revelled the rest of the night. Two or three overseers from the next estates went up but had not arms sufficient to pursue them. They could only convey the manager away from his bad quarters naked.

'I happened to be in Roseau as well as the next neighbour Curry and on Sunday an express was sent for me to dress his wounds. The Sunday morning would have been a most proper and fit time to have pursued them, as they must have been greatly fatigued and very sick from their debauch. But through stupidity and inactivity it was omitted. In about ten or twelve days thereafter a party of six, armed, came past my dwellings in the night time. I don't apprehend they came with an intention to attack me particularly but to reconnoitre and endeavour to gain intelligence, if any people had been sent out after them.

'A party of the coloured people with some French deserters were ordered into the woods after the runaways but they mutinied and deserted before they got far into the woods, the expedition of course ended and nothing further has been yet done. I sleep armed every night as well as everyone in Layou valley. I am given to understand that our legislature are proposing to put martial law in force and to send out the militia with some of the King's troops after the runaways. If so, we shall have very hard duty, for my part, although I hate walking and climbing, I shall have no objection. Especially if we can get good guides to carry us to these rascal camps, and I daresay there will be a little blood spilt as they are well supplied with powder and ball. In their marches it is surprising with what caution and prudence they proceed, as much so as ever Washington did.'[35]

Within days of the attack on Cassada Garden Estate, a large group of Maroons attacked F. Vidal's Estate at Macoucherie. The planters at that time were on heightened alert and succeeded in capturing six Maroons. Five were banished and one condemned to hang, but pardoned on promising to guide a party into the camp of Pharcelle, of which he has been a soldier. A detachment equipped under the 27 March Act went on the expedition. The guide, true to his word, led them to Pharcelle's camp. A fire fight ensued, and under the cover of darkness the Maroons made good their escape. 'They suffered no losses, but killed the guide and another of the party, and wounding several, who, with the rest returned dispirited to Roseau.'[36]

In revenge, Pharcelle led an attack against the estate of Mr. Vidal's plantation on 18 August 1784, burnt all his negro huts and outhouses, and rifled his dwelling house. The Vidal family just narrowly escaped death as repeated vollies were discharged at them. The Maroons carried off a large sum of money, everything moveable, and destroyed all they could not use or take away. In frustration, Vidal abandoned his estate and would never return.

The Maroon raids would continue unabated. Just a few weeks later, on 5 September 1785, a large party of the Maroons, again led by Pharcelle descended on Coolete's estate at Mount George. They immediately opened fire on the negroes working on the estate, killing several. The Maroons then proceeded to kill a great number of horned cattle, which they were forced to leave behind. As they left, they set fire to the negro huts, damaging every other thing of value that they could lay hold of. More and increasingly violent attacks would follow.

On 12 October 1785, between the hours of eight and nine that night, a party of Maroons, numbering up to 100, came down on the estate of Thomas Haddock Esq., at Tarreau. After plundering the stores of a quantity of liquor and provisions, they burned the dwelling and still houses, together with all the negro houses, except three or four. At the same time, some of the blacks belonging to another planter John Grey Esq., who had been on Tarreau estate, were pursued by the Maroons. They fired several discharges, wounded one of Mr. Grey's negroes and threatened to burn the estate. Two of Haddock's negroes were also wounded and one of them later died.

Other newspaper reports at the time indicated that the Maroons were heard to propose setting fire to the estate, which they could have done at the moment without any difficulty, but one of them said "no we have done enough this night, it is late this is a grand estate, and we will come another time and spend a night upon it." They then went to the Layou river and called out that the French settlers should not fear them, as their vengeance were directed solely against the English, whom they wished to extirpate from the country. They then returned to

Tarreau joined their companions and marched off with their booty.[37]

On 24 November, a group of around 60 Maroons attacked the estate of Langston and Dixon's at Mahaut, burnt all the negro houses, fired the dwellings, and attempted to kill Johnson Henderson, who with the manager defended it. In the process, he was severely wounded, but luckily escaped. The Maroons then spared the life of the manager. 'To the manager they gave his life saying he was a French man and that it was only against the English dogs that they directed their vengeance. They then carried off a great deal of stock, many firearms, ammunition, and sixty complete suits of negro clothing.

'While this was taking place on the estate, they sent parties to the mouth of the Layou river to prevent aid that might be sent from there, and at the same time to assure a certain French planter on the Northern point of that river that he might be at ease, they would not hurt a hair on his head. Following this attack, an alarm was given at Mr. Vance's estate at Layou, but the vigilance of the watchmen and sounding the conches from one estate to the other down the valley, put the whole quarter on their guard. The raid was aborted, at least for the time being.'[38]

The increasingly bold raids on the British owned estates drew the ire of the white planters who appeared unable to do much about it. The Maroon assaults were so effective that one English observer lamented, 'driven to the greatest distress and in dread of being destroyed by these cruel wretches, the English planters were constrained to abandon their estates and to retire with their families to Roseau.'[39] The worse criticism was however retained for the Governor and his seeming inability to bring the raids to an end, or for that matter capture the Maroon leaders. The frustration of the planters was captured in the following letter.

'The Maroon negroes of this island who during the French government were armed, disciplined and put under the command of several chiefs of their own lawless banditti by the Marquis du Chilleau [Duchilleau] as a scourge over the unfortunate capitulants of this devoted colony, has since the restoration of the British flag, through the influence of a party cabal and in direct opposition to repeated recommendations of our Chief Governor being suffered so to increase in numbers, arms, discipline and confidence that they have lately perpetuated the most unparalleled acts of cruelty and devastation in every quarter. The defiant settlements having no hope of security or safety, when those almost under the guns of Morne Bruce have been subjected and actually suffered desolation and ruin.

'It fills the soul with horror, cannot fail to excite, in the minds of the sufferers, a deep resentment against those who delayed the passing our Militia Bill and who by inefficacious temporizing acts have hitherto restrained the hands of government from effectually crushing them. From the commencement of his government and during these alarms our Chief Governor was increasing in his recommendation of a Militia Bill and for passing proper acts for the suppression of the runaways. Nevertheless, it was not until the 15th of March 1785 that the Militia Act passed. The colony was destitute of arms and accoutrements for them, and although they were as deficient of ammunition, they refused for some time thereafter a Powder Act which would have supplied them.

'They passed however some acts empowering the governor with advice of his Council to send out certain free people of colour, to arm them and to supply them with pay and provisions during their excursions but these powers could not be exerted for want of arms, ammunition and proper leaders. All these acts were revised some were amended but all inefficacious and objected to (though not navigated by the Governor and Council), as they were evidently unequal to the end proposed and whenever attempted to be carried into execution, proved instead of suppressing the means of giving numbers, and confidence to the enemy.' [40]

One of the acts referred to was passed on 23 November 1785, and was '*an act to suppress runaways by obliging proprietors of slaves to furnish, a proportion of their slaves, to be sent into the woods. To provide officers by engaging white and free people, and granting encouragement to apprehend and destroy runaway slaves; and to empower magistrates to search and examine vessels, suspected of holding correspondence with them.*'[41] Governor John Orde argued that the acts were necessary to protect property, silence the opposition, and to minimize the danger, which threatened every individual in the colony.

Further, the laws would 'enforce a conviction of the necessity of taking the most decided measures against the Maroons.' In just two weeks after legislation to form the militia was enacted, armaments were sent to the various camps, and seven days later, all stations were considered completely secured, fortified, and hutted with provisions and ammunitions for two months. The militias were given strict orders to act either conjointly or separately in order to force the enemy from their stronghold.

'The parties formed and patrolling on the different coasts must prevent their retreat at the several estates in every quarter associated, armed and vigilant, will prevent surprise and at the same time pick up the dispersed stragglers. Every possibility of their getting supplies is cut off by the other prudent arrangements, which have been taken and there is every reasonable ground to hope, a few weeks will put an end, to one of the greatest evils that every cursed an unfortunate colony.'[42]

Notwithstanding the formation of the militia and the various acts to restrict the activities of the Maroons, the open rebellion and attacks on the plantations continued unabated. The indignation and fury among the white inhabitants would continue to build as the spate of attacks progressed. Many continued to lament the lack of more stringent 'measures for the reduction of these daring villains and exemplary punishment of some of them, have not been prosecuted with more vigour and expedition as a timely exertion would have prevented several of their late atrocious acts.'[43] In November, additional arms and ammunition was shipped from Antigua to the Rangers. The successful Maroon raids on the West coast under the guile and leadership skills of Pharcelle,[44] would be a prelude for what was to come on the South East coast, at the end of the first week in December 1785.

5

Balla and the Royal Rangers

Balla was among the earliest blacks to arrive from Africa, after the British began importing slaves into Dominica in 1763. He was born in Guinea, and like the two Princes of Calabar, he too was born to a ruling family. According to *The Public Advertiser*, 'the chief of the runaway negroes is named Balla, a native of Guinea, and a Prince in his own country, who was brought to this island twenty years ago, and immediately on being landed made his escape, and could never afterwards be caught.' [1] Indeed, Balla successfully eluded the authorities for over twenty years, while he built up a large and committed group of followers. 'He has been exceedingly zealous and active in seducing his brethren to join him, and assert their liberty,'[2] the paper concluded. Such was Balla's influence that he would rise to become the Chief of the Maroon chiefs, and was often referred to as their general. Sometime in 1768, Balla would be joined by Jacko, who would eventually succeed him as the supreme Chief upon his death.[3]

By December of 1785 and with the Maroon war in full swing, there were eight major Maroon camps in Dominica that were known to Governor John Orde and his rangers. In the heights between Colihaut and Morne Diablotins, one headed by Pharcelle; in the heights of Castle Bruce another headed by Grubois; between Layou and Rosalie one headed by Balla and Congoree; and in Grand Bay one that was headed by Pangloss. In addition, the rangers determined that there were at least four additional camps around Grand Bay.

An unknown colonist writing to a friend in the United States in a letter later reprinted in *The Pennsylvania Packet* newspaper was moved to remark that: 'these runaways have been particularly fortunate in their choice of station. Nature has so broken and crumbled the island that there are more than a hundred places almost inaccessible to any but themselves. To add to their calamity, it is a melancholy truth that there are in the island, a set of wretches who supply the banditti with ammunition and provisions, and which there is every reason to believe are conveyed to them by their good neighbours the French.'[4]

The Rosalie estate, located some eighteen miles across thick mountain ranges from Roseau the capital city, was particularly vulnerable to attack. Owned in part by Lieutenant Governor Stuart, the owners spared no efforts in building up the estate defences. By December 1785, there were a total of 180 slaves, who were considered to be faithful negroes, with five white men at their head, along with 36 stands of arms, a double fortified four pounder, and two swivels and stone works with plenty of ammunition. Also, on the property were several muskets, which provided an air of invincibility to the white plantation owners.[5]

Weeks before the attack on the Rosalie estate, there was an air of foreboding among the owners, made worse by the growing string of attacks throughout the islands. To begin with, the threat to the estate was well known. Some of the faithful negro slaves had secretly informed the manager that an attack was eminent. Just three days before the actual attack on 6 December 1785 a runaway negro was captured by the 'Rosalie Negroes' and immediately taken to Roseau to stand trial. He had been sent by Balla on a mission to gain additional information about the layout of the estate for a planned attack. Convinced that the captured Maroon would be forced to reveal details of the plan, before being put to death, Balla immediately hastened its execution. He would eventually be joined by Jacko, Congoree and other Maroons before descending on the Rosalie estate

The day of 6 December 1785, started like most other days before it on the Rosalie estate. The field slaves awoke at the crack of dawn and made their way to the fields of sugarcane. On that particular day the focus would be on the clearing of the sugarcane fields. Two days later, news of the historic sacking and destruction of the Rosalie estate, headed by the feared Maroon leader Balla, and his faithful deputy Congoree (Congo Ray) and his son, would spread across the island, and ultimately be exposed to the British public.

This particular event elicited a great deal of fear and dread in the hearts of the white planters, and a vow of revenge and retribution from Governor John Orde and his Deputy Stuart. The event was retold in harrowing detail by the house slave Catharine, and Mr. Dunche, one of the five white men lucky enough to escape with his life from the carnage. Their account of the actual attack was reprinted in several newspapers including *The Independent Gazetteer* of 4 March 1786 in Pennsylvania, United States of America; an account of which is given below.

'At about seven in the evening near grass throwing, the negroes not having come from the field, Mr. Gamble, the Manager, who had been bottling off a cask of Madeira sent Catharine to the kitchen to light a candle; that on her way she received a shot in her arm, on which she ran back to the manager's house (a turret detached from the dwelling house), crying out that she was wounded by the runaways. Mr Gamble immediately ran out upon the steps before his door, and called out to the negros at the works to come up: that in this act, he received a shot in his left breast. It appears to be at this stage of the melancholy business that Mr. Dunche made his escape, as he was unacquainted with the entrance of Augustine the driver, and other circumstances in the early part of this unfortunate affair.

'This faithful slave hearing Mr. Gamble call for assistance forced his way through the runaways, into the house, as did also a negro named Robert, the property of Mr. Gamble – but the latter was killed in the attempt. It appears that Mr. Gamble on finding himself wounded, snatched up a musket, with which he brought down one of the runaways, as did Augustine the son of the chief Congoree (Congo Ray], with another. Mr. Gamble then took a second piece [firearm] with which he killed another of the runaways. At this time three white men who were employed on the estate, forced their way into the house, and finding no more ammunition they attempted by slashing some of the priming of the swivels, which were in the house, in the pans of their muskets, to discharge them but in vain.

'Mr. Gamble then sent a Negro who was in the house to the kitchen for a brand of fire, with a promise of a considerable reward, if he brought it. But he had scarce left the house, before a shower of balls flew about him, which obliged him to flee, and it was with difficulty that he escaped the pursuit. He hid himself in the bushes, and was unable to return. The three white men who had last joined Mr. Gamble, now thought only of their own preservation, and attempted to escape by the windows. Mr. Armstrong a carpenter who first leaped out was shot and fell, on which one of the runaways ran a bayonet up through his throat, which pierced the upper part of his skull. Mr. Harton, an overseer, received a shot on leaping out and was pierced through the skull. And Mr. Leslie another overseer was shot as he was standing at the window, preparing to leap out.

The faithful Augustine now proposed to Mr. Gamble who knew to himself that he was approaching towards his last moments to suffer him to remove him to a place where he might breathe his last in peace, and his corpse not be subjected to the barbarity and indecent insult of these barbarians. But he replied that since it was to be his fate to die by dogs, he would face death on the spot. This worthy black then intimated an intention of endeavouring to seek his own safety by flight, at which Mr. Gamble now almost spent and faint said: "Augustine, will you leave me?" to which this faithful servant replied with a true greatness of soul, worthy of one in a higher sphere: "No master we will die together."

'This was alas their fate for at this moment the murderers rushed in and shot him. Mr. Gamble reeled to his bed and fell down on it, on which the savage leader Congoree with a leer of brutal satisfaction said: "That is what I wanted you are now in your grave – now my boys set fire." This, after plundering the house, they performed. Humanity revolts at the shocking sequence. After having given to their savage thirst of blood full scope they spread a long table in the dwelling house which they covered with the plate and cutlery of the honourable Lieutenant Governor Stuart and having killed all the stock they could find, they, whilst their drums were beating, and guns firing gave themselves up to every excess of riot and inebriety.

'Chief Balla had dressed himself in a uniform coat, with gold epaulets, which they had found among their plunder. But previous to this, Congoree, with a party had gone down to the bay, and began to spread fire and desolation around him. There they again found Catharine, in a house with her mother, and both her sisters whom they fired at --- and again wounded; they also wounded her mother and two sisters. Congoree then exultingly displaying a lock of hair said: "See here your manager's hair, go look at him now, how he looks. Your father killed my son but him myself dispatched." They then set fire to the store next to the crane and continued doing the same to all the other buildings, till the whole, except the dwelling house, or two or three of small importance were entirely consumed.

'They continued in riot and plunder until ten o'clock the next day when they departed, leaving an estate in point of buildings, one of the first in the islands, a heap of ruins. Mr. Gamble was a young man of an amiable disposition, universally regretted and his unhappy fate is by all lamented. Mr. Armstrong's body was found at some distance, to which he ran before he fell. They had heaped trash on him and endeavoured to consume it with fire and the mangled remains exhibited a shocking spectacle. Unfortunately, among other valuable articles of plunder a number of muskets and a considerable quantity of ammunition, fell into the hands of these miscreants. They were all completely armed with firearms and their number by all accounts was about 200. By the time the carnage was over, four of the five white men were killed, several of the loyal negroes were killed and wounded, and an unknown number opted to join Balla and his group in their mountainous hideout.

It is to be noted that only 50 slaves of the original 180 returned to the Rosalie estate.' [6]

Other eyewitness accounts reported in various news outlets at the time indicated that in addition to Augustine and another faithful slave killed that day, several negro children in the house with Gamble, also suffered a similar fate. On the side of the Maroons they suffered the loss of three dead including the son of Congoree. In addition, only the mill and the governor's house were saved from the fire. 'They also killed all the poultry they could find, and the total cost of the devastation was put at well in excess of ten thousand pounds.'[7]

A London newspaper, *The Public Advertiser,* in reflecting on the pain and humiliation, which was felt across the island, by the whites, following the attack noted: 'the dreadful catastrophe of Rosalie closes this shocking narrative. It is too faithfully and minutely related, in the public papers enclosed, to make it necessary for me to be distressed by repeating it…' The paper faulted the owners and managers for: 'leaving the canon criminally as fatally left an hour after sundown, without a single watchman on duty, without a rendezvous established in case of an attack, without a negro taught the use of a musket, or one who knew where to go for arms.' It continued: 'only nine muskets were loaded and two hundred ball cartridges, lodged in one place, and the firearms dispersed in many others unknown and unapproachable during the attack.

'No more than about 50 of the negroes are returned out of 180; where the rest are disposed, wounded, starving and perhaps dying; we know not. Many perhaps are carried off by the runaways laden with the plunder from Rosalie and such is the terror, which those here labour under, which they cannot for some time be prevailed on to return. Nor is it to be wondered at, while men are not to be found, for managers willing to risk their lives whilst those savages are in force—in a word whilst promising at least 200 hogheads of sugar are fit for the mill. The want of negroes, managers, works and stores will make it impossible to take it off and so expensive will be the repairs necessary to put the estate in order that I fear that I am but too well sounded in saying that those wretches have in one night destroyed a property that cost near 100 000 pounds sterling and brought ruin on all concerned with it.'[8]

Another newspaper, *The Freemans Journal or the North American Intelligencer* was somewhat more sympathetic to the plight of the Maroons, noting: 'however shocked we must feel at the recital of the enormities perpetuated by the Negroes in Dominica on the unfortunate settlers there, candor and impartiality must confess, that the severities and cruelties exercised by many white people on those creatures, are of equal weight, in the scale of reason and common sense. Ferocious, easily inflamed with passions, among which, perhaps, the most predominant and characteristic is revenge.

'It cannot excite much surprise that a repetition of such treatment should drive those ill-fated beings to madness. The declaration of one of the Chiefs, Congoree that the manager of the Rosalie estate had killed his son, and that he had dispatched him for it, is a convincing proof that a spirit of retaliation actuates them. The discrimination they make between the French and the English clearly shews that their steps are not marked by wanton undistinguishing fury, but that revenge for oppression is their grand stimulus.'[9]

A similar sentiment was expressed by a writer in *The Pennsylvania Packet*, where it was observed: 'the oppressions that the unhappy negroes endure in Dominica and the other islands, have occasioned their late excesses, and prove the absolute impropriety of tyrannising over that description of people....without trampling in such a cruel manner as is practiced upon every principal of equity and human tenderness, which, if not adopted, scenes of the most dreadful and shocking nature, will possibly, at some time or the other, be the consequences of their exertions for freedom, unless, a period shall arrive, when they will be placed on a footing of the other inhabitants of the world.'[10]

A report appearing in *The Pennsylvania Packet* in February 1786, demonstrated the extent to which the Maroons were feared. 'The depredations committed by the Negroes who reside in the mountains in the island of Dominica have been carried so far as to oblige the inhabitants to send to Martinique for soldiers, arms, ammunition. The negroes exercised the law of retaliation on many of their old masters, murdering and captivating many, and carrying off everything they could find.'[11]

Not surprisingly, the growing spate of attacks and in particular the destruction and havoc wreaked on the Rosalie estate did not go unnoticed, striking fear and consternation in the hearts of many within the colony. A letter written by an unknown resident on the day news of the Rosalie attack reached Roseau, and which appeared in a Scottish Newspaper *The Edinburgh Advertiser* a few weeks later echoed this sentiment, reading in part: 'The runaway negroes accounting for between four and five hundred are committing most dreadful depredations on the estates in the interior parts of the island; killing white people and negroes, burning and plundering houses, and destroying everything that come in their way. This evil is a legacy left the island by the French, who supplied these miscreants with arms and gave them every encouragement in their power. They have taken different positions in the country, have formed separate encampments, and elected chiefs and from thence send down small parties who have attacked the estates, drove away cattle, and done every mischief in their power.'[12]

Such was the dread and dismay created by the attack on the Rosalie estate that many white settlers seriously considered leaving the island altogether. In fact, at the time scores opted to board boats anchored in the Port of Roseau to make good their escape, while others retired to the forts.[13] They were further spooked by rumours that Balla and his group were marching on Roseau in the hope of exacting more revenge.[14] Notwithstanding that the 30th regiment and the local rangers were in swift pursuit of Balla, and had successfully paraded the heads of two of his men around Roseau, it would take several more weeks before the fears of the white settlers would be quelled.

By December 1785 when Balla successfully raided the Rosalie estate, there were no less than three hundred and forty eight well-armed Rangers, including whites, creoles and negroes actively seeking to exterminate the Maroons.[15] The white rangers were part of the 6 000 British loyalists who left for the British West Indies following the American war of independence. Many of the loyalists went to Jamaica and Barbados, but some made their way to Dominica. Earlier, in March 1784, members of the 30th regiment had arrived in Dominica from Jamaica.

In addition, some of the whites joining the rangers belonged to a number of 'distressed loyalists' who had arrived in Dominica in March of 1785 from East Florida. Governor John Orde had subsequently granted them a supply of provisions for their subsistence and some lands to settle on. The loyalists were also furnished with tools and materials for the building of houses on the land granted to them to an amount of 1 650 pounds. The Governor also advised that they focus on the planting of coffee and provisions.[16]

The Pennsylvania Packet commented on the change that the rangers could expect in the manner in which fighting was conducted in Dominica, noting that: 'the mode of action will be changed with them from bush fighting or a fair chance to curvetting and dodging among the pendulous rocks, where they may shoot a man across a ravine and it will cost them two hours to get at the body.'[17]

At the beginning of January 1786 the 348 strong ranger corps in Dominica were separated into three legions with the First Legion or Green Rangers located at the head of the Layou River in the centre of the Island and comprised of 102 men. The Second Legion or Northern Blue Rangers operated at the head of the Battiboo River on the abandoned lands of Nibber and Fallin [in Colihaut] and comprised 97 men. There was also the Third Legion or the Southern Blue Rangers comprised of 108 men and encamped to the West of Grand Soufriere. In addition, there were detachments of the 30th West India Regiment [Black and Creoles], with 16 and 14 men stationed at Point Jacko and Castle Bruce respectively. Finally, there was a detachment of 11 irregulars in the area of the track leading from Grand Fond to Laudat, known as the Chemin L'Etang.

More specifically, the First Legion was comprised of 85 men in camp as follows: 1 captain, (John Marshall); 2 lieutenants (John Egan 2nd in command and Mr. Peyton 3rd in Command Royal artillery); 1 surgeon (Dr. Ried); 1 sergeant, 1 corporal and 12 privates of the 30th West India Regiment; and 1 bombardier Royal Artillery, as ordinance store keeper. There were 5 acting sergeants, 5 acting corporals 1 volunteer guide all free people of colour and all completely armed and clothed; plus 5 negro guides and 50 black rangers armed and clothed. In addition to those remaining at the camp there were a corps of 17 reserves used mainly to escort provision, expresses etc., comprised as follows: 1 corporal and 4 privates of the 30th regiment; and 1 sergeant, 1 corporal, and 10 privates of the free people of colour armed and clothed.

The 84 men at the camp of the Second Legion were comprised as follows: 1 captain (Garett); 2 Lieutenants (Moore, 2nd in command and Todlumler, 3rd in command Royal artillery); 1 surgeon (Dr. Gayner); 1 sergeant, 1 corporal and 12 privates of the 30th Regiment; 1 bombardier Royal artillery, as ordinance store keeper; 5 acting sergeants, 5 acting corporals of the free people of colour, all completely armed and clothed; 5 negro guides; and 50 black rangers armed and clothed. In addition, there were a corps of 13 reserves to escort provision, expresses etc. comprised of 1 sergeant, 10 privates of the free people of colour; and two volunteers William Younger Esq. and William Dacody.

The 79 men of the Third Legion encamped West of Grand Soufriere comprised: 1 Captain (William Young Esq.); 2 lieutenants (Samuel Gray, second in command, and Mr. Kemp third in command); 1 surgeon (Dr Spencer); 1 sergeant, 1 corporal, and 12 privates of the 30th regiment; 1 bombardier Royal artillery, as ordinance store keeper; 5 acting sergeants, 5 acting corporals, whites and free people of colour, all completely armed and clothed; and 50 black rangers armed and clothed. There were also 1 sergeant, 1 corporal, and 6 privates from the 30th regiment. Serving as reserves to escort provision were 24 men comprised of: 1 sergeant, 15 privates, whites and free people of colour, 5 negroes to serve as guides.

In addition to the three major ranger camps, there were specific detachments of the 30th Regiment strategically place around the island. In order to prevent supplies from Marie Gallant and Guadeloupe and to assist the estates in that neighbourhood, 16 men were stationed at Point Jacko under the command of 1 lieutenant (Thomas Amkettle); along with 1 surgeon (Dr Little); and 1 sergeant, 1 corporal, and 12 privates. Fourteen men were stationed in Castle Bruce and Richmond comprised of 1 sergeant, 1 corporal, and 12 privates.

Finally, there was a detachment of irregulars in the St David Parish comprised of: 1 commandant (John Falvez); and 1 sergeant, 1 corporal, and 8 privates. The two last detachments were expected to protect the estates within their reach by patrolling on the outskirts and watching Grubois' camp in the mountains above Castle Bruce.[18] With the detachment keeping a watchful eye on sea traffic to the French islands in the North, His Majesty's Brig called the *Falcon* cruised on the South East Quarter to prevent supplies from the two French islands to the South, Martinique and St Lucia.

The encampments of the legions were set up at equal distances from each other from the southern to the northern extremities of the island. Frequent patrols were sent from camp to camp, to keep up a constant communication with each other and for the purpose of cutting off all supplies from the Maroons. Governor John Orde also greatly increased the rewards offered to those who would kill the Maroons. For every chief taken or killed £50 was offered, and for a male slave taken or killed £33 was the reward. Also, per day the commander of a camp received £1 and 13s; a surgeon £1, 4s and 9p, second in command 16s and 6p; sergeant 12s and 41/3p; corporal 8s, and 3p; private 6s; and negros 3s. They were also all provided with provisions and clothing.

Governor John Orde's attempt to exterminate the Maroons would prove to be an extremely costly exercise, forcing him to drastically introduce new taxes, including on slaves. He was convinced that the military arrangement put in place would 'pretty well secure the island against the future depredations of the Maroons, but it will be accompanied with an almost intolerable expense.' [19] More troubling was the fact that 'an eighth of the best negroes in the island are employed as watchmen and guards, plantation work is lessened one half, which will not only lessen this year's crop but prevent planting for the next. The Caribs in St Vincent were not one-tenth of a threat like the runaways yet it cost the government two millions to suppress them.'[20]

No sooner had news of Balla's attack at Rosalie reached the camps that the Legions launched a series of assaults against the Maroon hideaways hoping to deal a decisive blow to them, and more importantly, exterminate their leaders. It would however take almost three months of near daily searches before members of the 30th Regiment and the Legions were able to finally register success in their capture of the feared Maroon chief Balla.

The same day of the Rosalie attack on 6 December 1785, and with those lucky enough to escape the carnage relaying the harrowing details, the detachment of the 30th regiment encamped at Castle Bruce sprang into action. At the same time, Captain Marshal, who commanded the First Legion encamped at the head of the Layou river, made a bold attempt to intercept Balla and his followers as they retreated from Rosalie. This was just the beginning of the hunt.

On 9 December Captain Marshall wrote to Governor John Orde to demonstrate that he was taking decided and immediate action to hunt down and kill Balla. The letter was transmitted by express to Roseau, through one of the 17 members of the corps reserved explicitly for this purpose, and read in part: 'Sir, Yesterday I moved with what could be spared from the camp, to intercept Balla in his return from Rosalie, on our march through his old camp ground, Charles, the negro your excellency sent me, being advanced in our front some distance, perceived two sentries posted there, and he from that was sure, Balla was then in his camp, we immediately marched for it.

'After very hard labour we came to a mountain near 400 feet high, which we ascended by the assistance of the vines and descended in like manner, we immediately got sight of the camp, and saw some few take to the woods. We fired several shots and a few were returned: we set fire to the camp and found a small boy of three years old, a woman was also shot, many different articles were found, such as a new militia jacket, a new coverlid, and some blue jackets, and many small things, 4 fire locks were taken and six destroyed, a few pounds of powder we got.' [21]

Later Captain John Marshall would be joined by a contingent from the Northern rangers as they scoured the forest in search of Balla, Congoree and the over three hundred Maroons, comprising men, women and children, who were with them. Balla and his followers, however, appeared to have been swallowed up into the vast Dominican forest, and in the process, taking his pursuers almost two weeks before accessing his camp. By the time the rangers arrived, Balla and his followers had vanished and were nowhere to be seen.

The second account of any kind of success by the militia in catching a glimpse of the Maroons responsible for the devastating attack at Rosalie, appeared in a local Dominica newspaper, which was later reprinted in *The Independent Gazetteer* of Philadelphia. In the letter, written by Captain John Marshall, he recounts meeting an almost deserted camp and killing and beheading two runaways, and capturing one more, whom he hoped would lead him to Balla. The letter is addressed to Governor John Orde, and reads; '*Balla's Camp, Friday December 23, 1785.*

'Sir, after refreshing the detachment of the 30th Regiment your Excellency sent me, I moved out with them and a detachment of the Legion, at 9 o'clock yesterday morning, our disposition being made to surround the camp and to cut off every retreat. But in getting out of the wood into the clear ground, we found the whole encampment had moved. Captain Garrett with one Lieutenant and twenty-six North rangers joined me this morning at nine o'clock. I had just sent out a detachment to find a track the run-aways had taken. They were absent about half an hour or better, when we heard the discharge of three or four guns. The guide of the above detachment returned with an account that they had fallen in with a guard of the runaways, had shot two and taken one.

'We immediately moved out and at our arrival at the spot where they were posted, I examined the prisoner and find by his intelligence, Balla, Congoree, Jacko, Mabrie, Colligrie and Jack are the Chiefs, who command about a hundred men; of whom Balla is the General; that they had taken post at Terre Firme, at a distance of about six hours march. As the provisions were insufficient to supply the detachment, it was thought advisable to return to this encampment for the afternoon and send for a fresh supply to Olive Hill, which will be received tomorrow, we shall then move to beat up Balla's encampment at Terre Firme. The prisoner Gabriel is the property of Mr. Vance, and one head whose name was Stephen, was the same property who had been six years absent.

The other head was Augustine, the property of Mr. Loraine, who had also been six years absent. I send the two heads to the magistrate at Layou, by this escort to be forwarded to Roseau. The prisoner Gabriel promises to conduct me into Balla's encampment. After he has done that, I shall send him to your Excellency. He is much burnt being in one of the huts that blew up when we set this encampment on fire. Should your Excellency think proper to order any execution of him in the field, I shall wait your commands. I have the honour of being, Your Excellency's Humble Servant, JOHN MARSHALL, Commanding the Centre Legion of Rangers.

'P.S…The fate of Charles is known; on coming down the hill, we found him shot in several places, and from the report of the prisoner Gabriel, we find he had been executed by Balla. They are very much distressed for want of provisions. This party of the guard hut has not had anything for four days. They sent a man to Balla's camp this morning for provisions and he is expected back this evening. The mode of executing sentence of death when produced by Balla, as it is curious, we shall give some account of it: it is simply thus….the victim is fixed at a convenient distance, by way of a target, at which each man in the encampment tries his hand in order to improve himself as a good shot. This was inflicted on Charles, and his body exhibited the appearance of a mere honeycomb.' [22]

One week later, Captain John Marshall wrote a second letter to Governor John Orde in which he laments the fact that he was unable to make much progress since the prisoner Gabriel seemed unwilling or unable to take him to Balla's camp. A copy of that second letter was partially reprinted in *The Pennsylvania Packet* a few months later, under the heading: *'Extract of a letter from Captain Marshall to the Governor John Orde , Castle Bruce 30th December 1785.'*

'Sir, agreeable to my last letter to your Excellency, I marched for Harris plantation on Tuesday morning where I remained all night and next day set out for that camp of Balla's, where the prisoner Gabriel had left him. Captain's Garret legion led the front, the detachment of the 30th regiment led by me in the centre, and the green legion in the rear. In this order we marched until 8 o'clock when the advanced guard observed six runaway some distance to their front of which Captain Garret gave me immediate information.

'I ordered him to push on with Lieutenant Egan and a party of the free legion, as fast as he could, and if possible, to take them before they could alarm their camp. He soon after, saw seven more loaded with provisions, who were so closely pursued that they threw down their load and cutlasses. The prisoner informed Captain Garret that he was near the encampment that he had left them in.

'He immediately ordered a party to secure a pass on their left, while he pursued on the right. I marched up the main path with a detachment of the 30th regiment and the green legion. Captain Garret very soon entered the encampment, which he found abandoned. Being very much disappointed, I sent for Gabriel, and told him, that if he did not give me every information in his power, I would immediately put him to death. He said that at a good distance up the hill, there was formerly an old encampment, and where he supposed, as it was very difficult to get at, having one pass into it they would be found.

'We immediately marched for it and when the party got some distance up the hill the sentinel was seen. From the situation of my post it was not in my power to surround them. I therefore ordered captain Garett to immediately take the hill and force into the camp, which he and his party, notwithstanding being exposed to all their fire and having a path where only one man could march in front with great bravery got into (under cover of a fire which I had previously concerted against the party, where the enemy might be expected to oppose them), without any party being wounded, although obliged to hand up their muskets as they gained the top.

'On entering it he found a young girl, between two and three years old, the rest all got away by scrambling higher and getting to the skirts of the mountain Diablotin. Captain Garett pursued a mile and killed one man, the head of which, and the child I brought to the honourable general Bruce's, to be forwarded to Roseau. Meeting with precipices' impracticable to get down, the party returned. So soon as we got into the post, I ordered out scouting parties, and patrols during the night, the rest of the party remaining in the camp.

'Early in the morning I sent fresh scouting parties and patrols who returned about ten o'clock, without being able to see any of them, and the next day was obliged to give the party only half allowance owing to the impossibility of carrying a sufficiency with the carriers for so large a party, for any length of time. I therefore ordered fire to be put to their camps, first securing about fifty or sixty pounds of very fine glazed powder, about nearly the same weight of ball, slugs and shots, about a dozen and a half of bill books and some axes.

'We broke about a dozen of iron pots, not being able to carry them with us. We also found three militia regimentals, and two other coats, with some negro clothing, and shorts belonging to Rosalie. They had thirty-five huts, which seemed calculable to hold four men each. There were no provisions and from all the information that I can collect, they exist only on what is brought in by their scouts. After I had seen all the huts burnt, having scarce any provisions, I desired captain Garret to march for general Bruce's estate while I followed with the detachment of the 30th centre legion and baggages.

'He arrived here last night and myself this morning; where we found all our wants immediately relieved and the party all comfortably lodged with plenty of provisions (great part dressed) for our reception. We are all under very great obligations to the general for his very particular attention in person to every individual of the party. As they are all very much fatigued, he has advised me to remain here tomorrow, and next day in order to refresh them. I shall then advise with him, what is best to be done to get at them again. The whole party are much in want of shoes. The general very kindly gave me and captain Garret a pair each: we had walked three miles with very bad ones till we met him. I have the honour of being, Your Excellency's Humble Servant, JOHN MARSHALL, Commanding the Centre Legion of Rangers.' [23]

With 1785 drawing to a close, the rangers were no closer to finding Balla. They however were determined to find him at all costs, and would spare no efforts in so doing. As days turned into weeks, their daily patrols in search of Balla proved increasingly futile. It would not be until 21 January 1786 that members of the 30th regiment would set eyes on Balla, and that with the help of a former runaway by the name of Frank. He was determined to cash in on the hefty reward being offered to anyone succeeding to capture the most feared of the Maroon leaders. Much of the details of the events of that day is contained in an express from Rosalie to Governor John Orde. The letter was written on 22 January 1786, by Mr. Colin, who since the events on 6 December 1785 had taken over as manager of the Rosalie estate.

The express arrived in Roseau on 25 January and provide the following details, which were later reproduced in *The Pennsylvania Packet*: 'On 21 January John Richardson commanded a small party, which left Rosalie in search of Balla's camp. It was made up of four whites, three of whom came from the 30th Regiment, and seven negroes, including Frank, the former runaway slave who would act as their guide. After leaving Rosalie, Richardson immediately divided the group into single file and tried his best to separate the blacks from each other to prevent the negroes from speaking to each other, and making any noise.

'They headed towards Grand Fond, above which Balla's brand new camp was presumably situated. After several hours, they came upon a watch house with a fire going. Continuing their march, they suddenly heard the cry of children, at which point Richardson immediately ordered the guide to the rear, and put him in care of a negro. They were within sight of Balla's camp.

'On examining the camp ground he found it very high and no passage to it but one, which was round a point cut in very high steps not more than four inches broad from the precipice; so that it was with great difficulty a man could pass with his musket. The upper step was at least three and a half feet high. He advanced and the party following close, he jumped upon the top and sat down upon a small bush (the only one there). He then beckoned to one of the Negroes to follow, but observing him to make a long face, he beckoned to him to send up one of the 30th (Farl) who immediately mounted, and sat down behind him; he then beckoned to the Negro again to mount, which he did. He then ordered him to fire upon the first negro he saw, which he soon had an opportunity of doing.

At the first sound of gunfire the camp erupted and its occupants began to scatter in every direction. Richardson claims that he got a glimpse of Balla as he hastily fled the scene. The entire party then mounted the pass towards the houses, even as they continued to fire. As they chased after Balla looking for an opportunity to fire upon him, Richardson claims that Balla dropped his hat. It was immediately picked up by Corporal Hammond, who put it on over his own. 'Suddenly, two shots rang out from the hill above the camp. Hammond received one in his left arm, and the other passed through the rim of both of the hats he had on.' The party was then instructed to scour the bushes in different places, where they suspected any of the Maroons may be hiding. At the sound of any rustling, they would immediately fire about five rounds, in the direction from which they heard a rustling. 'They saw only one negro with a blue and another with a red jacket.'

'The ammunition of our party being nearly expended, and the day far advanced, they could not attempt to pursue them any farther. Balla at first fled but in about half an hour he stood on a hill with a white shirt on and called out in French "*O you thieves, you come like thieves, that's not fair*." Richardson then said "Come in, boys, you have your pardon." [*To which he answered in terms of indecency and brutality, with which we cannot stain this paper*]. Richardson then called out "Captain Marshall to the left a little and you will have him." Balla set off instantly and about an hour afterwards he appeared on the other side of the hill and repeated as before: "*Oh you thieves, you come like thieves, that's not fair*."

Richardson then called out "Captain Garret, a little lower down;" on which he again made off. They are almost sure some of them must be killed, and wounded being so near, and so many good marksmen, and they might have fallen down the precipice. They pursued Balla so closely as to take his gun, powder horn, bag of balls his silver mounted ivory handled cutlass and all his OBEAH, which he was to perform, such wonders with and three dollars in the Obeah bag.

Balla's camp consisted of ten large houses, which was built to hold 10 persons each. With the light rapidly fading and low on ammunition, the whites surrounded the camp, and kept a look out in case Balla and his men reappeared. The blacks were then instructed to rummage through the houses, and turned everything out of doors. Their search revealed five children; two boys and three girls, whom they immediately seized.[24] Frank assured them that one of the boys was the son of Mabuyah[25], who was Balla's second in command. He had replaced Congoree, who had taken another large group of Maroons, further into the interior, closer to the Boeri lake.

The search complete, they immediately set fire to the ten large houses, which 'entirely consumed all their pots, calabashes, bills, hatchets, two muskets, and one axe. All the salt was destroyed, except only about two handfuls, which they must have been supplied with from some estate, as it was herring and beef salt.' Before setting the fire, they retrieved Gamble's [the murdered manager of Rosalie estate] regimental coat, a pistol and about four pounds of powder, four pounds of small shots and forty balls, which had been cut off cast nets, ten pounds of French soap, and six muskets (kept four). 'One of the guns taken is a fowling piece belonging to Governor Stuart, or the late Captain Clarke. They were short of flints as they were under the necessity of cutting some of the country stone for flints to their guns.

'Richardson says Corporal Hammond, Farl and Coil, of the 30th Regiment behaved most admirably, and none of the blacks were in the least backward; it was with difficulty some of our negro lads could be prevented killing the children, after they were taken. The runaway Frank, upon the whole behaved very well. He lost the path two or three times but with the assistance of a Rosalie negro, called Little Jem, was set right, by very narrowly observing the tracks.

'The Obeah apparatus has been brought into town. It consists of some human hair (a white's) bound up in a kind of scalp, with clotted blood, supposed of the unfortunate Gamble, a part of his buckle, and other heterogeneous materials known only to the savage fabricators and characteristic of their brutal disposition. This Obeah, he persuaded his followers was to procure him constant success, but as Mr Richardson and his party have battled the power of his incantations, it is to be hoped that Balla's fortune and influence are on the decline.'[26]

6

The Death of Balla

By early 1786, newspapers were awash with reports out of Dominica on the exploits of the Maroons. By that time news of the mayhem visited on the estates by them in late 1785 had steadily made their way to London and elsewhere. One such account in *The Edinburgh Advertiser* read: 'They have taken different positions in this mountainous strong country, have formed separate encampments, and elected chiefs; and from thence send out small parties, who have attacked the estates, drove away the cattle, and done every mischief in their power. The measures adopted for the suppression of these villains are as follows, viz – four parties of his Majesty's 30th regiment, about fifty of the island militia, and two hundred negroes completely armed, the whole equally divided, and three of the parties commanded each by an officer of the 30th regiment, and the other party by Mr Young formerly a Colonel in the Carolina militia.

'They are to form different encampments at equal distances from each other, and for the purpose of cutting off all supplies from the insurgents. And in case an opportunity should offer of striking a blow with success, the whole may be easily collected on one spot. The legislature has offered great rewards, to whoever kills any of those miscreants.'[1]

Meanwhile, there was growing disillusionment among the planter class in Dominica, particularly over the inability of the rangers to capture the Maroon leaders. Planters grumbled openly about the decided lack of success in blunting the Maroon attacks. This frustration was echoed by an unknown writer, from

Dominica, in a letter penned on 5 February 1786 and later reprinted in *The Times of London* in April 1786. He lamented the fact that on the same day Balla destroyed the Rosalie estate on 6 December 1785 that there were over 300 men in the woods engaged in the search for Maroons. 'Three strong parties went into the woods the 6th of December against the Maroons; the party to the Northward commanded by Mr. Garret, an officer of the 30th regiment, that from Layou commanded by Captain Marshall of the same regiment, and the party to the Southward by Colonel Young, a gentleman from North America. They went out as above mentioned on the 6th, and that night the Maroons destroyed Rosalie estate on which there were 180 slaves, and murdered four out of five white men, that were upon it the fifth having made his escape with great difficulty.'[2]

The frustration was clearly palpable with the letter continuing: 'those three parties consisted of 300 men (negroes), and from that force we had great hope of the reduction of the Maroons, but I'm sorry to say that we have been much disappointed, as there has not been above twenty of the Maroons killed, or taken prisoners, since these parties were sent out, and those were chiefly women and children. One of the Chief called Farcelle [Pharcelle], whose party is above 100, had proposed to surrender, but though the time for it has elapsed, it has not taken place.'[3]

In an issue of *The Times of London* just two days earlier, and quoting from an extract of a letter penned on [7 February 1786], another unknown writer, attempted to explain the reason why the rangers had failed so miserably in capturing the leaders, noting: 'very little has been done by the parties sent out against the Maroons, their movement have been conducted with too much caution, the gentlemen who commanded were not accustomed to traveling in our woods, were totally unacquainted with the country, and with the manners and disposition of the negroes under their command.'

The writer also expressed deep frustration with the rangers failure to get Pharcelle to surrender. 'We have been a week past in a state of suspense and great anxiety, by terms of a pardon having being settled with Farcelle alias Pharceillé, the Chief of a camp above Callipaut [Colihaut], for the surrender of that camp said to be above 100 in number. As this desirable event has not taken place, we are apprehensive there has been something wrong in conducting the business, and the more so, as the public has no great confidence in the present negotiators.'[4]

In that same month of February 1786, several newspapers were reporting on the fact that the rebellious negroes had resisted the most vigorous efforts to reduce them to obedience. 'That they had sheltered themselves in the inaccessible eminences of the island, from whence they were continually defending in predatory parties, and upon all occasions manifested the most inexorable cruelty, sparing neither sex nor age.'[5] To better survive the onslaught, the Maroons had adopted a new strategy that of breaking up into smaller groups of less than ten persons and remaining dispersed, while being constantly on the move. With their ability to mount major attacks against the plantations waning, however, some in Dominica were prepared to declare them vanquished and announce victory.

This was exemplified in several letters coming out of Dominica during February 1786. Two such extracts of letters dated 6 February 1786 appeared in *The Belfast Mercury or Freeman's Chronicle* in April. The first one read: 'After infinite hardships and fatigues through the most impracticable country in the world our legions have already brought the runaway war to a happy conclusion without the loss of a single life or limb by sickness or wounds. There are of the runaways many killed their heads exposed on the public roads and their bodies hanging on trees in the woods. Balla's party the most bloody and daring villains have been driven from various camps, many of them killed and taken their arms and ammunition in great quantities with clothing and all their other conveniences taken from them, carried or burnt; the remains are now starving and dispersed and every day some heads brought in. Pangloss in the South Quarter is killed with several of his party; many have been found after their several action crushed to death by their fall from precipices in their flight, the rest are also dispersed and starving.'[6]

Another extract read: 'after a variety of skirmishes with the runaway negroes and taking possession and burning their camps I am happy to inform you that the rebellion is now nearly quelled by the gallant and judicious behaviour of the 30th Regiment. We expect this day the surrender of Pharcelle a runaway negro chief with around 140 of his party and 20 of Balla's men who has been treating with his Excellency for a surrender on their being pardoned. About three weeks ago his majesty's sloop of war the *Unicorn* captured a French sloop from St Anne Grandterre on board of which were found a chest of muskets a quantity of powder ball and other articles which rendered her errand suspicious considering the situation of this island.'[7]

Notwithstanding the limited success at making inroads against the Maroons a triumphant entry in *The Times of London* around that same time boasted of the remarkable gains made by the rangers against them. '..After infinite hardships and fatigues, the rebellious negroes have been quelled in all quarters, without the loss of a single life on the part of the inhabitants; but that many of the runaways had been killed, and the heads and bodies exposed on the public roads. That Pangloss, one of the leading rioters, is killed and his adherents destroyed: and that Balla and Pharcelle, the two other principals, have been totally dispersed, and their parties taken, killed, or reduced to obedience; for that everything is at last restored to tranquillity and good government.'[8]

Claims of the quelling of the Maroon uprising in early 1786 would prove to be premature and far from the truth. The reports sounded more like propaganda pieces aimed at boosting the morale of the local white population. At that time, Pangloss still was very much alive and responsible for scores of Maroons around the Grand Bay area. This would, however, not be the last time such an outrageous claim was made as the authorities struggled for over more than fifty years to reign in the Maroons and their continuing quest for freedom.

New chiefs would emerge to lead the struggle, while the more seasoned campaigners would continue the fight. Ultimately, the brutality exercised by the rangers only appeared to strengthen the resolve of the Maroons and to encourage other slaves to make good their escape.

It was a fact that two months after his audacious attack on the Rosalie estate the rangers had failed to capture Balla, although their persistent raids had resulted in the capture of a few mainly Maroon children and women. They were either tried, convicted and sentenced to death, returned to their owners or sold to plantations in other Caribbean islands. One such Maroon captured during February 1786 was Cicero, or often referred to as Essex. He was a dedicated helper to Balla and served as his gun bearer. Known as a master strategist, he had also been instrumental in setting fire to the Rosalie estate during the attack, and had worked closely with Pharcelle and Congoree. However, he was betrayed by another slave called Petite Jacques and was eventually captured by Augustine, a free Negro, in Mahaut.

The authorities, anxious to prove that they had not forgotten or given up on exterminating those who participated in the Rosalie attack, arranged a hasty trial for Cicero, and condemned him to death on the testimony of Petit Jacques, who detailed his involvement in a series of Maroon attacks conducted during July to December 1785. On 25 February 1786 in just over an hour, he was found guilty and sentenced to be gibbeted alive at Woodbridge Bay, which was carried out one week later on 4 March. [9] Right on time, he was hung by the neck at the public square in the Roseau market.

Even the Maroons that were sent to other islands continued with their rebellion. Nowhere was that better exemplified than in the case of a captured Maroon, who in February 1786, was sold into slavery to a plantation owner in St. Kitts. Within a week of arrival in St. Kitts that spirit of resistance, rebellion, and the yearning for freedom borne out of living free in the mountains of Dominica, manifested itself with deadly consequences. Closely observing the movements of his master, he waited until he left home, broke into his chambers, and took a large broad sword. He then entered into a home near that of his master, which he found empty.

Undaunted, the Maroon then crossed the street into a school, which was being presided over by an elderly lady. It was still early in the morning, and only a few students were present. He then encountered 'the only daughter of a Mr. Moore, and her he butchered in a most shocking manner.' [10] The next to die was the daughter of Dr. Duplesor, who was killed in a similar fashion to the first child. Two other children present tried to escape, and they too were struck down. Both would later die of their injuries.

The Maroon then jumped over a fence, and entered through the back door of a white man's house named Fautoran, who was at breakfast with his family, including his elderly mother. A house negro, in hearing the commotion observed the Maroon's entrance. Acting quickly, he grabbed a hatchet, and crept up behind him delivering a severe blow to his temple, just as he raised the sword over the head of Fautoran, to deliver the fatal blow. The Maroon fell to the ground and was instantly seized by the house negro and turned over to the white authorities.

Two days later, he was tried for the murders and 'condemned to suffer the rack and gibbet.' Before being put to death a week later, his arms, legs, wrists, and thighs were broken off. It was reported that 'he bore it all without a groan, a sigh, or even the trembling of the flesh.' [11] His head was then cut off and his body burnt. A witnessed to the grisly event later remarked that 'never did I see a man die with such resolution.'[12]

Meanwhile in Dominica, contrary to claims of the surrender of Pharcelle, he would remain a thorn in the flesh of successive governors for at least another fourteen years. Similarly, Pangloss survived and would go on to join forces with Pharcelle in later exploits. Another leader Jacko would survive a further twenty-six years exemplifying the spirit of resistance. Meanwhile, the unrelenting search for Balla would continue, and it was not long before he would be captured and killed by his nemesis within the green rangers.

On 17 March 1786, Lieutenant John Egan, Sergeant John Bernard, Corporal Jack Worden, and ten privates of the Green Rangers, along with a negro guide, left the center region camp at Olive Hill, taking with them five days provisions. For the past two months they had been hard on the trail of Balla, after having captured and killed several of his men, and sending others to sham trials in Roseau. They were determined to get rid of the General, the Prince, the Chief of Chiefs who had created so much havoc and convinced so many negroes to leave their masters estates.

By nine o'clock on Sunday morning, they were just about three miles from the second branch of the Layou River, where they found a track, and there met Captain Garett of the Northern Blue Rangers, from whom they soon separated. They continued on that track for a further four hours until about one o'clock when they heard the noise of some strokes of a bill, or hoe. Lieutenant John Egan immediately dispatched four men to investigate. Approaching a small clearing in the woods, they discovered a young woman tilling the ground. The men silently crept up behind her, one immediately put his hand over her mouth to prevent her screaming, while another grabbed her by the arms. She was then swiftly carried to Lieutenant Egan for questioning.

In the meantime, Sergeant Bernard, and one of the privates named Marley, along with two others, had been ordered to pursue the track. They soon discovered some smoke, upon which Bernard sent Marley immediately to inform Lieutenant Egan. Upon hearing of this development, Lieutenant Egan sent out orders for Sergeant Bernard to re-join him. He had very little trouble in making the woman talk, and could barely believe what he heard. She informed him that Balla was indeed in the camp along with two children where Bernard had seen the smoke. In addition, there were two negro men and five negro women who were out seeking provision, whom they would be able to take at sundown; as they would then be returned.[13]

The men conferred quickly about whether they should attack immediately or wait for nightfall when the others returned. They soon decided against an evening attack after the woman under intense pain inflicted by her captors revealed that: 'Balla had two guns and plenty of powder and balls, and might probably, when joined by the other two men kill someone of the party. Besides that, the darkness of the night might favour their escape.' [14] However, it was the thought of taking Balla dead or alive, which drove them to agree to attack immediately. Afterall, getting their hands on the prized trophy was far more important than capturing all of the Maroon party.

With the decision made, and confident in his plan of attack, Lieutenant Egan ordered that the baggage and provisions be thrown down, the white feathers to be taken off of the men's hats and the party to advance. The woman was then quickly tied up, and left besides the baggage and provisions. Her life would be spared because of the valuable information she had provided, but she would be kept as a prisoner. With that small matter dealt with, the men crept steadily forward, on their hands and knees in the direction of the camp, and hopefully Balla. Lieutenant Egan and four men went to the left of the camp and the corporal and six others went to the right, while Sergeant Bernard with the guide and the other two approached the front of the huts.

Bernard had not gone far when he discovered Balla between two large trees, in the front of the hut armed with two guns and his powder at his side looking most alarmed as if he had not heard their approach. Bernard levelled at him and found himself at too great a distance, he therefore threw himself again upon his hands and knees, and advanced about fifty or sixty paces. One of the other party named Hilliare then raising his head above the bushes saw Balla levelling his piece towards them and said to Bernard; "Maître Balla voir vous,…laisser moi passer pour tirer"[Master Balla sees you…let me pass to shoot]. At this moment Balla cocked his gun, Hilliare heard the click of the cock, instantly fired, and lodged his discharge in Balla's thigh, at about 40 yards distance. Balla then fell, and notwithstanding he could not get on his feet, still scrambled on the ground, presenting his piece as if he determined to let fly at the first one whom approached him.

'On this Bernard ordered his party to fire on Balla, reserving his own. Neither of the sots struck him but lodged on the other side of him. Bernard instantly sprung behind a tree, and levelling at Balla's body lodged three balls in his belly on which he fell flat to the ground. They then rushed in upon him, and found him not quite dead. For when Bernard endeavoured to take a large knife from him, he struggled hard to get it back. All the party were by this time come up then they tied his hands behind him. Egan would later relate that: "he begged to loose him, and he would tell them all he knew.' [15]

In answer to their questions among other things, Balla revealed that he had fought alongside Pharcelle about four months ago, had not seen him since, but believed him to be at the Trois Pitons. That Congoree was in the heights of the Boeri Lake, with five negro men, five women and two children; but that he has no guns or cutlasses. Mabuyah is to the North of Terre Firme with three men, three women, two children and has two muskets and that Curry Greg is around the area of Boeri Lake, with seven men, three women, two children and seven guns.

Balla also revealed that all the plunder, which they have got is in the possession of Mabuyah, except some money, which his wife Canda had about her; and that all the rest of his party are either killed, taken or surrendered. The men gave Balla some rum on three different occasions as he grew faint, hoping that it would enable him to keep speaking. Balla then requested of them that they would bury his Obeah before him since he was certain that he was himself dying. Balla then called out several times, as long as he was able, "*Canda, Canda, femme moi! Venne rendre, Bois pas bonne encore... Balla il pris.. Balla va mourir*" ["Canda, Canda, my wife, come and meet me, the Tree is no longer good...Balla is gone...Balla is going to die"]. He then died. And so, it was that about 2 o'clock on Sunday 18 March 1786, the most feared Maroon leader in Dominica, Balla died in the forest of Dominica, less than two miles from the Layou River.

A party which had been stationed close to the camp, returned at the rising of the moon, to see if any of the women, or any others had come back but found everything just as they had left it, and supposed the firing may have frightened them away. Egan would later declare: 'they appear to have been destitute of every necessity. Balla being so reduced in clothing that he had on a woman's old blue jacket, and an old ragged shirt and trousers. He also had a red silk scarf, which served him as a sling for his gun.' [16] The woman prisoner who was earlier captured was said to be Zabeth, the property of Diana Cubbin. She has been in the woods two years and has during the time nursed Balla's child by Canda, called Laurent, who is brought in together with Jean Baptiste, another child.[17]

Although dead, Balla's ordeal was far from over. No sooner did he breathe his last that his chest was split open, his heart pulled out, and then his head was cut off. After taking his guns, about ten pounds of powder with some other trifles, and the two children including his son, who had witnessed the whole affair, they left the spot. One day later, the head of the once feared Maroon Chief was exhibited on a pole, in the marketplace in Roseau. News of his death quickly spread across the island, and scores turned out to stare at a man who for over twenty years was just a name to many. Throughout Dominica and as word of his death spread the Maroons and slaves on the estate would sing the sad mournful song, 'Balla mort, bois gatay' ['Balla is dead, the tree is spoilt']. To countless blacks caught in the yoke of slavery, he evoked aspirations of lasting freedom, but to many whites his memory was one of pain and dread.

An unknown commentator on seeing the head of Balla stuck on a pole would remark: 'This day was exhibited on a pole, in a marketplace of this town, the head of the notorious runaway Chief Balla who was surprised by a party of Captain Marshal's Legion, under the command of Lieutenant Egan. He received four balls above the groin, which caused such an effusion of blood, that it was impossible to remove him alive from the spot, and prevented the public indignation being gratified by a striking spectacle, being made of that daring villain, who has so long caused alarm, and spread such devastation in the colony.'[18]

Two days after Balla's death, on 20 March 1786, Lieutenant John Egan of the Northern Rangers, from his base at Camp Olive, wrote this letter to Governor John Orde: 'Sir, I have the honour to inform your Excellency, that at two o'clock yesterday,

I was so fortunate as to fall in with Balla and some of his people --- The former was shot, one woman and two children taken prisoner, one of whom is Balla's son. I am sorry the father's wounds were so bad as to not to admit him being sent alive to Roseau. Prior to his death, he informed me that Congoree was in the Grand Bay area. Mabuyah and Curry Greg with others in the Terre Firme mountains and Farcelle in Trois Pitons.

'I also took two guns about four pounds of gunpowder, an iron pot, his silk sash and Obeah, which I send with the head and prisoners to your excellency. I shall march tomorrow morning to meet Captain Marshall and Garett at the head of Papa River. I have every reason to suspect, some of the other parties have fallen in with the runaways as the report of several guns were today definitely heard here. I have the honour to be, with the utmost respect, Your Excellency's most obedient servant, JOHN EGAN Lieut. Center Legion.[19]

A little less than a month later on 16 April Governor John Orde, still basking in the popularity derived from the demise of the most feared Maroon Chief to date, wrote to the British Secretary of State Viscount Sydney, to give his own account of Balla's death: 'good fortune has given us possession of the Principal Runaway Chief, Balla, many of his followers are killed and taken, many have surrendered and the rest are greatly dispersed and distressed … Balla … would not suffer himself to be taken until so wounded that he could not fly,' he wrote.

Governor John Orde continued, 'the behaviour of this deluded wretch at his death proved him as hardened as previous conduct had done—he refused answering almost any questions that were put to him, though perfectly in his senses—he called upon his captors repeatedly to cut off his head, telling them that they might do so, but that Balla would not die—his obi or charm and his child were the only things that he expressed much anxiety about. The former he wished to bury, the latter, a boy of about 5 years old he bid to remember, the Beckeys or White Man had killed his father.'[20]

Following the death of the acclaimed Maroon leader Chief Balla, the authorities continued their unrelenting search for other leaders such as Mabuyah, Pharcelle, Curry Greg, Jacko, Congoree, Mabrie and Colligrie. In the process, scores of Maroons were captured and executed, with the government admitting to have killed 'over one hundred men, women and children.' Governor Orde and the white establishment were beginning to sense victory, or at least talking like they believed that the uprising was over and the Maroons sufficiently subdued. However, the claim made by the Governor that 'everything is at last restored to tranquillity and good governance,' could not be further from the truth.

In May 1786, some in the Colony were warning that 'the insurrection of negroes at Dominica is likely to produce very fatal effects, and if not seasonally and radically stopped will certainly communicate its contagion to St. Vincent, in which Island the Caribs are well informed by the priests.'[21] However, Governor John Orde appeared not to be worried. He penned an open letter to Captain Marshall and others responsible for the relentless pursuit and killing of the scores of Maroons. The 3 June 1786 letter from government House, stated that 'the revolted negroes being now no longer formidable, and many of the parties serving against them of course called in, his Excellency the Commander in Chief takes this opportunity to acquaint the officers who commanded the Colony Legions, with what must be most commendable to them --- His Majesty's most gracious approbation of their conduct, signified to him by letter received yesterday, from Lord Sydney, one of his Majesty's principal Secretaries of State.

'His Excellency at the same time begs to refer his thanks, to the Captains Marshall, Garret and Young; to the Lieutenants, non-commissioned officers, and men employed on that service, for the zeal, resolution and perseverance, with which they have prosecuted to the point of success, at which it is now arrived. His Excellency has strongly recommended to the Assembly, the providing of funds for the payment of arrears of wages that are due; and he will at all times have real pleasure to being useful to those to whose exertions he considers himself and the colony so much obliged.'[22]

The House of Assembly, for its part, still exulting in the death of Balla, passed the following unanimous decision on 17 August, 1786:

RESOLVED UNANIMOUSLY that the thanks of this House be given to Major Campbell to the officers, non-commissioned officers, and private men of the thirtieth Regiment to Captain Hamilton the officers non-commissioned officers and private men of the Royal Artillery, for the exemplary manner in which they presented themselves to his Excellency the Commander in Chief to be employed in the service of this colony, against the runaway slaves at a time when the lives and property of the inhabitants were threatened with the most imminent danger.

RESOLVED UNANIMOUSLY that the thanks of this house be given to the Captains Marshall, Garret and Young to the officers and private men of the legions for the indefatigable exertions, good conduct and gallantry, which they exhibited during their campaign, in the woods, in pursuing the runaway slaves through an almost impenetrable and inaccessible country, in attacking them wherever they could be found, and in effecting so general a dispersion of them, that among the killed, taken and surrendered, we number one of their principal and most daring chiefs, and upwards of one hundred of their men, women and children, and which, in its consequences, has afforded a more perfect security to our lives and properties, and will we hope, have the effect of preserving us, from the future depredations of this barbarous and savage banditti.

THOs BEECH, SPEAKER

Thos Beech, the Assembly speaker followed this up with a personal letter to Captain Marshall in which he again commended him for his gallantry and expressed the gratitude of an entire colony. However, the official and public pronouncements on the demise of the Maroon revolt was not backed up by events on the ground. Sensing their tenuous grip on the revolt, the House of Assembly, in the same month in which it claimed that the onslaught 'has afforded a more perfect security to our lives and properties,' moved to pass an Act on 26 August 1786 '*to establish a corps of Rangers to act against runaway slaves*' and to repeal that of November 1785.

DOMINICA.

By his Excellency Sir JOHN ORDE, *Baronet, Commander in Chief of the Iſland of* Dominica, *&c. &c. &c.*

Proclamation.

WHEREAS ſeveral *Gangs of Slaves*, within this Iſland, are in a State of *Inſurrection*, and may receive great Succour or Aſſiſtance from an improper Communication of *Foreign Veſſels* with the *Out-bays* of this *Iſland*. *I have, therefore, thought fit*, by this my Proclamation, to call upon and require all *Magiſtrates*, and *Other* his Majeſty's faithful Subjects, within my Government, to detain all *Foreign Veſſels* that may be diſcovered landing or taking *any Thing* from any of the *Out-bays*; and to deliver up ſuch Veſſels to any Commander of his Majeſty's Ships of War, or to any Officer of his Majeſty's Cuſtoms.

Given under my Hand and Seal at Arms, in the Town of Roſeau, this Twentieth Day of January, One Thouſand Seven Hundred and Ninety-One; and in the Thirty-firſt Year of his Majeſty's Reign.

J. ORDE.

By his Excellency's Command,

M. S. WALROND.

Duly Proclaimed, in the Town of Roſeau, this 20th day of January, 1791.

GEORGE BRUCE, *Deputy Provoſt Marſhal.*

ROSEAU: Printed by MATHEW GALLAGHER, in *New-lane*.

7

The 1791 New Year's Day Rebellion

As the months wore on following the death of Balla, some of the Maroons being displaced sought refuge in Martinique. *The Pennsylvania Packet* reported that 'the Count d'Amas governor of Martinique gave strict orders to all parts of the islands for the searching of canoes, pettyaugres, that might arrive [from Dominica] as he strongly suspected they [Maroons] had arrived that way and he wanted to send them back.'[1] The authorities also all but declared complete victory over the Maroons. In September of 1786, a member of the rangers wrote to his friend in London that 'the runaway Negroes are not yet extirpated; but I believe are hard pressed for provisions and ammunitions.'[2]

Another member in a letter written around the same time observed that 'on Monday the troops fell in with Mabuyah and made prisoners of several runaway negroes. This has almost put an end to the insurrections, which have for so long disturbed this island. The following vote of thanks has been given to the troops who have with the greatest alacrity suffered much fatigue in pursuing the rebellious negroes through almost inaccessible mountains.'[3]

The sense that the authorities were gaining the upper hand was reflected by the extent to which they made light of the Maroon experience by having their own 'marooning' parties. One such party was held for Prince William Henry, younger brother of King George II when he visited Dominica in February 1787. The marooning party was described in the *Times of London* as follows: 'a select number of ladies and gentlemen assemble together and proceed up the country to some sequestered retreat, near the confines of a wood, and bothering on such part of the sea shore which is calculated for fishing; while one party is employed in drawing the nets for sea fish, others are engaged in catching mullet, in the little rivulets, with which those islands are intersected.

'Servants that is negroe men and mulatto women attend on the occasion with a cold collation, consisting of ham, poultry etc. and decorate the table for dinner, under some tamarind tree, whose branches are more extensive than those of the English oak, and afford a better security against the showers of rain that are so prevalent. Gentlemen or ladies who chose to regale themselves with punch have it in the highest perfection… what with temperature of the climate, the harmony of the music, the sweet society of the tropical fair ones and the unanimity which usually pervades these festive entertainments they may be said to excel the splendour of a court, or the tumultuous noise attendant on European pleasures.'[4]

Notwithstanding the seeming dismissal of the Maroon population their numbers continued to grow as they consolidated and intensified the relationship with the men and women on the estates. This growing relationship and the continuing defection of slaves from the estates did not go unnoticed by the authorities. In late 1787 the planters out of desperation, demanded that the governor procure additional troops from Grenada,[5] ostensibly to help in curbing the Maroon influence.

In February of 1788 their growing numbers were discussed by the government's Privy Council. The minutes of one such meeting recorded the following: 'small parties of these people [runaways] were still appearing and holding considerable correspondence with the estates….'[6] Even Governor John Orde lamented the fact that 'some small bodies of these banditti, still continue together and that they receive supplies from and have considerable correspondence with the different plantations.'[7]

The continued relationship between the Maroons and those on the estates ensured a consistent supply of provisions as well as a gradual addition to the numbers of those seeking refuge in the forests over time. During that same period, the rangers continued their relentless search in the various hiding places of the Maroons, and in the process recording the occasional success. Samuel Gray, a ranger with the 30th regiment sent a letter to the governor regarding their success against the Maroons. 'Sir I have the honour to inform your Excellency that Sergeant McDonald returned to camp last evening from the quarter of Grand Bay and reports that on Sunday morning last he fell in with a runaway camp on the head of a river that runs through Mitchin's estate,' he wrote.

Gray continued, 'the Camp consisted of ten large huts. One of the villains who had a riffle locked stood to fire but as he raised his piece was shot down by one of the rangers. All the rest made their escape except a child about six months old who was thrown away by its mother. The man killed named Bazil, the property of Mr. Morfon had been a long time in the woods. There was taken in the camp, one gun, one cutlass, two bayonets, some powder and lead, rice and farine, and five fowls. The man shot said, before he expired that it was Pangloss's camp and that they were supplied with farine by a negro man who just left them. McDonald took also in their camp, six Obeahs two of which I cut up and found in one a gold ring set in topaz stone, in another gold ring also a gold breast pin, and some silver with many other curiosities.'[8]

In late 1789, Governor John Orde took a leave of absence from Dominica to make his way to England, ostensibly to deal with personal issues. On this voyage, Orde took with him the son of Balla, who had been captured on the day that his father was killed. Following his capture, Orde kept him as his slave raising him as his personal pageboy at Government House. Although Balla's son disappeared from the record soon after arriving in London, it is believed that he was afforded an education and like the Princes of Calabar before him became an exotic character in the London social scene of the late eighteenth century.

Weeks before the governor's departure for England, the Dominica Council in a letter dated 14 August 1789, praised the efforts of the governor at maintaining security on the Island. 'As your Excellency's government has been distinguished by a vigilant regard to the internal security of the Colony, a steady attention to the impartial administration of justice, and an ardent desire to protect and promote the real commercial interests of the mother country and colony we doubt not, but your Excellency, will receive the entire approbation of our gracious sovereign. By having persevered with zeal in acting up to the high obligation of public station and character, your Excellency must secure the applause of the well-meaning part of every community,' James Bruce President of the Council wrote. [9]

Eight months later in April 1790, the Assembly wrote a letter to His Majesty King George III, expressing sentiments completely at odds with those shared in the Council's letter. They thanked His Majesty for granting a leave of absence to their Governor John Orde. The Assembly noted that since his departure the inhabitants have enjoyed that peace and concord, which for three years they were strangers to during his government. Further, during that time, commerce was oppressed, the courts of justice improperly interfered with, and a numerous train of evils experienced by the harsh, unconstitutional, oppressive, arbitrary measures of the Governor.

These measures they thought were detrimental to His Majesty's service and the true interests of the Colony. 'Filled with dreadful apprehensions of the return of the said Governor John Orde, the Assembly humbly implores that His Majesty, from his paternal regard to the happiness, peace, and comfort of his subjects, will appoint another governor to the Colony.'[10]

Far from agreeing to the request of the Assembly for a replacement governor, the King on 27 July 1790, granted '*the dignity of a Baronet, of the Kingdom of Great Britain, to Governor John Orde Esq. Governor of the island of Dominica, and captain in the Navy and the heirs male of his body, lawfully begotten.*'[11] This elevated status to knighthood was clearly an attempt to reward Governor John Orde for his decisive actions taken against the Maroons and for returning the colony of Dominica to some semblance of normalcy. It also meant that the request of the Assembly to have him replaced was roundly rejected by His Majesty, and Governor John Orde returned to Dominica in October 1790.

Fuelled by the ongoing revolts in the neighbouring French Islands, and the growing allure of living free of the bondage of slavery in the forests of Dominica; the slaves on the plantations, in particular those on the Western side of the Island were prepared to act. This desire and yearning were heightened by rumours that the slaves were to be granted three days off each week, and paid two shillings for the days that they worked. In fact, rumours began to spread throughout the island that the main reason why the Planters were opposed to the return of Governor John Orde was that he had been given orders by the King to improve their conditions and that the Planters were against such action.

When the slaves eventually determined that this was not true, many started to abscond from work nonetheless. However, their actions were generally disorganized during most of 1790, until the feared Maroon leader Pharcelle hatched out an audacious plan for his followers to execute on 1 January 1791.[12] It had been more than four years since the death of Balla, and despite the Rangers best efforts they had not succeeded in detaining or killing the one who had apparently replaced Balla as the Chief of Chiefs. For this they would pay dearly.

To aid in his bold plan, Pharcelle would rely on the mulattos coming out of Guadeloupe and Martinique. The presence of the mulatto[13] among the Maroons was by no means surprising. In June 1790, the Martinique authorities had brutally supressed a mulatto uprising linked to the revolutionary fervour that had gripped the French colonies. On 3 June 1790, the insurrection among the mulattoes and people of colour led to an attack against a fort in the town of St Pierre that resulted in the death of the captain of the guards. In response, the authorities ruthlessly hung and gibbetted one hundred and thirty mulattoes.[14] Following the action by the French authorities, many whites and mulattoes, including the leaders, fled the island; with some taking refuge in Dominica. That same month, Martinique's French governor the Viscount de Damas warned

Dominican Lieutenant Governor James Bruce that the rebels were coming to Dominica.[15]

Among the mulattoes arriving in Dominica from Martinique was Jean Baptiste Polinaire, a fiery rebel who arrived on the island in June 1790 with his wife, child and father in law. Although not the one who initiated the uprising in Dominica, Polinaire drew on his experience in Martinique and the network of mulatto friends, who had joined forces with the Maroons, to keep in touch with Pharcelle and the other ringleaders. Over a period of time, he was able to gain the trust of the plotters and was furnished with details of the plot and how it was to be carried out.

One pamphlet printed in French, *l'Ami de la Liberte l'Ennemie de la Licence*, was addressed largely to the newly arrived mulattoes. It exhorted them to conceive of a free society where they were no longer bound by oppressive authority but could engage freely in the bountiful islands and demonstrate to all the world their capabilities as free and independent people. One such publication read in part, '*my dear brothers, what are we waiting for? What reflections do we still have to make? Arise and abandon your chains; and this wretched state of slavery! And with our hands let us help one another create a new and agreeable chain of unity and brotherhood; and with united accord we repeat, arise, arise and grasp that liberty!*[16]

Over the years, Pharcelle from his base of operations in the heights of Morne Desmoulins had been in frequent contact with the free people of colour in Martinique and Guadeloupe. This he accomplished through frequent visits to those islands with the use of small vessels from Dominica. In December of 1790 he was spotted along with some of his followers returning from Guadeloupe, a situation that was, at the time, noted by the authorities.[17] A few days later he was seen together with Pangloss and several other Maroons, all armed, when they came down at noon to the springs in Mr Laronde's coffee, a plantation on the South East coast of the island. They were observed by Janvier, a slave belonging to La Ronde and a Carib named Bigaire who lived on the La Ronde's estate.[18] No sooner was

Pharcelle back in Dominica that he began his plan to completely expel the white planters from Dominica. In order to do this, it was important to spread the word through to the slaves on the various plantations.

Pharcelle was aided with his plan through an extensive network that his notoriety as a *Neg Mawon*, had enabled him to build up among the plantation slaves over the years. He engaged with his key collaborators mainly in the South East part of the island. At the Rosalie estate, there was Charles the Driver, Jack Sailor, John Baptiste, and New Tim; at Sorhaindo's estate there was Richard, Jernel, Hippolite, and Juliann. Enslaved on the La Ronde plantation was Paul, Janvier, and Michel. Further South on Charles Bertrand's plantations were Edward, Charles, Negro Ned, Billy, Bobadil, Apollo, and Paul; while Jappa and Renault, belonging to Anthony Bertrand would all play crucial roles in the plot.

On New Year's Day 1791, as blacks and whites across Dominica celebrated the festive season, word of the uprising was quietly spread. Pharcelle despatched three of his trusted followers, armed and carrying rum, to the Sorhaindo plantation. At the same time, Bobadil delivered rum to Bertrand's plantation and Edward did the same at Rosalie; where he gave the news to Charles the Driver. Their message was a simple one, the Negroes were dissatisfied with the inaction of their Masters and intended to rise up, under the trusted leadership of Pharcelle. More importantly, 'they were not satisfied in having the three days that were talked of to be allowed them, but would have their full liberty.'[19]

Moreover, Pharcelle did not limit his contacts simply to the estates in the South East, he also called on more of his network on the Petit and Grove plantations, further South of the island. This included trusted slaves such as Cudjoe, Toussaint, Narcisso, and Louisson. Everywhere the message was the same that the slaves should be ready to rise up to claim their freedom from work, and that they were in fact ready to rise, under their commander in Chief, Pharcelle.[20]

The following week on 9 January, under the guise of delivering rum, Pharcelle's emissaries delivered the news that the plan was still on. In fact, contrary to rumours being spread, Pharcelle was alive and well[21] and waiting for the correct time to spring into action. At the Rosalie estate, Edward and Jack Sailor quietly spread the news to other trusted slaves that they should not trust the whites to give them their three days off, and as such, all the whites should be put to death.[22]

At the same time, Pharcelle and his Maroon band regularly frequented the estates on that part of the island, known as the French Quarter; where they would receive regular supplies of provisions. As word of the pending uprising spread among the slaves, many of them simply absconded from work on the plantations, and joined the Maroons in the various camps across the island. It was during that time that Primus a slave who belonged to Mr. Renault escaped with six others from the estate. Primus would later go from estate to estate spreading the word of the uprising, and in the process would become very familiar with the leaders. At the same time, the sudden disappearance of so many slaves, so quickly, did not go unnoticed by the authorities. As early as 13 January, Governor John Orde was informed of the growing 'gangs of negroes' making good their escape,[23] a situation which greatly alarmed him.

In preparation for the attack, the Maroons continued to carry out surveillance on the various estates. On 17 January, the owner of Hartford estate in the Mahaut area reported that one of his trusted slaves had encountered a group of seven runaways and one mulatto, who were all armed with guns and cutlasses.[24] They reportedly told the slave that they were not about to rob the white man, but they were prepared to defend their mountain hideouts.[25] The slave, fearing for his safety, informed them that he belonged to a French owner, and was allowed to continue on his way, after taking his possessions.

Meanwhile plans for the attack continued and by mid-January there was a growing sense among the plotters that everything was in place. To begin with, 'Jappa belonging to Mr. Anthony Bertrand was the commander in chief who said that he sent to consult Pharcelle in the heights above Morne Desmoulins. That each plantation was to have had its chief and that at the hours of supper the negroes were to put their masters to death, while they were at table and they were also to assassinate the free people of colour who should speak of the matter.' They also agreed that 'the negroes to take the Windward part of the island for themselves from Grand Bay to Lasoye, except that Governor Bruce and some other gentlemen who were good to their negroes were to be permitted to remain on their estate and that those of the whites who were not killed were to have the Leeward of the island.'[26]

By that time it was clear that the enslaved across the island knew of the plot, even those of Roseau who sent news to those of the Windward of the island. Pharcelle was considered to be the mastermind behind the plan. The chiefs were organised by Edward, from Charles Bertrand's estate, who served as the ringleader among the enslaved, and the liaison between the Maroons and the plantations. Paul was the chief on La Ronde's estate, Richard on Sorhaindo's, Edward on the Rosalie Estate and a driver of Mr Gally was to be chief from his estate, but did not come when the time came, but stayed on his master's estate.[27]

The stage was now set to begin the attack on Monday 17 January. On the Saturday before the battle, Paul from La Ronde's estate sent for Polinaire, and told him to go with him to Charles Bertrand's estate. Subsequently, Polinaire and two other Martinique mulattoes accompanied Paul to the estate. There they met, among other plotters, Edward from the Rosalie estate, whom, as part of the planning was requested to go back to Rosalie on the following morning, and to take 24 muskets as the battle was to begin on the Monday following.

At Rosalie, they were to send forward only one of their party to retrieve the muskets, while the rest were to remain on the other side of the river. They were further instructed that if the overseer saw them and wanted to prevent them from taking the muskets, they were to tie him and not let him loose until they had crossed the river. Those present generally agreed that they should move forward as soon as possible. [28]

The following day Sunday, the key plotters, again met, with the exception of those from Rosalie, using the cover of a public dance, to put the finishing touches to their audacious plot. On Monday night the slaves from the Rosalie Estate were to march about three miles to the Charles Bertrand Estate, where Edward, Bobadil, Negro Ned, and Apollo would be waiting. Here, they would combine to begin killing of the whites.

Once complete, those from Rosalie were to join with the nine slaves from Bertrand's estate and then travel the short distance to the Sorhaindo plantation, in order to kill the whites while they were at supper. From here they would move together to the Boetica River, before joining others including some mulattoes, and among them Polinaire, at Point Mullatre, a further two miles away.[29] From here, the group would systematically move from plantation to plantation murdering the whites, and would be joined at the south of the islands by other Maroons and slaves.

The absence of the plotters from the Rosalie Estate should have served as a warning to the remainder of the group because on the Monday morning they did not show up as planned. Instead, when the rangers showed up at Rosalie a few days later they were all found drinking while crowded in the home of the manager, Orr who had hastily left the estate when he learned of the impending attacks. It is not clear why the Rosalie slaves backed out from the plan but it was later revealed that Jack Sailor told Polinaire that 'at the last Runaway War, when Rosaly was burnt, the Negroes of that Estate had got a bad name, and that, therefore, this time they would not begin.'[30]

Meanwhile, unbeknownst to the plotters, the authorities had just the day before captured Primus, the Maroon, who had a few days previously escaped from Mr Renault's estate but who also had intimate knowledge of the plot through his contact with Pharcelle and the other chiefs. The authorities were astounded when Primus revealed that Pharcelle was at the centre of a plot, together with the enslaved negroes to kill the white planters.[31]

Wasting no time, rangers were immediately despatched to the Charles Bertrand plantation, where they detained and questioned Negro Ned, early Monday morning. From him they learned quickly that the free mulattoes, including Polinaire, at least two of Sorhaindo's Mulattoes, and a great number of 'Negroes in the woods' were expected to join in. He however denied that either himself, or any of the slaves on Bertrand's estate, were part of the plot.[32]

The rangers quickly moved on to the Rosalie estate, where that afternoon, they detained Charles the Driver, Jack Sailor, New Tim, and John Baptiste. Under intense questioning, they admitted that Pharcelle and Edward from Charles Bertrand's estate were the ringleaders of the plot, but had no knowledge of the involvement of any mulattoes.[33] Based on this information, Edward was then swiftly detained and confirmed the involvement of the mulattoes in the plot, including Polinaire's role.[34]

A white man and two negroes were immediately sent out to apprehend Polinaire. Alone in his house and awaiting the night time to begin the raids, Polinaire, had already received word that Edward had revealed his involvement in the plot. Through a hole of his door he saw the men approaching. 'Upon which he took his [sable] and went out by his back door and went into a piece of manioc and staid till they were free. That Christophe belonging to Mr Charles Bertrand had told Mr La Ronde's negroes that Edward had accused the examinant and that Mr La Rondes negroes had informed him first.'[35]

That night the remainder of the plotters, including Polinaire, proceeded with their plan. Of some concern was the fact that, Pharcelle and Pangloss the two Maroon leaders appear not to deliver on their promise to make available the weapons. Their carefully laid plans were now not only known to the authorities, but key aspects were unravelling. 'That they expected Pharcelle with three hundred muskets, and Pangloss with two hundred muskets; *which did not come.*'[36]It was not made clear why Pharcelle and Pangloss failed to show up that night as previously planned.

Polinaire's party consisted of approximately fifty men, including Jean Baptiste from Guadeloupe, two mulattoes from La Ronde's estate, Paul and Michel, and another mulatto Cocque from Laseuillee's estate. [37] The chief from the Sorhaindo estate Richard, had thirty followers, so too did Paul from La Ronde's estate.[38] Similarly, another mulatto from Guadeloupe had at least thirty mulattoes under his command.[39] On that Monday night, Polinaire was the undisputed head of the group, assisted by Paul ranked second, and Edward was third. Nevertheless, it was estimated that in total there were about two hundred fifty conspirators.[40]

For now, undeterred, the plotters ably led by Polinaire, pushed on with a plan to systematically force the planters away from their estates. News of the uprising in Dominica spread quickly soliciting fear and horror among the planters both within and outside of Dominica. A planter in Barbados wrote to his friend in England on 18 January that 'last night brought us very alarming accounts from Dominica respecting the negroes; several about the North part of the island have taken up arms and refused to work particularly not more than three days in the week. Several of the estates have all their negroes deserted, and the accounts say they dread the consequences. I hope they will be quelled as two regiments the 13th and the 15th left this town two days ago for the island.'[41]

Over the next three days, Polinaire and his party succeeded in forcing the planters on the Windward side to abandon their estates in fear, and liberating the slaves, thus quickly adding to their numbers. Among those fleeing for their lives was plantation owner Charles Bertrand and his two sons who sought refuge at the home of Alex Ross.[42] By 20 January, Edward had escaped his captors at Rosalie, and joined Polinaire and his men who had taken over the home of Bertrand. There, they slaughtered a cow and prepared dinner in honour of Pharcelle and Pangloss, who surprisingly did not show up. That same day, another planter William Oliver, wrote to Governor John Orde, pleading with him to send a party of rangers to the rescue, where already 'seven or eight of the French gentlemen from Windward were obliged to quit their estates and leave.'[43]

Meanwhile, outraged by the events surrounding the insurrection, Governor John Orde issued the following proclamation on 20 January 1791 in response to the New Year's Day rebellion:

> *Whereas several Gangs of Slaves, within this Island, are in a State of Insurrection, and may receive great succour or assistance from an improper communication of foreign vessels with the out-bays of this Island. I have, therefore, thought fit, by this my proclamation, to call upon and require all Magistrates, and order his Majesty's faithful subjects, within my government, to detain all foreign vessels that may be discovered landing or taking anything from any of the out-bays; and to deliver up such vessels to any Commander of his Majesty's ships of war, or to any officer of this Majesty's Customs.*
>
> *Given under my hand and seal at arms, in the town of Roseau, this twentieth day of January, one thousand seven hundred and ninety-one; and in the thirty-first year of his Majesty's reign.*
>
> *J. ORDE*
>
> *By his Excellency's Command,*
>
> *M.S. WALROND*
>
> *Duly proclaimed, in the town of Roseau, this 20th day of January, 1791.*

Two days earlier as soon as news reached Roseau of the insurrection, the 30th regiment under the command of Captain John Marshall and his deputy Urquant were mobilised to counter attack Polinaire and his men. Just five years previously, Marshall had led repeated raids against the Maroon strongholds. Elements of the 30th regiment were supported by a detachment of the 15th regiment under the command of Captain Combe.[44] The combined commands of the 15th and 30th regiment were under Colonel Myers, who won praise for his efforts, and would go on to become the Quarter Master of all His Majesty's navy.

[45] The regiments travelled through the Chemin L'Etang road and the village of Grand Fond, arriving on the night of the 20th, the same day that Polinaire took over the house of Charles Bertrand.

News of the owners abandoning their estates did not sit very well with the rangers who were now forced to fight to regain control of the estates. Captain Combe, soon after his arrival wrote to Governor John Orde thus: 'Mr Bertrand has been the most deceived man alive with regard to his own people in this late affair. Messrs Sorhaindo, Le Ronde, Gallée, Le Fevre and Roche are the gentlemen who, I believe are not now at their estates, and I am well persuaded that their returning immediately would be attended with infinite advantage.' [46]

Polinaire and his men for their part, were expecting the troops from the two regiments having being warned by some of the slaves that they were coming. However, Polinaire claims that he did not believe it to be the governor's troops but rather those of the old regiment that had before been paid by the planters. He assumed that they had deserted and were coming to attack them on behalf of the planters.

No sooner were the soldiers spotted that Paul and Richard began to fire on them. Polinaire claimed that at time he did not fire, but kept himself at a distance, 'not being willing to fire on his fellow creatures.' That one of the soldiers being advanced before the rest was first killed by Bicque belonging to Mr Lafueillie, that the others were killed by Mr. Sorhaindo's negroes at the river, named Charles, Lumel Thomas, Michael and a big Bourrique [donkey] negro who came with the clothes and accouchements of the deceased soldiers. The negroes that killed the soldiers took their arms and gave their own old ones to others.' [47] In all, there were sixteen other muskets among the negroes, and some cutlasses. During that first pitched battle all the negroes escaped, including Locque, Bourrique negro, Abraham Compagnion, Michel and Gros Thomas, and Demba. In the days ahead these and several others would be either captured, killed or taken prisoner.

That night, the troops of the 15th and 30th Regiments surrounded the house of Charles Bertrand, and after an initial confusion as to whether Polinaire should be taken alive, if inside, they opened fire. In the ensuing confusion, one mulatto soldier and three blacks from the estate were killed; three were wounded with one later succumbing to his injuries.[48] Polinaire had quietly slipped out on the arrival of the troops.[49]

On 21 January, the House of Assembly met in session and put out a bounty on Polinaire's head.[50] '*Resolved that this House will make good any sum not exceeding the sum of two hundred pounds currency to provide for the reward that may be offered by His Excellency the Governor to any white person or Free Person of colour or to purchase the Freedom of any Slave who may apprehend or kill the Mulatto Man named Paulinaire, now at the head of a Party of Rebellious Slaves*.'[51]

Over the next few days, Captain Marshall and his men, gradually wore down the resistance of Polinaire's party, taking many prisoners and killing others. Without the active support of the Maroons, Marshall was confident that they could be defeated. At the same time, Governor John Orde carefully guarded the coastline in order to prevent the mulattoes from heading to Martinique. Polinaire for his part attempted to get a boat from Grand Bay but finding the bay guarded was forced to return to the woods. At the same time, the authorities seized his wife and child, hoping that this would force his surrender.

Towards the end of January with the rebellion largely contained, Governor John Orde addressed the Dominica Legislature where he called for the arming of the militia and imposition of harsher laws in the colony. 'Mr President and Gentlemen of the Council; Mr Speaker and Gentlemen of the Assembly, Gentlemen. The particular and alarming situation of public affairs have occasioned me to call you together at this moment regardless of every other circumstance. You will not I am confident defeat my expectations and intentions in this measure. Let every private concern be suspended for the present: exert all your wisdom and power to meet and counteract the pending mischief: enable the Executive Government to avert similar evils from you in future, or to concur them if they occur, by passing such salutary and perpetual laws as the judgement of the Legislature may think necessary for that purpose –arming and frequent meeting of the militia (which at present is on the worse footing).

'Empowering the Executive Government to regulate the entry and residence of foreign vessels with the out bays and coasts of the island--- passing such laws, which will enable the Commander in Chief to call out the whole military force of the colony and to provide them with quarters, slaves, convenience, and recompence by better regulating by acts of the colony the government of slaves, and providing for their prompt and exemplary punishment in such cases as the present.

'Checking by wholesome and moderate laws the licentiousness of printers; to one of whom the author of *The Caribbean Gazette*, a great deal of the insubordination now prevailing in the colony, is to be inputted; and providing more perfectly for the protection of the officers of government, particularly of the revenue, and the due punishment of those who molest them in the execution of their duty, are, I conceive, the principal objects for your immediate attention.

'Gentlemen, the particular and meritorious activity of Captain Murray of the Royal Navy, and the commanders of the King's ships and other vessels now here, employed in the service of government, and the unprecedented exertions of the whole garrison particularly the 15th and the 30th regiments under the able command and direction of Colonel Myers, on the later occasion (though encountering circumstances of some discouragement), have called for my warmest thanks.

'Allow me to recommend the better corps in the strongest terms to your grateful attention. Since your last meeting I have found it my duty, with the advice of his Majesty's Council, to incur some expense on the part of the Colony, in providing quarters and other accommodation for parties of the King's troops sent to protect the different parts of the Colony, on the late alarm and also to offer considerable additional rewards to those who take the rebel Pharcelle. I rely on your providing for payment as soon as circumstances will allow. Mr President, there never was a time when unanimity and confidence were more necessary for the good of the colony than the present.[52]

The response by the Speaker of the House to the Governor, while suggesting possible support for tightening up on law and order was somewhat less sympathetic to his hostile position concerning the Printers. 'The situation of this unfortunate Colony for a long time past under all the dreadful apprehensions arising from a revolt among the slaves afforded no small degree of concern to the representatives of the people, which was augmented by the reflections that in consequence of the prorogation of the House of Assembly in the first week of their session their constituents were denied of that benefit to be expected from the exercise of the Legislative power, and that at so awful a moment, when the lives and fortunes of the inhabitants were known to be in imminent danger, and every evil was to be apprehended from its suspension.

'The members of the House of Assembly however, at all times ready to discharge the important duties annexed to their public as well as private situation, returned with the greatest alacrity, the exercise of their functions, as soon as they were permitted by your excellency, notwithstanding the difficulty of convening a sufficient number who could with common prudence quit the more immediate defence of their properties, and the House have endeavoured and will continue to provide such remedies as appear to them most likely to remove the impending danger, and to avert as far as depends on them, similar evils for the future.

'In averting to your Excellency's recommendation to check by wholesome and moderate laws the licentiousness of printers, it occurs to this House, that the laws of Great Britain are of themselves sufficient for the punishment as well as protection of her immediate subjects, and as any attempt to influence the minds of those whose duty it may be to assist at the trial of persons under criminal prosecution pending the suit is subversive of the principles of justice, and consequently unlawful, any steps taken by this House to interfere with the editor of *The Caribbean Register* while under a prosecution for a libel against your Excellency, would be prejudging the cause, by which they would be guilty of an act of the highest oppression nor has it appeared in any writ to this House that the general consequences deduced by your Excellency in this publication have prevailed in the community.

'The House at the same time are ready to allow, peculiar local circumstances make it necessary for them to avail themselves of the capacity in which they act as the grand inquest of the country to retrieve such evils and to provide a punishment for such crimes as are not immediately cognizable by the laws of the mother country; and it appears to them that one of the principal causes to which the present disaffection among the Negroes are attributed, is the publication of a French Gazette, printed for some months past, in the town of Roseau under the title of *l'Ami de la Liberte l'Ennemie de la Licence*, in which such encouragement is given to slaves, and opinions promulgated in their favour, so dangerous to the lives and properties of their masters, as by being industriously distributed among them and enforced by the example of several ill-disposed free people of colour, who have lately come over from Martinique, could not fail of producing, we have at this day so much reason to lament, and this House trusts that your excellency, as the executive power will give such force to the remedy that may be applied to this evil as shall most effectually remove it.

'The activity of Captain Murray and the officers and seamen of his Majesty's navy and the captains and seamen of the merchant ships in the harbour as well as the exertions of the whole garrison, and particularly of the 15th and 30th regiments under the able command and direction of Lieutenant Col. Myers, merit our most grateful acknowledgements and your Excellency cannot doubt the inclination of the House of Assembly to give the 30th regiment such marks of esteem, as their long and meritorious services to this Colony so justly deserves. The expenses incurred by your Excellency in providing quarters and accommodations for his Majesty's troops, will be taken into consideration as soon as they can be laid before this house and provision shall be made for the payment of the reward, which your Excellency has offered for the rebel Pharcelle.

'It is with regret that the House are obliged to make any observations in reply to your Excellency's speech that may not be relative to the immediate and important objects of their present deliberations; but it would be unjust to the character and credit of their constituents, if they passed over in silence the necessity your Excellency conceives there may be to provide more effectually for the protection of the officers of the Revenue and for the punishment of those who molest them in the execution of their duty. The House of Assembly knows of no instance wherein the laws already existing have been inadequate to that purpose, nor has there occurred, within our knowledge any subject of complaint.

'The inhabitants of this island are not more distinguished for their steady and affectionate loyalty to the King and to the British constitution than they are for a prompt and dutiful subordination to the laws of their own community, and flattered as we are by the confidence which they have reported in us by a delegation to represent them in our public capacities, and which alone has entitled us to your Excellency's attention, we have the conscious satisfaction of having never derogated in any action of our own, from the character either of good citizens or good subjects.

'It will be our duty as it is our inclination, to concur with your Excellency and the Hon. Board of Council in every measure that may tend to preserve and promote the blessings of harmony and good order amongst all ranks of people. The welfare and happiness of all are the sole objects of our deliberations, and a uniform and steady exercise of our legitimate powers in a constitutional manner are the means we shall make so as to accomplish them.'[53]

Finally, on 1 February with the others in his party either having being killed or captured, Polinaire himself was taken prisoner. His end came after a Kalinago man offered to lead Colonel James Bruce to his hiding place, around the Castle Bruce area. The man was promptly offered 5 Joes, the equivalence of two hundred pounds for leading Colonel Bruce to Polinaire. Within a short time, Bruce commissioned several slaves noting that "I had twelve of my best people armed with every firelock that could fire." Shortly thereafter Polinaire was found hiding in a cave close to the plantation, taken into custody and put in chains. He was later transferred to Roseau via a coastal sloop to await trial.

Three days after his capture, and in trials lasting nineteen days, nineteen of his co-conspirators including Paul, Richard, Edward, Michel and Demba were all condemned to death and executed for their roles in the insurrection. Just six days after being detained, Polinaire himself was put on trial for being the ring leader of the revolt, he was found guilty and executed on 1 March 1791, one week after the executions of Cyrus, Hannibal, and Renault. Though ultimately short lived, the insurrection on Dominica's South East coast would send shockwaves through the British establishment and hasten the introduction of a Bill in the House of Commons to abolish the Slave Trade.

Following the brutal suppression of the insurrection, there was a flurry of correspondence out of Dominica to Great Britain. The British public had gained a renewed interest in the subject given the brutal suppression of the insurrection and the increasingly vocal Society for the Abolition of the Slave Trade, which included William Wilberforce, Granville Sharp, and Thomas Clarkson. A letter written from the Committee of Correspondence in Dominica to the Agent W Knox in London gave additional information on the matter. 'Soon after Christmas the negroes in different parts of the island began to show signs of discontent, and threw out hints that government had determined to free them, that their masters were to pay them for their work that Governor John Orde had bought out such powers with him and that on communicating to the assembly, they would not hear of it, and he had quarrelled with them with several other such extravagant ideas as designing people had put into their heads.

'And about the tenth of January the negroes on Mr. Mair's estate absolutely left off work, while the liquors were boiling in the coppers and insisted that the managers should allow them three days in the week to work for themselves at the same time that other gangs in the neighbourhood seem only waiting for the success of this demand, to make the same, or more extraordinary ones. Themselves nearly at the same period eleven of Mr Wenstone's negroes, on his Rosehill estate absented themselves, and those on the French estates, in what is called the French Quarter, were daily going off and collecting themselves together, were using all possible means to persuade others to join them, and committing depredations upon all the property adjoining.

'Towards the 14th the insurrection had got to some height and accounts were coming in from the country truly alarming. Captain Urquart who commanded the light company of the 30th regiment many of whom had been employed on former expeditions against the runaways waited on the governor on the 14th with his lieutenants and Major Campbell, who commanded the regiment, and offered to go out against the insurgents without fee or reward. Things were daily growing worse and worse; several respectable French planters to Windward had abandoned their estate to save their lives; some of them had their whole gangs in rebellion, when on the 29th the Governor accepted of Captain Urquant's offer, and sent his company to Rosalie and other parties to Grand Bay.'[54]

On 18 March 1791 about 100 members attended a meeting of the Association of West Indian Planters and Merchants[55] in a London Tavern, for the purpose of taking into consideration the alarming situation of slave insurrection in the islands, and providing for their safety. The meeting paid particular attention to a letter dated 3 February 1791 from Dr Clark of Dominica and addressed to Mr. Baily in London. Along with a detailed account of the recent insurrection in Dominica, the letter noted that 'the ruin or the prosperity of the island was now at hand.' The meeting concluded with a resolution for the appointment of a committee, consisting of Lord Penryhn and the agents of the different islands, to present a proposal to Lord Greenville, to request that a military force be sent to the islands to protect the whites and keep the blacks in subjection, during the present very critical stage of the Slave Trade Bill.[56]

A few days later, the Association wrote their memorial to Lord Grenville, the Secretary of State, which read as follows. 'That your memorialists feel the greatest alarm at the account lately received, respecting an insurrection of negroes in Dominica, an insurrection which appears to have been founded upon no pretence of ill treatments as to food, clothing or other particulars, but to have occurred in pursuit of what they term their "Rights", which in their interpretation, extend to an exemption from labour, during four days out of seven; although they are supported during the whole seven days, and during infancy, old age, and sickness, at the charge of their masters.

'That your memorialists learn, with the utmost concern that these doctrines, which are novel among the negroes, have originated from the new language and proceedings heard in this country respecting the slave trade; information of which has been disseminated, by various channels, among the negroes. That these doctrines on the subject of the slave trade have been countenanced by persons in such high authority at home, that, without due and immediate attention, they are likely to spread more and more among the negroes in cases where they have not operated already; it been found easy, by various experience, by means of such examples and discussions, to infuse a spirit of disquiet, among persons who were before disposed to rest contented.

'That one of the surest symptoms, of danger, upon the current occasion, appears to have been the aptitude with which the negroes have believed and spread reports on these subjects. That, while the principal persons pleading here for the Abolition of the Slave Trade, affect to stop short as to the Abolition of Slavery in the islands, the colony negroes (who will feel distress, instead of benefit, from a diminution in the importation of slaves) apply the arguments and authorities, which are advanced on these occasions in such a manner as solely to favour their own emancipation.

'That the topics thus inadvertently urged by persons living at home and at a distance from the state of danger, tend to produce the most disastrous consequences in the islands; not only by exposing the lives and properties of the colonists in every shape to destruction and checking the great work of cultivation, which this country is bound by good faith and various Acts of Parliament and Charters severally to protect; but by hazarding the lives of the negroes themselves, in case it shall be found necessary to act against them for self-preservation.

'That although the revolt in question at Dominica is at present stifled, yet the principles are not settled upon which it is understood to have taken place, nor are they confined to Dominica. That these principles are both permanent and general in their operation, and that none can tell when and where they will next appear in action. That it is clear that if it will be too late to apply a remedy when the evil which is feared shall actually have manifested itself in overt acts; since more mischief may be done during a single night than it is possible ever after to repair.

'That the late tranquillity of the islands, which has far exceeded expectation furnishes no argument that the fears of your memorialists will not be speedily realized; for, while this tranquillity proves that the Colonists have been cruelly slandered when they have been charged with provoking their negroes to revolt, by their inhumanity, yet it by no means prove that the negroes will not revolt, in consequence of the new temper and ideas, which they have thus suddenly imbibed whenever they find opportunities.

'That it is a strong presumptive fact upon this occasion, that the negroes in Dominica shewed no previous symptoms of their designs, although it is said that they were prepared, upon every estate in that island, to take advantage of any success, which might have fallen to the share of the revolters. That your memorialists without attempting anymore to appreciate the value of the colonies to the Mother Country and without repeating any of those arguments in their favour which they have found of late years to be so constantly ineffectual, claim as British subjects that the most prompt and ample protection may be afforded them, against the present urgent dangers, which the peaceful establishment, usually allotted to the islands, is so badly unable to insure to them.' [57]

Meanwhile in Dominica there was growing tension between Governor John Orde and some of the inhabitants of the country with their interactions growing increasingly hostile. A report in *The Independent Gazetteer* observed that 'between the Governor and the inhabitants of Dominica, the old disputes are revived and carried to a greater length, and with more animosity than ever.'[58] Part of these 'old disputes' had to do with the Legislatures' attempt to keep him away from the island, when he returned to London in 1789. Worse, Polinaire, when he was questioned after the insurrection stressed that the Legislature's behaviour towards the governor, and their attempts to keep him away from the island, contributed to the revolt. The legislature was clearly not happy with Governor John Orde.

'That the origin of the revolt was that Mr. Ankethell accompanied by Mr. Hall and afterwards another gentleman came to the Windwards of the island to get the signatures of the planters, to prevent the return of Governor John Orde to this country. Saying that if Governor John Orde returned to this country he would protect the negroes and mulattoes, which would make as much trouble here as at Martinique. That the negroes understood that it was the intention of the inhabitants to fire on the first that Governor John Orde should come and sink him sooner, than let him land if they knew the vessel,' Polinaire noted.

He continued 'that since the arrival of Governor John Orde, the negroes had heard that he Governor Orde had given orders that the planters should give to their negroes three days in the week and that the planters had refused to do it but on the contrary, were more strict upon them. And that as the planters had refused that to Governor Orde they were all resolved to take that time themselves, and that the free people of colour who should refuse to assist them should be put to death, upon which their fight began.'[59]

Another of the governor's problems arose from his attempts to blame the press for the state of affairs on the Island, after he was roundly criticized for encouraging the uprising in Dominica. In his speech to the Dominica House of Assembly on 28 January 1791, he stated that 'checking by wholesome and moderate laws the licentiousness of Printers; to one of whom the author of *The Caribbean Gazette*, a great deal of the insubordination now prevailing in the colony, is to be inputted; and providing more perfectly for the protection of the officers of government, particularly of the revenue, and the due punishment of those who molest them in the execution of their duty, are, I conceive, the principal objects for your immediate attention.'

The governor was also immediately criticised by the Speaker, himself having openly shown his disdain for his leadership, and having led the effort to stop the return of the governor to Dominica a few months earlier. 'In averting to your Excellency's recommendation to check by wholesome and moderate laws the licentiousness of Printers, it occurs to this House, that the laws of Great Britain are of themselves sufficient for the punishment as well as protection of her immediate subjects, and as any attempt to influence the minds of those whose duty it may be to assist at the trial of persons under criminal prosecution pending the suit is subversive of the principles of justice, and consequently unlawful, any steps taken by this House to interfere with the editor of *The Caribbean Register* while under a prosecution for a libel against your Excellency, would be prejudging the cause, by which they would be guilty of an act of the highest oppression nor has it appeared in any writ to this House, that the general consequences deduced by your Excellency in this publication have prevailed in the community.' [60]

All through the first half of 1791, the pressure continued to build on Governor John Orde. A writer in *The Independent Gazetteer* opined, 'what construction is the world to put on that part of Sir Governor John Orde's speech to the legislature of Dominica....The obvious one is unfavourable in every point of view to his Excellency. He pays but a sorry compliment to the understandings of the inhabitants at large. In ascribing so extensive bad effects to the publications of any individual, and he certainly recommends to the Colonial Legislature what has been deemed unnecessary in England, where such freedoms are daily used with the characters of the first personages in the kingdom.

'Had his Excellency given this matter that consideration and attention, previous to him thus committing himself to the public, which its importance merited, he would have learned that since the year 1694, no attempt has been made in the mother country to impose any restraint on the press by statute --- and that the liberty of the press is regarded by the most enlightened of mankind, as essential to the nature of a free government.

'The common law allows ample redress for wrongs which individuals may suffer from the abuse of this liberty; and it cannot for one moment be supposed that throughout the colonies, there is to be found a Legislature who could so far forget what they owe to themselves and their constituents, as to attempt the least injury to this Palladium of British freedom. Perhaps it would be difficult for Sir John to explain what he means by the 'insubordination' that he complains of. He certainly cannot wish to introduce the rigid rules of military discipline into civil government; and to make it as criminal in a citizen to scrutinize the conduct of those intrusted with power, as it is in a soldier or sailor to disobey the orders of his commanding officer.

'The recommendation, has however, the merit of being unique; of being perfectly unprecedented. But the Baronet[61] has shown himself a very indifferent politician, in descending from the dignity of a Royal Representative, to make so humble a character as the editor of a newspaper the object both of personal resentment and legislative attention.'[62]

For the second time in as many years the British authorities questioned the actions and behaviours of Governor John Orde, when on 22 June 1792 the Lords of the Privy Council met in the council chamber to proceed in the consideration of the complaints against him.[63]Although the results or the inquiry by the Privy Council was never made public, Governor Orde, after serving nine years as Commander in Chief in Dominica, ultimately relieved command in December 1792, paving the way for Thomas Bruce to act as governor until the naming of Henry Hamilton in 1794.

Years later in 1813, Archibald Gloster by then the Chief Justice of Dominica would write of Governor John Orde's reign that 'a sanguinary warfare prevailed between the runaway slaves and the inhabitants, their masters, which spread destruction in many quarters of the colony, and dismay throughout all; … I have always understood, that the whole white and free coloured population of the island, was for a long period actively engaged in quelling these daring insurgents, and that it was only accomplished after a great sacrifice of lives, and a ruinous expenditure of the public funds…Independent of the evils necessarily attendant upon internal insurrection, unpleasant political animosities subsisted between Governor John Orde and the inhabitants, which continued until he left the command in December 1792.'[64]

A black ranger of the 8th West India Regiment in Dominica.

8

Struggle to End the British Slave Trade

On 18 April 1791, thirty-two year old William Wilberforce introduced the first Parliamentary Bill in the British House of Commons, to abolish the slave trade.[1] *The Independent Gazetteer* described that moment thus. 'Wilberforce, steady to his purpose, undaunted by the opposition of interested men, and confident of the goodness of his cause, he proceeds to shew first, that the mode of procuring slaves in Africa was replete with cruelty and misery, and to prove his assertions on this head, he relates a number of striking accounts, by which it is clearly demonstrated that the traders on the coast and the Princes with whom they contracted, were so accustomed to this cruel traffic, that every spark of humanity, every idea of honour appeared extinct in their hardened hearts.

'Secondly after feelingly describing the miserable state of the Negroes in the middle passage, he refutes the argument that the Negroes in their own country were doomed to misery and drew a pleasing picture of their quiet occupations, and peaceful habit of life in Africa when not irritated against each other by the Europeans. Wilberforce by espousing the cause of suffering humanity, endeavoured to show the injustice and cruelty of the trade.'[2]

Wilberforce, for his part, in his impassioned plea to end the slave trade intoned: 'Some people indeed, have found out, an excuse for the treatment, which the Negroes experienced at our hands; for they represented them as a race of beings suffering under the particular displeasure of Heaven, branded by wrath and doomed to bondage and infamy. If those who urged this doctrine were sincere in it, he would feel himself disposed to respect their zeal, however mistaken it might be. The dispensations of Providence were incomprehensible; nor could man discover, by dint of reason, why moral evil was suffered to exist in this world with moral good. Until God himself should reveal the cause, man must submit to what he cannot comprehend.

'But when he heard people urge the supposed displeasure of the Almighty against this unfortunate race of men, merely as an excuse for those cruelties which their passions prompted them to exercise upon the Negroes, he felt his indignation rise against those who had the audacity to add blasphemy to barbarity and endeavour to make the common Father of mankind the accomplice, or rather the author of their cruelties.'[3] Wilberforce ended his remarkable speech by moving 'that the Chairman be directed to move for leave to bring in a bill for preventing the further importation of African negroes into the British colonies and plantations.'[4]

Time and time again throughout the course of the ensuing debate, mention would be made of the insurrection in Dominica, with harsh criticism reserved in particular for William Wilberforce. Member of Parliament Colonel Tarleton stressed the link between the Dominica insurrection and the move to abolish the slave trade. 'To what could they impute the last insurrection at Dominica? – which island the governor lately pledged himself to hold in subjection, without the assistance of the military, but which was lately saved, from horrid carnage and midnight butchery, by the adventitious preference of two British regiments?[5] To what he repeated could Gentlemen impute this insurrection but to the question of abolition?'[6]

Another member of Parliament, Mr Stanley, who firmly opposed abolition, stressed that the insurrection in Dominica 'was greatly to be attributed to what had passed in this country, from whence everything was translated into French, and sent to Martinique and from thence to Dominica.'[7]William Pitt observed he could 'prove that a system of moderation and of mercy, would contribute more, even to the worldly advantage of the planters than the present horrible practice of cruelty which set at defiance the precepts of religion, which destroyed the sense of justice, and eradicated the feelings of humanity.'[8]

Nine days earlier on 9 April 1791 at the seating of the House of Commons,[9] Lord Carhampton reiterated that the insurrection in Dominica had taken place after the slaves received a report that the Governor had received orders, which he had refused to make public, from the Parliament of Great Britain and from Master King Wilberforce, for their freedom. As a result of this insurrection the blacks had resolved not to work more than three days during the week and to be paid for each day two shillings. Worse, they had resolved on a fixed night to cut the throats of all the whites on the island.

Lord Carhampton went on to note that it was fortunate that the insurrection was suppressed by the regiments on the island, but it was only after the destruction of many negroes, and the wounding and killing of many in the military, one of whom, being taken by the blacks, was cut into pound pieces while alive. He said that he thought it his duty to state the facts to his country "that the blessed effects already procured by the Right Honourable Gentleman's (Wilberforce) black humanity, might be well understood and generally known.'[10]

Wilberforce in his defence replied that he considered it unfair for Lord Carhampton to attribute the insurrection in Dominica to the measures that he had introduced in the House to end the slave trade. He noted that insurrections had taken place in Dominica long before his having thought of the abolition of the slave trade. To the contrary, his resolutions would not be calculated to promote insurrections, but rather to quell them, and if it was imagined that such motion was to go to the emancipation of the blacks, now on the island that such opinion was mistaken. His only intention was to put an end to the slave trade.[11]

One of those rejecting the arguments of Wilberforce was William Young who argued that the accounts, which had been given of the suffering of the slaves in the West Indies, were 'incredible, and must be greatly exaggerated.' He further argued that if the trade was abandoned it would produce great evils. In his view many parts of Africa were extremely populous, and the devastation of the fruits of the earth so great by the locusts and other insects that all the horrors of farming were to be apprehended unless part of the inhabitants were carried off.

Another member Mr. Francis, contended that: if the arguments of Mr Wilberforce had not convinced every one of the propriety of the abolition of the slave trade, 'no human reasoning ought ever to be allowed to have any weight.' Whatever had been said in favour of the trade, no one had asserted that it was not criminal, and he doubted much, whether it was even profitable.

Meanwhile, outside of the House debate, the Association of West Indian Planters and Merchants had come to the conclusion that it was not practical for Britain to send out a sufficient force, as in the island of Jamaica alone there were 270 000 blacks and only 25 000 whites. They therefore resolved 'that the most proper mode of keeping our West Indian islands in safety and peace, is to bring Mr. Wilberforce Bill, now pending in the House of Commons to an immediate termination, and that the administration of this country ought, for the safety of our possessions, to oppose the abolition of the slave trade.'[12]

Already, the lobby to prevent the end of the slave trade was gaining in importance. The Association could rightly depend on several House members to support them in their quest. Finally, when the vote was taken at the end of the debate on 20 April, the *Bill for preventing the further importation of African Negroes into the British colonies and plantations*, was eventually defeated by 163 (Noes) to 88 (Yeas) votes. Final passage would have to wait a further sixteen years until 1807 to witness the successful enactment of any such Bill to abolish the Slave Trade in the British West Indies.

After the rejection of the Bill in 1791, the Independent Gazetteer launched a scathing attack on those who voted against the Bill. 'Notwithstanding the decision of the majority in the British Parliament against the abolition of the slave trade, yet in the eye of reason – the injustice, the iniquity, the impolicy and the national disgrace, must remain unlessen and perhaps, may (for the present) be unhappily increased in some respects, by the melancholy decision of that important question.

'Nevertheless for the honour of humanity, let it be known to the whole world that eighty and eight members of that honourable body, continued to a late hour in the night (when the house was comparatively thin), and gave their decided vote for a total abolition. I felicitate them on the satisfaction they must experience, in consequence of the part they have acted, and on the honour done their cause, by noble speakers on their side of the question. For those gentlemen, I feel a respectful sympathy, on account of the affecting subject with which their minds must have been agitated; and (on behalf of the oppressed) I return to them my hearty thanks for their humane exertions.'[13]

However, wwhen news of the failure of the act reached Bristol, 'the bells of the city were a ringing, the workmen and sailors got half a holiday, a number of cannon were discharged, a bonfire and fireworks were given in the evening, and Mr. Wilberforce in effigy, was hanged and burnt.'[14]

On 26 April 1791 at a meeting of a society instituted for the purpose of effecting the abolition of the slave trade, which was Chaired by Granville Sharpe, it was resolved that the thanks of the committee be respectfully given to the illustrious minority of the commons, who lately stood forth the assertors of British justice and humanity, and the enemies of a traffic in the blood of men. 'Resolved that acknowledgements are particularly due to William Wilberforce Esquire, for his unwearied exertions to remove this opprobrium of our national character, and to the right honourable William Pitt, and the right honourable Charles Fox, for their virtuous and dignified co-operation in the same cause.

'In addressing a free and enlightened nation on a subject in which its justice, humanity and wisdom are involved, we cannot despair of final success; and we do hereby, under an increasing conviction of the excellence of our cause, and in conformity to the distinguished example before us, renew our firm protestation, that we will never desist from appealing to the consciences of our countrymen, till the commercial intercourse with Africa shall cease to be polluted with the blood of its inhabitants.'[15]

Even before Wilberforce introduced his Bill for abolition of the slave trade, the House had sought to gain evidence pertinent to the trade. In '*An Abstract of the Evidence Delivered before a Select Committee of the House of Commons in the years 1790 and 1791, on the part of the Petitioners for the Abolition of the Slave Trade*,' crucial information on the means of capture, and the shipment of the slaves were chronicled. In one instance, a witness to the trade Mr. Dyrample observed that 'the great droves of slaves brought from inland, by way of Galam to Senegal and Gambia were prisoners of war. Those sold to vessels at Goree, and near it, were procured either by pillage or by robbery of individuals. Grand pillage was usually executed by the king's soldiers numbering upwards of three thousand who attack, set fire to a village, and seize as many people as they can. Private robbers also lay in wait to capture unsuspecting villagers and then sell them.

'Other testimony revealed that "children are torn from their parents; parents bereaved of their offspring, wives from their husbands, and husbands from wives; and in a manner the most diabolical: in order to sweat and toil for their oppressors, without the comforts much less the rewards of labour and fatigue…the evidence uniformly agrees and incontrovertibly proves the iniquity and cruelty of the trade in its commencement.'[16]

Almost a year later, on 3 April 1792, Wilberforce, undaunted by his earlier failure reintroduced a motion in the House to abolish the slave trade. For over three hours he presented an eloquent case for ending the slave trade, ending with, 'that it is the opinion of this committee that the African slave trade ought to be abolished, and that a bill be ordered to be prepared for the same.' This produced a long debate in which William Pitt in an eloquent and dispassionate manner called for the immediate abolishment of the slave trade.

Other members spoke both for and against the abolition of the slave trade. However, when the vote was taken for immediate abolition, 193 members voted against and 125 voted for the motion. Eventually, Dundas moved as an amendment, that 'it is in the opinion of this committee, that the trade carried out by British subjects, for the purpose of procuring slaves from Africa, ought to be gradually abolished.'[17] At seven o'clock on the morning of 4 April 1792, and after a protracted debate, lasting almost a day, a bill was ordered to be brought in accordingly, with 230 members in support, and 85 against.[18]

Following this vote, the House once again transformed itself into a committee on Monday 23 April to consider the best means of effecting a gradual abolition of the slave trade. On Wednesday, the committee voted on an amendment proposed by Lord Mornington that the period be extended to 1 January 1793. 109 members voted for the amendment and 158 against. On Friday, Mornington again offered an amendment, this time to abolish the trade by 1 January 1795; this was again defeated with the ayes at 130 and the noes at 161. A further vote was taken on setting the abolition date to 1 January 1796. This time it was passed with 151 ayes and 132 noes.[19]

The Bill was then sent on to the House of Lords, but it was blocked after certain members claimed that it was received too late to be considered during the current session. On 26 February 1793, Wilberforce rose before the House of Commons to move 'that the House will on Thursday next, resolve itself into a Committee to take into consideration the present state of the Slave Trade.' [20] He was immediately challenged by William Young who proposed that 'instead of Thursday next' be inserted 'this day six months.' He observed that since last session he had been to the West Indies and had found 'the condition of the slaves very easy and comfortable, not only those who were young or might have arrived since the subject had been under Parliamentary investigation, but likewise those who had been long established on estates.'[21]

Young was of the view that with some regulations the slave trade would of itself gradually decrease, and he 'hoped to see the time when only one ship would be employed in that service,' but, he should not wish the trade to be totally destroyed. His arguments were countered by Wilberforce who said he was determined to persevere, and never to rest, till this trade, which was a disgrace to the British nation and to human nature, was finally and completely abolished. He was determined to employ the talents which had been conferred upon him by his Maker, to his honour and the happiness of his fellow creatures. Wilberforce and the other abolitionists would, however, need to wait a lot longer to get the bill passed. By a vote of 61 ayes and 53 noes the House agreed to set aside consideration of the bill to abolish the slave trade for a further six months.

During June 1793, a fitting tribute appeared in *The Ipswich Journal*, in support of those, including Wilberforce on the side of abolition. 'The man to whom Africa and Europe owes much has been calumniated and abused, but his mind conscious of rectitude, fears neither the envenomed shaft of ridicule, nor the silent progress of abuse. The friends to the abolition have been twice defeated in the Commons House of Parliament… Let us then hasten to rectify the error. Is liberty no longer desirable to the African? Are the cruelties and the horror of the traffic removed? Or is the right of man to buy his fellow creature and doom him to perpetual slavery yet ascertained? If these queries must be answered in the negative let us hasten to renew our exertions….. and may they be crowned with success.'[22]

Meanwhile, on 1 February 1793, France had declared war against Great Britain as part of the French Revolutionary Wars,[23]which would drag on until 1798. Following the outbreak of war between the two nations, various versions of the Bill were debated in Parliament, although no real progress was achieved during that period. On 17 February 1796, Wilberforce tried unsuccessfully to present the question of the abolition of the slave trade before the House of Commons. He noted that it was not any temporary operation on his feelings that had induced him to undertake the task 'but a rooted hatred and abhorrence of the barbarities exercised on his fellow creatures;' and nothing should ever deter him from continually bringing the business before the public tribunal until he had obtained the abolition of a trade which disgraced the character of Englishmen.[24]

With the war ended, on 1 March 1799 Wilberforce once again rose before the House to put forward his motion for the abolition of the slave trade. He noted that he had so often brought this subject before the House that it would be putting himself to much needless pain, and giving the House much unnecessary trouble to go into it at any length during the present occasion. Events, had in fact, so changed since he first brought the subject to the House 12 years ago, that he could not entertain much hope of success from anything he could now say.

Wilberforce further noted that he could not grudge the many days and months and years that he had devoted to pursuing this cause, for his labour "was cheered with the expectation that a time would at length arrive when it would be no longer tolerated." He went on to bemoan the fact that a few little islands, which were mere specks on the ocean, were the cause of all this widespread misery and desolation. He could hardly find terms, in which to express his abhorrence of such an iniquitous system, nor his surprise that it should for a moment find an advocate among any who valued, or pretended to, the feelings of humanity. After an impassioned debate, the House voted 54 ayes, and 84 noes, against the motion brought forward by Wilberforce.[25] Four months later on 11 July 1799, the House of Lords consented to the Slave Trade Regulation Act, which restricted overcrowding in the slave ships.

In November 1799 Reverend Charles Peters, rector of the Parish church of St George in Dominica personally delivered to Wilberforce written notes on the treatment of slaves in the country, which he had observed or heard of during three trials for masters charged with cruelly killing their slaves.[26] Upon delivery to Wilberforce, Reverend Peters told him: 'if, Sir, the documents which I leave with you be, in your opinion, at all likely to answer the purpose for which they were intended, I empower and request you to make whatever use of them you please, without regarding, in the least, the manner in which their Author may be eventually affected by their publicity.'

The account of the trials, related by Reverend Peters provided excruciating details of the cruel treatment meted out to both captured Maroons and the enslaved, at the hands of their masters. This included days of prolonged torture in every manner imaginable, including being kept in chains, excessive floggings, and denial of food that from time to time left the victims either dead or seriously maimed.

The first trial related was that of Cordelia, a free woman of colour who was put on trial for the murder of her female slave. Dr Johnstone, a medical doctor testified at trial that 'on examining the body, he observed marks of recent and of former violence on almost every part of it, viz that the legs were much swollen, and deeply ulcerated ; that the head, neck, and the whole of the back exhibited little else than one continued bruise; that the skin was, in various parts, irregularly blistered, in consequence (this deponent swore) either of boiling water poured on it, or of some other external application of an injurious nature; that the face was bruised all over; and that the deceased had further received a severe wound in her upper lip, occasioned evidently by the teeth having been driven through it; which wound from its fresh appearance must have been inflicted within three hours before death. This deponent added that the skull also appeared to him to have sustained a material injury…'[27] Notwithstanding the testimony of several witnesses, including that of Dr Johnstone the defendant was found 'not guilty'.

In the second trial, Caesar More, a free man of colour was charged with immoderately flogging his slave to death. A witness testified that the slave had received 150 lashes of the whip and that when he visited him at his master's home he found 'the Negro Charles lying on the floor, with an immoderate iron collar around his neck, connected with a chain proportionately large, which chain was fastened to a block of more than 100 pounds weight…discovered on inspecting his body that from the lower part of the back, down to the extremities of the thighs, there was one continued wound, encrusted entirely over with clotted blood.'[28] Caesar More on this occasion was found guilty and charged twenty five pounds.

Finally, there was the trial of a free mulatto John Stewart, charged for the cruel treatment of his female slave, which resulted in her death and whom he accused of being a runaway. The court heard that the girl was beaten over and over by Stewart to the point where he had to be physically restrained. Stewart in his defence noted that it was 'his unquestionable right to treat his own property as he pleased.'[29] He was ultimately found 'not guilty' by the court.

Reverend Charles noted that although the persons brought to trial were coloured the whites were just as equally guilty. 'I conceive sufficient for me merely to observe, that whenever men, on whom it is officially as well as socially incumbent to protect and redress the injured, by punishing the guilty, either totally acquit the notorious delinquent, or treat him with such inhumane lenity as can tend only to legalize oppression, they become, through their neglect, joint partakers in his guilt, and ought, therefore, equally to partake in the ignominy which should accompany it; since by thus shewing mercy, without judgement, they manifest, to the discerning eye, that radical effect of steady principle which must infallibly incline them, at other times, to exercise judgement without mercy.'[30]

He concluded by saying that he does know of too many and too well authenticated instances of inhumane acts by white people on the island 'as would extract (were he but permitted to relate them) tears of mingled pity and indignation from the eye of every reader not altogether callous to sympathetic and virtuous feelings.' Reverend Charles then related the case of a young negro girl who was punished by her white master over a trivial matter. Her punishment included the use of the 'Barbados glove,'[31] which after one night of application resulted in the amputation of her hand just above the wrist. The detailed descriptions of the severe and inhumane treatment to which the slaves were subjected, given by a credible witness such as Reverend Charles, was used by Wilberforce to further bolster his case for the abolition of the slave trade.

In addition to providing concrete evidence of the mistreatment of slaves in Dominica to Wilberforce, Reverend Charles also directly appealed to the British Parliament to end the slave trade. 'The abolition, the speedy abolition of the slave-trade, is a measure intimately connected with the welfare and the morals of those Negroes who are already here. I build my opinion in this respect on the following grounds, the sufficiency of which I doubt not but every impartial and considerate person will readily acknowledge. All slaves brought to these islands from Africa arrive in a state of barbarism, arrive, I mean, with minds scarcely at all influenced by a sense of moral obligation, uninstructed alike in the principles of natural and of revealed religion, regardless of the laws by which property is secured, and totally inattentive even to external decency. ….the British Legislature must interfere, it must first abolish the importation slave-trade, and then extend its benevolent attention to the situation of those unhappy beings who have already been imported.'[32] It would however, be a further four years before Wilberforce could again face Parliament and an additional three years before decisive action on abolishing the slave trade was taken.

On 21 May 1804, Wilberforce again rose in the House to announce his intention to put forward the motion for abolishing the slave trade. He lamented the fact that 'unhappily, a shameful, nay criminal, indifference has for some time prevailed upon a question, which formerly awakened every just, generous and noble feeling of the human mind, and the history of it, we fear, furnishes but too certain a proof, that the operation of the selfish and sordid passions is constant, steady and persevering; but that the movements of virtue are fickle, transient and illusory. It is a melancholy instance how apt people are to grow weary of well doing. An obscure handful of avaricious, unfeeling dealers in men have, for near twenty years, laughed to scorn the virtue, honour and character, and even the pledged faith of the British empire.'[33]

Uppermost in the minds of the House members were the events in Haiti in 1802 and ongoing Maroon insurrections in

Dominica. *The Morning Chronicle*, in commenting on the motion before the House noted: 'it is impossible that the proceedings either in the Leeward Islands or in the French Windward Islands, can remain unknown to the Negroes in the other islands; and this knowledge is like that of good and evil; the Negroes must see their servile state; they are conscious of their shame and nakedness; and they must be ready to enter into any measures, the object of which is to change their condition. In addition to this they have seen the successful resistance of their brethren to the finest armies that ever went from Europe, and the superstitious reverence for whites, and the belief for their superiority, must be greatly weakened, if not extinguished forever. The greater the number of able bodied Negroes, smarting with the injury of being transported or kidnapped, from Africa, that is introduced into the islands, the greater will be the danger to the peace of the colonies, and the greater will be the force of the Negro insurrection.' [34]

Wilberforce formerly presented his motion to abolish the slave trade to the House on 30 May. In speaking against the motion, Member of Parliament Fuller noted that the slaves in the West Indies were very well treated. The Maroon War, he said had been alluded to during the debate and had been described in very favourable colours. He begged to state however, 'that in that war only eight or ten individuals joined the Maroons.' This however, could not be further from the truth but it showed the length to which those opposed to abolishing the slave trade were prepared to go.

After several hours of debate, the bill to abolish the slave trade was passed in the House of Commons on 30 May 1804 with 124 voting ayes and 49 voting noes. The period within which the slave trade would cease was however left for further discussion.[35] Unfortunately similar to what happened in April 1792, its passage was deemed too late to be debated in the House of Lords. Reintroduced into the British Parliament one year later in April 1805, the bill to abolish the slave trade was rejected by a vote of 70 ayes and 77 noes. It would take an additional two years before it was reintroduced.

On 2 January 1807 Lord Grenville, presented a Bill to the House of Lords entitled simply '*an act for the abolition of the Slave Trade*', which ordered that the traffic should be abolished, as contrary to justice and humanity, and that after the passing of the bill, it should be unlawful to fit out any vessel for the carrying on of this trade. On 6 February the House resolved that the General Abolition of the Slave Trade by law would take place on 1 January 1808; and after 1 May 1807, no ships are to clear out from Great Britain to the coast of Africa. Then on 23 February, almost two weeks after receiving the Bill, the House of Commons voted on abolishing of the slave trade, with 283 members in favour of abolition and 16 against.[36]

When finally passed by both houses in 1807, the bill to end the slave trade had taken just over sixteen years for eventual passage through the British Parliament. The abolitionists like Wilberforce and Sharpe, had exhibited much tenacity in their quest to see the end of the slave trade, which was borne out of a conviction to resist the scourge of slavery. For the abolitionists the Parliamentary victory planted a solid path to the eventual abolition of slavery itself, a journey that would last for an additional 26 years. To the Maroons scattered in the mountains of Dominica the end of the slave trade provided a much needed boost in their pursuit of lasting freedom.

9

Maroons and French Republicans Collude

A black soldier in Victor Hugues army.

By the end of March 1791, Governor John Orde, with the support of the 15th and 30th regiments, had successfully suppressed a major uprising that threatened the very existence of the plantation system and slavery in Dominica. In the months that followed, the colony appeared to experience a time of relative calm with very little Maroon activity reported. The two most noted leaders at the time, Pangloss and Pharcelle, after their famous non-appearance on the Windward coast to assist in the New Year's Day uprising, seemingly retreated to the relative safety of their forest hideaways. The authorities had started to sense complete victory with Governor John Orde commenting frequently on the state of tranquillity that pervaded over the island, and the fact that 'the negroes appeared completely subdued.'[1]

All that good sentiment and feeling of ease drastically changed around November of 1791 as echoes of the slave uprisings in St Domingo, and ensuing unrest in Martinique reached the shores of Dominica. The authorities' complacency was replaced by growing concerns that the agitation in those islands would take hold in Dominica. Governor John Orde in a letter to Henry Dundas, British Secretary of State for the Home Department, communicated his disquiet at the events taking place in the two countries.[2] Orde followed this up with a presentation to his administration in which he stressed the need for vigilance in preventing those coming from Martinique to 'be secured and prevented from improper communication with the Negroes in this island.'[3]

The governor's concerns, however, appeared to be unfounded as 1791 ended without further incidents followed by a similar year in 1792, where no major disruptions, on the part of the Maroons, to the plantation system was reported. The year 1793 would, however, would realise the worst fears of the planters and authorities on the island. On 1 February 1793, France declared war on Great Britain and Holland, and as before, given the proximity of the French Islands of Guadeloupe and Martinique to Dominica, this declaration of war had an immediate impact on these islands. Just a few days after the declaration, more than twenty slaves absconded from the John Greg estate and set up their own camp in the heights above Layou. This would prove to be the largest single number of slaves leaving the estates since the uprisings in January 1791.

Also, there were reports that a 'fleet of man of war had landed troops on Dominica on 16 February 1793 and were encouraging the slaves to revolt.'[4] In March, rumours also persisted of the French menace to Dominica society with an article in *The Aurora Advertiser General* noting that 'the numerous French immigrants settled there [Dominica] has been ordered to depart by government. This it seems has given the utmost offense and so far, has the indignation of some being roused, as to declare, that they would return thither in force, and mark the principal promoters of this measure for vengeance, and set fire to the town of Roseau. Every necessary precaution will be taken to prevent this insolent menace from being effected.'[5] In May, the Legislative Assembly following up on their fears passed '*an act to prevent the residence of His Majesty's enemies in this island.*'[6] The enemies referred to in the act were clearly the French from the neighbouring islands, and French nationals residing in Dominica who were considered to be hostile to the British interests.

That same month of May, Pharcelle, determined to take advantage of the turmoil and uncertainty on the island, made a surprised offer to the authorities. In exchange for the granting of a pardon to him and his complete freedom and that of other Maroons, he would surrender himself and serve the colony by taking in and bringing in other runaway slaves. This bold offer effectively offered a chance for the authorities to once and for all quell the Maroon revolts. The announcement of such an offer was first revealed by the Privy Council.[7] While the authorities seriously considered the offer and dared not refuse, it was Pharcelle himself, whom, at least for the time being, reneged on his offer.

Meanwhile, Lieutenant Governor Bruce realising that the Maroons were gaining in strength and confidence worked with the House of Assembly to enact legislation that would serve to improve the conditions of the slaves and another aimed to organise a ranger force to hunt down the Maroons. On 15 March 1793, '*an act to revive and make perpetual an act for the encouragement, protection, and better government of slaves, was enacted.*' The act had earlier expired and was revived and passed. That same day, an act to reconstitute the ranger force was also revived,[8] namely:

'An Act to establish a company of rangers, for the apprehending and suppressing of runaway slaves, and for obliging the proprietors, renters or employers of all slaves belonging to or employed on the several plantations and lands in this Island to furnish a proportion of their slaves to be sent into the woods after and in search of runaways; to provide officers for such company, by engaging such proper white

persons and people of colour as may be disclosed to be employed on the said service; and for granting encouragement for the apprehending or destroying of any of the runaways; and to empower magistrates, on the requisition of the commanding officer of the said company of rangers, to issue their warrant to call to the assistance of the said company of rangers a certain number of slaves from the neighbouring plantations in cases of emergency, and to prevent the importation of slaves convicted or known to have been guilty of murder, insurrection, or other capital offenses, and to prevent the sale of gunpowder, firearms or other offensive weapons to runaways.'[9]

By the second half of the year, the flare up of tensions between the Maroons and the authorities, and the fear of a French invasion, appear to have both subsided significantly, prompting Lieutenant Governor Bruce to confidently state in a letter dated 1 June 1793 to Secretary Dundas that 'the island continues in a state of tranquillity, trade is tolerably brisk in that and neighbouring countries.'[10] All that would change, however, when, emboldened by the successes of the slaves in St Dominique, and in a throwback to the attacks of 1785-86, 50 armed Maroons, at the dead of night, raided the Hampstead estate in August 1793, thoroughly ransacked it, and took everything they could carry away, along with nineteen slaves.[11]

That same month on 29 August French Republican commissioner Léger Félicité Sonthonax extended the rights of freedom and equality to all slaves and their family members in the whole of St. Dominique, a privilege which he had previously extended to those who fought on the side of the French Republic. By early 1794, that privilege was extended to all the slaves on the other French Caribbean territories. By April 1794, the English fearing that the revolutionary fervour that had resulted in the freedom of the slaves in the French West Indies, would spread to the British colonies, attacked and occupied Guadeloupe, Martinique and St Lucia; the three French territories closest to Dominica.

This strategy however appeared to have backfired as several of the revolutionaries from those islands made their way to Dominica. There they would further swell the ranks of the Maroons and continue to push for complete freedom for those still enslaved on the island. More worrisome to the authorities though was the fact that they now linked up with Pharcelle; the one Maroon who had for over a decade, so decidedly resisted enslavement. Sightings of armed mulattoes in Dominica became a near daily occurrence. In one such instance, French Planter John Trotter wrote to Lieutenant Governor Bruce to inform him that he had received intelligence from three negroes who disclosed that close to seventy mulattoes were seen armed with muskets and cutlasses around Dominica. He was also informed that 'the mulattoes had made arrangements to meet up with 'General' Pharcelle somewhere in the area of the Indian River in Portsmouth.'[12]

One such mulatto residing in Dominica, Joseph Durand, attempted to write a letter to Pharcelle in which he praised his efforts and also conveyed his best wishes to 'all the citizens of Pharcelle's camp.' He also promised to meet with him in person in the future. Unfortunately, 'a negro by the name of Belfast,' given the responsibility for delivering the letter turned it over to the authorities. Subsequently, Lieutenant Governor Bruce directed the arrest of Durand, and he was held for questioning.

Just days after Durand's arrest, on 15 October 1794 the government, fearing the worse from Pharcelle, and recognising his ability to bring together the Maroons and the mulattoes, met in the Legislature in order to reconsider his earlier offer of surrender. On that day, members of the House, with a renewed sense of urgency, proposed that the government allow Pharcelle his wish of crown lands and a full pardon in exchange for his help with the capturing of Maroons. The full resolution of the House in that regard read as follows:

'Resolved, that the commander in chief be and is hereby authorized to employ proper persons to treat with Farcelle, a black man, supposed to be at the Head of the Runaway slaves in the woods, for the purpose of making him and such other runaways as many be agreed upon with him free persons, under an Act of the Legislature to be passed....if such treaty shall take

effect, the Board and House recommend to His Honour to grant to the said Farcelle and his party, so to be made free, or to put them in possession of Lands belonging to the Crown in convenient situations in the woods, to cultivate and improve and constantly reside therein and, not themselves, the whole our condition that the said Farcelle and his party...shall consent faithfully to employ themselves for ever hereafter in searching for and apprehending all such slaves as may desire the service of their owners and retire to the woods, the said Farcelle and all Party to be allowed and paid proper rewards for such runaway slaves in their delivery to the Provost Marshal of this Island.'[13]

A house committee was then composed to continue negotiations with Pharcelle. Then on 6 December 1794, the House of Assembly hoping to capitalise on what they hoped would be collaboration from Pharcelle passed an '*act to enable the commanding officer of the corps of rangers employed in suppressing the runaway slaves, to procure such slaves for guides as he shall think best qualified to discover the camps or places of resort of the runaways in the woods.*'[14]

Pharcelle was later called to attend a meeting with the Assembly after word was received that he had agreed to the deal. In the agreement, eventually signed by Pharcelle it was made clear that he along with his two wives, Martan and Angelique, and six other Maroon men and their wives would be set free under the terms, which he previously proposed.[15]

Three days later, in an attempt to stem the flow of correspondence like the one which led to Durand attempting to contact Pharcelle, the House passed an Act '*to oblige the owners of negroes and persons of colour plying as porters, canoe and boatmen, to carry letters into the country, to give their names to the Treasurer, to have tickets and badges as porters, to regulate their conduct and hire, and to put them in due subordination.*'[16] Pharcelle's seeming defection to the colonial government appeared to have very little impact on the vast majority of the Maroons, who continued in their quest to win new converts from the plantations and to live free in their mountain hideouts of Dominica.

May 1789 witnessed the start of the French Revolution, where the old regime was abolished in favour of a constitutional monarchy. Almost immediately there was an outbreak of fighting and conflict, which became known as the French Revolutionary Wars lasting until 1802. September 1792 saw the constitutional monarchy being replaced with the First French Republic, which led to the execution of King Louis XVI, and an extended period of turmoil throughout the French empire. The French Republicans were now firmly aligned against the royalists, and the animosity and strife spread to the West Indian colonies. By late 1792 however, royalists were still firmly in control of Martinique and Guadeloupe forcing republicans including thousands of *gens des couleurs* (coloured people) to flee to the relative safety of Dominica in October of that year.

'These republicans-in-exile decided that since they had stayed true to the French government by fleeing royalist control, they were the legitimate representatives of the islands of Martinique and Guadeloupe, and were entitled to carry out the overdue election of parliamentary representatives. When they gathered to do so, a number of *gens de couleur* took advantage of the rights granted to them in April of 1792 to participate as electors. They were fairly well-represented (15% of the electors presented themselves as *gens de couleur*), and one of these chosen as a representative was a *homme de couleur* from Martinique, Jean Littée.' [17] Another *homme de couleur* selected during that time was Louis Delgrès who would go on to lead the resistance against the reestablishment of slavery in Guadeloupe in 1802. Once selected the representatives then travelled to France to take their seats in the National Assembly.[18]

By 1793, however, the situation was reversed, when, with the royalists losing ground to the republicans, between 3000 – 4000 royalists from Martinique and Guadeloupe made their way to Dominica, this time fleeing republican aggression. Their foray into Dominica was however short-lived as many died from a massive outbreak of yellow fever upon arrival. In early 1794, the British, exploiting ongoing events in France surrounding the French Revolutionary Wars, launched invasions of Martinique and Guadeloupe. The British found many sympathisers among the French planter class who resented the fact that the French Constitutional Assembly had passed a law abolishing slavery in the French colonies on 4 February 1794. That same day, royalist planters of Martinique signed an accord in London on putting Martinique under British jurisdiction. Soon after that declaration, the remaining royalists who had survived the yellow fever outbreak returned to Martinique.

Then, on 19 February the British invaded Martinique and it was finally captured on 24 March 1794. A few weeks later, on 10 April the French garrison in St Lucia surrendered peacefully to the British, with 'not a man killed or wounded.'[19] However, British rule over St Lucia did not last long. 'Emissaries were sent among the slaves and the poorer part of the French colonies to excite them to a universal and simultaneous insurrection. In St Lucia the project succeeded completely as the English troops were taken by surprise and overpowered. The main fort, after a blockade of three months, was compelled to surrender. Such of the British, as were not butchered, were shipped off the island and the tri-colour flag and the red cap of liberty, the new mumbo jumbo of the African slaves were erected triumphantly.'[20]

Meanwhile on Guadeloupe, negotiations were being conducted with the French planters, Ignace-Joseph-Philippe de Perpignan and Louis de Curt, who were desirous to gain British protection, and hence maintain the system of slavery on the island. On 11 April 1794, British troops led by General Charles Grey and assisted by a fleet led by Admiral Sir John Jervis, landed on Guadeloupe. Just thirteen days later, final French resistance crumpled, when French General and Governor Henri Victor Collot[21] surrendered the last stronghold at Basse-Terre, handing the island to the British and the French royalist supporters who opposed the French Revolution spearheaded by the republicans.

Just one month later, on 21 May 1794, French Republican Commissioner Victor Hugues landed on Guadeloupe with a small force of 1150 soldiers. Hugues was born into a rich Marseille family and had earlier migrated to Haiti. He was however, forced to return to France with the onset of the Haitian Revolution. Now firmly on the side of the revolutionaries in France, he was sent to Guadeloupe to reinforce the declaration of freedom for the slaves on that island.

No sooner had Hugues landed on Guadeloupe than he proclaimed liberty for all the slaves on the island, thus gaining their immediate support and that of the mulattoes or '*gens des couleur*.' Within five days he had succeeded in retaking the capital Pointe-a-Pitre from the British. On 6 October 1794, bolstered by the support of the newly emancipated slaves and mulattoes, he forced the surrender of English Brigadier General Graham and his entire force of 1500 men[22] at Camp Berville, which included 800 French emigres and 900 soldiers of African descent. Hugues would later write to his superiors, 'I communicate to you today, not as formerly, a complete rout of our enemies, but the bloodless capture of a whole army; of a strongly entrenched camp, ...the enemy made not the least show of resistance.'[23]

Emboldened by his success, Hugues shortly thereafter issued a proclamation to all the neutral nations trading with the islands, in which he declared: 'eight hundred republicans and two French frigates have conquered the island of Guadeloupe: eight thousand men, chosen troops, six line of battle ships and twelve frigates must yield to that courage, virtue and love of one's country that animate a Republican breast. With so inconsiderable forces, but entirely devoted to the triumph of liberty and equality, we have overcome all obstacles, and finally drove from this fertile, and now free country the remainder of the English pilfering horde....Have not our sloops of war, and other armed vessels, within these few months, taken, sunk or burnt eighty-eight of their vessels?...Are we not ready to attack their own colonies, and there convince them of the impossibility of such a blockade.

'But rob they must! That is the great principal of the English military service....We do therefore from our side formally declare, that we shall never deviate from the principals of equity and benevolence, which have directed all our operations, during and after the taking of this island: and that all neutral vessels shall be well received, and protected as far as it lies in our power; we assure them that the English rhodomontades inspire us only with perfect contempt, and that our enemies shall soon have reason to repent of their rashness and insolence.'[24]

Seven months after Hugues successful capture of Guadeloupe, Henry Hamilton was sworn in as Commander in Chief and governor of Dominica. When Hamilton was appointed, Fort Matilda in Guadeloupe was then besieging by the republicans and its proximity to Dominica would keep the governor and inhabitants continually on alert. Archibald Gloster would later write that 'in fact the war soon raged most violently throughout all the Antilles, and the French republican Chief, Victor Hugues having succeeded in forcing the British to evacuate Guadeloupe, commenced hostilities against the English settlements, into many of which he carried rebellions, murders and devastations.'[25]

With Hugues determined to spread his revolution throughout the islands, he seized an opportunity to do so by throwing his support behind the slave uprising in Grenada. On 3 March 1795, the rebellion started when Julien Fédon, a French Mulatto planter, freed his slaves and encouraged them to overthrow the British colonial regime. Within a few days, Governor Home was taken prisoner and the rebels were in control of most of the island, with the exception of the capital St Georges.[26]More than 7 000 of the close to 30 000 enslaved persons on the island together with the French republicans actively participated in the more than sixteen month uprising.

Just days after Hugues joined forces with the revolt in Grenada, a distraught captain of His Majesty's vessel *The Scorpion* sent a distress letter to London stating: 'the French have taken Grenada and Montserrat from us, and no reinforcements had then arrived from England. If they are not expeditious, we shall shortly be without an island, as nothing can save them but a large body of troops. Victor Hugues the French

Commissioner at Guadeloupe has distributed proclamations, declaring all negroes free who will take up arms for the French Republic; and I suppose there is no want of disaffected persons, in all the islands, to stir up sedition and join him in his plans.'[27]

A similar situation of Hugues' support for rebellion against the English played out in St Vincent and the Grenadines. Just days after the outbreak of the rebellion in Grenada, governor James Seton fearing the worse, declared martial law. On 8 March, the black Caribs[28] of St Vincent with the support of the republicans began attacks on the British plantations. The black Caribs numbering around 2 000 were unable to get the support of the more than 12 000 enslaved blacks on the island due to lingering animosity between them. Consequently, the uprising was far less successful than in Grenada. As early as August of that year there were reports of the Caribs being defeated.

The *Northern Star* reported that 'at St Vincent, the resurrection was quelled entirely; the last body consisting of about 500, being either killed or taken, and examples made of the ringleaders. A part of the militia was dismissed; and just as the island began to assume a tranquil appearance, another party of French desperadoes, consisting of 150, suddenly landed and renewed the confusion. A desperate action soon took place between them and an equal number of our troops, which finally ended in the defeat of the enemy, the greater part of whom were either taken or destroyed; the remainder fled and took refuge in the mountains.[29] It would take a further two years before the British succeeded in completely crushing the revolt and expelling the black Caribs from the island.

An anonymous writer out of Martinique on 20 April 1795 described Hugues actions thus: 'Hugues has formed the plan for destroying the English colonies, and the execution of this plan is the object of the agents he keeps in the different islands, of the parties he entertains, and of the insurrection he excites in them. His means are much greater than it is believed in Europe. At Guadeloupe he has about 6 000 white people, 1000 of whom are national guards, and the rest consists of those who left the other islands, or who were imprudently banished from

Martinico without being sent to Europe.

'The latter to the number of 3000, although they have left their families and property as pledges here, are the most implacable of our enemies, and breathe vengeance and extermination. Fifteen hundred of them are well mounted, armed and equipped... He places much confidence in the insurrections he excites in the English islands, which he thinks must considerably weaken our force, by obliging us to send thither numerous detachments. Besides the white people he has armed 10 000 negroes; but on these he relies very little.'[30]

All this time, Hugues had his sights set on the capture of Dominica, strategically located between Martinique and Guadeloupe. He however adopted a decidedly different approach to that employed in Grenada and St Vincent. In Dominica, his plan focused on engaging the Maroon population and enlisting the support of French sympathisers and inhabitants on the island. Much of the French inhabitants were concentrated around the village of Colihaut and the neighbouring coffee plantations on the North West coast of Dominica. To further encourage the support, of in particular, the wary French planters suspicious of his plan to free the slaves, Hugues issued a proclamation inviting the true Frenchmen on the island to join in the invasion. He also threatened to put to death those who did not cooperate along with their families.

Consequently, by early June 1795, Hugues had already colluded with a number of the many French inhabitants of Dominica on his plan to expel the British, including the hundreds of republicans who had remained on the island after arriving two years earlier. As part of the plan, the French inhabitants would provide the Maroons with weapons and they would join the group of Hugues' invading party after his men landed on the island. By that time, there were an estimated 1,236 Europeans in the island, 14 967 slaves and 445 free people of colour.

Starting on 4 June 1795, Victor Hugues rather than opting for a large frontal attack on Roseau began landing groups of men along various points on the North of the island. The plan was to join with the Maroons and march against the militias defending key areas in the island. The first landing reportedly took place on the evening of 4 June, when 5 boats containing 50 men attempted to land on the North Eastern village of Woodfordhill. They were however repulsed by militiamen controlling the gun battery on La Soi Point.[31]

On 6 June a further 200 men landed at Batibou Beach and made their way unopposed to Pagua, where they took over the Hatton Garden plantation, making it their main base. That same day, another force comprising 400 men landed at Batibou Bay and advanced towards Woodfordhill. By that time however, news of the invading forces had reached Roseau and Governor Hamilton mobilised about 200 militiamen from the St George's and Pointe Mitchel regiments, the Coloured Fusiliers, the Coloured Artillery Company, the Black Rangers, the Light Infantry Company and the Grenadiers, who immediately set out in two different directions in an attempt to encircle the invaders.[32] British ship Captain Caswell who travelled from Martinique to London just days after the French invasion reported that: 'the French from Guadeloupe had effected the landing of 400 men on Dominica, who had marched back of the island, and fortified themselves, and who were receiving continual reinforcements, by the revolting of the negroes: In a short time they were expected to begin operations against the English, and would soon possess the island.'[33]

However, the reality on the ground was somewhat different. Without the availability of a charismatic leader like Pharcelle it was difficult to rally the full support of the Maroons. For the second time in four years, Pharcelle mysteriously disappeared when the revolt against the British commenced. Without his leadership and as in the Windward Island uprising, the plan to effect a revolt quickly unravelled. Just six months before, Pharcelle had seemingly accepted the Legislature's offer for crown land, freedom for himself and his wives, in return for his collaboration. So by the time Hugues was ready to attack, he lacked the superiority of numbers he had hoped for coming from the support of the Dominica Maroons.

To make matters worse, the hastily assembled militiamen put together by Governor Hamilton with the guidance of trusty slaves successfully encircled the main force in Hatton Garden while hunting down others in the woods. By 16 June it was all over. British retribution was swift and uncompromising. Confirmation of the French defeat would later appear in United Kingdom newspapers including from *The Gentleman's Magazine*, which stated: 'Captain Elmshie left Dominica on July 13 1795 and confirms the account of the defeat of the French who landed in that island, except a few stragglers who had fled to the mountains. Dominica was entirely freed from them. The plan for taking that island appears to have been conceived between Victor Hugues and the French inhabitants of the island who were very numerous.

'Many of them who were wealthy planters, armed their negroes and put themselves at their head to join their countrymen. A number of the most active of the French planters have been tried. Eight were hanged. Several more were on their trial and there was no doubt they would in a few days share the same fate. These French planters all possessed handsome properties. Governor Hamilton finding that no confidence could be placed in the French inhabitants has sent upwards of 600 of them to England. There was only one company of regular troops in Dominica so that the island has been saved chiefly by the spirited exertions of the English inhabitants and their faithful slaves. The enemy fortunately remained a little time on the island before their defeat that they did very little damage to the plantations.'[34] It would take a further two years before Hugues would attempt another attack on Dominica.

Indeed, several of the French inhabitants involved in the conspiracy were subsequently captured, tried under court martials set up for the purpose; some were executed for their role in the attempted revolt.[35] Among those executed were Robert Motard and Henry Petit a white and coloured respectively, who were considered to be French spies. In addition, more than 95 men, women and children, mainly whites and mulattoes, were banished from Dominica.

Archibald Gloster in reflecting on this situation observed that 'Dominica from its value and proximity, did not escape his [Hugues] vindictive vigilance. — By his emissaries he corrupted and alarmed some of the French planters and on the Fourth of June 1795, an invasion was attempted; but a brave and energetic resistance on the part of the inhabitants principally under the auspices of Governor Hamilton, compelled part of the enemy to fly, and the rest to surrender, and from urgent necessity, the only law that continued to exist for a considerable time after, was, the *Law Martial*.'[36]

More than eight years later in 1803, the Legislature in Dominica passed an Act '*to prevent a return to this island of persons who were banished thereon by sentences of general courts martial held in the year one thousand seven hundred and ninety five [1795] for the trial of sundry persons charged with high treason, and to prevent aliens as well whites as free persons of colour, possessing sentiments inimical to His Majesty's government from introducing and establishing themselves in this colony and for other purposes*.'[37]

The preamble of the act also provided additional details on the 1795 uprising. 'Whereas sundry persons natural born or adopted subjects of the King, or owing allegiance to His Majesty residing in this island, did some time in the year 1795, when this colony was invaded by the enemy, rise in open rebellion against His said Majesty, with intent to favour the designs of his enemies in invading and conquering the same. And whereas, sundry of the said rebels and traitors having been duly apprehended, were brought to trial by and before certain courts-martial held in the island (the same being then under martial-law), for such their said crimes, and being thereof duly convicted were adjudged some of them to suffer death, who were executed accordingly, and others of them to banishment from the colony, some of them for a certain period, and others of them whose names are inserted in the schedule, hereunto annexed, for and during their respective lives.'[38]

Although the plan to invade Dominica with the help of the Maroons proved unsuccessful in June 1795, the clear threat posed by an alliance between them and the Guadeloupe and Martinique republicans would be used to good effect by the French against the British. Playing on this fear, a deliberate ploy employed by the republicans in Martinique seeking to retake control of that island from the British, was hashed out later in the year. In November 1795, word went out that a group of mulattoes had landed on Dominica, joined with some of the Colihaut rebels and a large number of Maroons, and formed a large camp. The Dominica authorities immediately sent for help from their troops stationed in Martinique, and a large force was despatched to seek out the rebels. After searching for ten days they were unable to discover any of the group from Guadeloupe.

It turned out to be a deliberate ploy to get the British troops away from Martinique. No sooner had they left than the Guadeloupe republicans landed on the Southern end of Martinique. They arrived on the island undetected, with four field pieces and 700 pieces of arms and a great deal of ammunition. Lord Dalhousie, the British commander on the island immediately attacked them along with the 70 men at his disposal. In the course of the attack, 15 British soldiers were killed and several wounded; while 80 of the attackers were reportedly killed.[39]

To the British authorities the knowledge that the Maroons and the enslaved population understood the ideals of the French Revolution served to create further fear and anxiety among them. So it was that as the Maroon rebellion continued with increased violence and determination, the planters ascribed this escalation of the struggle to their adherence to the principles of the French Revolution. To back up their claim, they pointed to the French gazette, '*L'Ami de La Liberte'*, which at the time was printed in Roseau, as a major source of this influence. The Legislative Assembly pointed to the fact that the gazette was extremely dangerous and served as a corrupting influence, for in it, such encouragement is given to slaves and opinions promulgated in their favour so dangerous to the lives and properties of their masters.

All together the year 1797 proved largely uneventful,

except for news of the discovery of a plan by Victor Hugues working with a republican sympathiser, Monsieur La Coste to take over Dominica in the early part of June. La Coste,[40] who was residing in Dominica, kept in close and constant contact with Hugues and eventually provided him with a list of all of the British troops on the island, and their various positions. In addition, he provided to the Guadeloupe Governor the best day to attack the island. 'From every information, there was no doubt, but that the Island would become an easy prey to the enemy, who were anticipating in idea the plunder.'

La Coste's plans were ultimately revealed to the authorities by a soldier whom he had entrusted with the secret, and he was immediately arrested. The authorities in Dominica were clearly rattled by the French attempts to take over Dominica and the seeming ease with which local French sympathisers well entrenched within Dominican society appeared willing and able to aid in those efforts. Consequently, following La Coste's arrest, the Legislature swiftly passed an Act on 16 June 1797 '*to declare the law concerning the cognizance trial and punishment of spies, and to enable the governor to issue warrants to hold court martial for their trial, to prevent foreigners from landing or remaining in the island without licence, and to punish inhabitants receiving or concealing such foreigners*.'[41]

The condemned spy La Coste was summarily tried and condemned. It is said that 'he met his fate with uncommon fortitude, and seemingly rejoiced in his attempt to serve his countrymen. He ascended the ladder with spirit and alacrity, he exclaimed publicly, 'France will not condemn my conduct. Whatever hypocrisy may be necessarily assumed, every Frenchman, be his political opinions what they may, wishes well even to New France. There are thousands of Frenchmen, if an opportunity occurred, who would be guilty of what is now called a crime.' After praying some time with the priest, La Coste was launched into eternity.[42]

On the same day of his execution on 22 June 1797, someone in Dominica addressed a letter to his friend in England, in which he indicated that: 'we have been on the brink of destruction here.

A Frenchman by the name of La Coste, had laid a plan for an insurrection, and to have all the English put to death. It was to have taken place in a few days, but was providentially discovered, and this day he is to be hanged.'[43]

Reflecting on the conquests of Victor Hugues, Phillip Stanhope would later write: 'Victor Hugues at Guadeloupe displayed a true Jacobin energy turning his views of conquest to the English islands, he succeeded in kindling the flame of revolt among the negroes, the Maroons and the Caribs. With their aid the French gained possession of St. Lucia and St Vincent. In Grenada and Dominica their attacks, though at first successful, were finally repulsed.'[44]

As for Hugues, his reign as governor in Guadeloupe would come to an end when he was replaced and sent as governor of French Guinea. By 1802 Napoleon successfully reimposed slavery on the French colonies, including Guadeloupe. Hugues would later lament that 'the men who have got possession of power at Guadeloupe are the same who for eight years have distinguished themselves as the enemies of the Mother Country, and the instigators of every disturbance….These men will never pardon me for having always shewn the greatest reluctance to raise to military or civil rank, the negroes or men of colour.'[45]

In 1808 Hugues while governor of French Guinea capitulated to the English and in 1810 was court martialled in Paris for 'not having done his utmost in defense of the colony; and secondly of having capitulated with the Anglo-Portuguese in order to save his own plantations and property.'[46] At the end of the trial, Hugues was acquitted of all charges and ordered to be restored to his duties. He returned to French Guinea where he remained as governor for a period of time. Hugues died on 12 August 1826, at the age of sixty-four, in Bordeaux France.[47]

10

The West India Regiment

Great Britain, conscious of the ongoing threat posed by the Maroons and other slave rebellions across the Caribbean,[1] was anxious to find ways to protect their slave interests. To help accomplish this, they turned to a cohort of slaves and African recaptives, organised into a regiment. It consisted of white sergeants, corporals, drummers, and officers. They became known as the West India Regiment and would be used to fight against the Maroons, provide protection to the plantations, and quell rebellions on the estates. Up to this point there was heavy reliance on white troops permanently stationed on the islands or those who were rotated from Britain on a regular basis. Initially, the West India Regiment consisted largely of creoles but later came to be dominated by blacks born in Africa, emanating mainly from the Gold Coast and the West Central Africa area.[2]

In support of this new recruitment drive, the Dominica Legislature on 16 October 1794, passed an act '*to authorize the Commander in Chief to employ armed parties of white persons, free persons of colour, and slaves with proper officers, to discover and apprehend runaways, and suspected white and coloured persons, and for the purpose of payment of such parties.*' [3] Two months later, Governor Henry Hamilton arrived in Dominica to replace Governor John Orde, following his departure in 1792, and whose position was temporarily filled by Lieutenant Governor Thomas Bruce. Within days of Hamilton's arrival, another Act was passed, this time on 6 December 1794 '*to procure guides to discover runaway camps and places of resort in the woods.*'[4]

Increasing evidence of the fear existing in Dominica concerning the potential for the Maroons to illicit the support of the mulattoes, was demonstrated that December, when, in addition to the two laws enacted to stifle Maroon activity;

another was passed directed at curtailing any interaction with the mulattoes from the neighbouring countries. The Act sought 'to authorize the governor to order pettyaugres and small craft to be detained to prevent improper communication with the enemy and to press the same into service if necessary.' [5] As far as the authorities in Dominica were concerned, the threat posed to the plantation system by the Maroons was far from over.

Early in 1795, the first group of slaves to serve in the regiment were purchased for around 70 pounds on the coast of West Africa and transported to Dominica in regular slave ships. They were initially housed at Charlottesville (Newtown), near to Fort Young in Roseau. This first and subsequent groups were finally brought together under the command of Lieutenant Colonel John Skerrit and named the 8th West India Regiment on 15 September 1795. Later, a 9th West India Regiment would be added. These 'slaves in redcoats' as they were often referred to were allowed to receive the same allowances as the whites serving in the units. They would later be more commonly referred to as the Loyal Dominica Black Regiment.

The British response to Hugues tightening his hold on Guadeloupe was to consolidate their own grip on Martinique, which was done with the appointment of Sir Ralph Abercrombie in command of the affairs of the Windward Islands. He was stationed in Martinique, and had orders to retake Guadeloupe and St Lucia.[6] In Dominica, the Assembly realising that the 25 000 troops available to Abercrombie were insufficient, passed an act in Parliament to make available more able-bodied men; and to that end they turned to the slaves.

An act '*to appoint a committee of the Legislature to select healthy male slaves from the estates, to act as pioneers against the French, in Sir Ralph Abercrombie's army, to appraise the same, regulate the hire, and make good their approved value to proprietors in case of death, or wounds and not returned to their owners,*'[7] was passed on 7 November 1795. One month later, on 3 December 1795, another Act was passed '*to raise a corps of healthy male slaves, to act as soldiers in defence of the colony, for a limited time, appraising, regulating their hire, and for other purposes.*'[8]

By January of 1796, in Dominica, the slave population was estimated at 13 500[9] and that of the Maroons at several hundred. The latter continued to be entrenched in the mountains of Dominica and to pose a serious threat to the very survival of the plantations as they successfully lured an increasing number of slaves away from the estates. This continuous depletion of slave labour prompted Lieutenant Colonel Johnstone, who was engaged in searching for the Maroons, to write to Secretary Dundas deploring the deteriorating situation. 'The Estates are daily decreasing in value, by the desertion of the Negroes belonging to the Estates, and other causes….,[10] Johnstone lamented. Interestingly, the situation in Jamaica was decidedly different where the West India Regiment set up in that country proved extremely effective in almost completely wiping off the Maroons. At the same time, the black Caribs in St Vincent were similarly defeated, and those slaves who tried to escape in Grenada, were similarly subdued by the West India Regiment.

Throughout the year 1796, the Maroons in Dominica continued to consolidate their numbers while the authorities were preoccupied with keeping the islands of Martinique away from the French, and at the same time attempting to retake St Dominique. That year, after serving as governor on Dominica for less than two years, Hamilton died on 29 September in Antigua, after a long illness. John Matson subsequently acted as governor for about a year before being replaced by twenty-nine year old Andrew James Cochrane Johnstone, by the King's appointment on 28 March 1797. Johnstone would eventually arrive in Dominica to take up his appointment on 9 September 1797.

Already, by the year 1797 the wisdom of using slaves to fight on the side of the British was being questioned, thus forcing Sir Ralph Abercrombie by then the Lieutenant Governor of Martinique, to write to the Speaker of the Barbados legislature in their defence. 'Sir, I have observed with regret the dislike expressed by the Legislatures in most of the British islands, to the establishment of a permanent body of Black troops for their defence—a prejudice allowable perhaps in them, may have operated in their minds; a more mature consideration of the plan will, I apprehend shew that it contains nothing injurious to their interests; that on the contrary it will lend considerably to their security and protection,' he wrote.

Abercrombie continued: 'from the information which I have received, Great Britain intends to keep up in peace and in war, a most respectable force in her sugar colonies, and it is proposed that a third part of this force shall consist of Black troops, who from experience have been found to be in every way qualified. In no instance has their fidelity been impeached during the course of this war. They are obedient, sober, hardy, and suited to those services which ruin European troops, in this climate, with whom, however, it is proposed that they should always be mixed in the proportion of one third Black and two-third European.

'The garrison will be frequently changed; no place of importance will be left to the Blacks; discipline and habit will alienate them from every connection with the people of their own colour; the officers and the greater part of the commissioned officers, will be British. The conduct of the Black corps serving at St Lucie and the island rangers at St Vincent and Grenada, has been most exemplary, and alone supercede all arguments. It has occurred to me that the mode established to raise recruits for the West India regiments may have been objectionable.

'I have on that account prevailed with Mr Boutien the contractor to give up his contract, and I'm ready to adopt any suggestion, or any mode more suited to the views of the colonies. If the Legislature will tax themselves with a certain number, I shall willingly receive them at the price paid to Mr Boutien, or if any particular person or persons are pointed out in the different colonies, they shall be employed. Having received His Majesty's instructions and knowing the wishes of his ministers on this subject, I cannot help expressing an earnest desire that the colonies may give into the measure; and feeling as I do, highly interested in everything that concerns the security of the island, will be very gratifying to me, if I shall be enabled to carry it into execution.

'I request therefore, that you would take the sense of the Legislature of the Colony, over which you preside upon this important business. A more deliberate investigation will, I am inclined to think, convince them who have hitherto opposed the question, that this measure is not only founded upon policy, but experience. I shall hope to receive from you such information upon the subject as I can report to government with satisfaction.

'In the meantime, if it meets with the success which I trust it will, no time should be lost. Whatever recruits can be raised, fit for the service, shall be received in charge by the Commanding Officer of His Majesty's troops in your island, and victualled from the day they are delivered; nor shall any other delay be made in payment than what is absolutely requisite.'[11]

The Dominica Legislature in the meantime moved quickly following the installation of Johnstone to shore up support for the 8th West India Regiment. An act was passed on 7 November 1797, ostensibly '*to declare when martial law is in force, to provide refreshments for militia on march, and slaves and mules to carry provisions and other necessaries, to have weekly meetings of militia, during war, to prevent, in martial law debtors leaving the island without payment or security, and to enable the judges and others to exercise their offices during martial law, and for other purposes*.'[12] This was quickly followed up by an act to fix the militia pay, passed on 15 December '*to provide carriers of ammunition and provisions for parties sent out by the Governor against runaways, to fix their pay or hire, and mode of payments*.'[13]

During the last three months of 1797, Johnstone continued his aggressive campaign against the Maroons capturing a large number and returning some to their masters. So relentless was Johnstone's campaign against the slaves that Reverend Charles Peters, rector of the Parish church of St George in Dominica, wrote: 'that the practice of *Marooning* among our West-Indian slaves, (at least in the island of Dominica), is occasioned chiefly by the fragrant and habitual cruelty of their masters, no dispassionate and experienced person will pretend to question, since nothing but the sense of extreme misery could ever prompt men to encounter voluntarily with the dangers and the hardships that are inseparable from such a course of life.

'The life of a Maroon, Reader, renders him liable perpetually to be hunted down (i. e. taken either alive or dead) by any military or civil sportsmen, who may be appointed, or who may feel disposed to engage in the pursuit. Of these unhappy beings, however, the small Island of Dominica was supposed to contain, in the year 1797, nearly 400. The danger naturally to be apprehended from so numerous a body, if permitted deliberately to form and execute their desperate schemes, imposed it, doubtless, as an indispensable duty upon the guardians of the colony, to adopt such measures as were best calculated to reclaim and subdue the fugitives.

'Those measures his Excellency Governor Johnstone did adopt, and that with such promptitude and judgment, that in the course of a few weeks every formidable party of Maroons throughout the island was dispersed, and a considerable number prevailed on to surrender.' Notwithstanding the relentless pursuit of the Maroons, most resisted to the bitter end. 'A great many of them however (according to the report of those who surrendered) persisted in their resolution neither to submit, nor to be taken….,' Reverend Peter stated. Many of the Maroons were shot by the Rangers, others who surrendered as well as those captured were meted out the most severe treatment including 150 lashes of the whip, with many dying from the inhumane treatment.

For those Maroons who survived the onslaught, including Maroon Chief Jacko, they consolidated their position in the mountains of Dominica, determined not to suffer the same fate as that of those in Jamaica, St Vincent, St Lucia and Grenada. Johnstone, however, continued to train and equip members of the 8th West India Regiment, with the ultimate goal of hunting down the Maroons, and registering the same kind of success as was accomplished in the other West Indian islands.

Then in January of 1798, the black regiment recorded a major victory when it discovered a camp of around 200 Maroons, proving that the Maroons were far from being wiped out or defeated. *The Times of London* described it thus: 'a camp of around 200 runaway negroes, at Dominica which had for some time been very troublesome for the Colony, has been broken up by detachments from the Loyal Dominica Black Regiment commanded by the Hon. Governor Cochrane Johnstone.

'By the success of this measure, many of these runaways have been got back to their owners, and it is expected that the whole of the remainder will be forced to surrender, as, besides totally destroying their camp, the banditti were forced to abandon all their provisions, which fell into the hands of the detachments. We have the pleasure to add that this important advantage has been obtained with the loss of only one private belonging to the Loyal Dominica Regiment and at an expense to the colony extremely trifling.'[14]The sighting by the regiment of so many runaways just in one camp underlined to the authorities that the Maroon threat was far from being over.

In reacting to this threat, the Legislature embarked on enacting a number of laws aimed at enhancing their ability to detain and otherwise disrupt the growing number of Maroons. More importantly, the Assembly would enact legislation to allow for the acceptance of the testimony of the black militia, many of whom were still slaves, against the Maroons. Two such pieces of legislation were enacted on 30 April 1798.

The first was an act '*to make testimony of slaves admissible in certain cases,*[15] *and under certain restrictions, for a limited time, to forfeit runaway slaves who have been absent from the service of their masters a certain time; and to oblige the inhabitants of this Island having intelligence of the situation, or motions of the runaway slaves to communicate the same to the persons and in the manner prescribed by this act; and to prevent persons from harbouring or employing slaves on their plantations without a written permission from the owner or person having charge of such slaves; and for other purposes*.'[16]

The other was '*an act for apprehending of runaways and to oblige the Provost Marshall to receive and advertise them, and if unclaimed within limited time, to oblige him to sell them for the public benefit; for appointing a committee of the council and assembly to inspect the common goal from time to time, and for other purposes in this act mentioned.*'[17]

By the middle of 1798 it was becoming increasingly clear to the Legislature that their attempts at securing 'healthy male slaves' to serve was not necessarily meeting with the anticipated results. Therefore, on 16 August 1798 less than three years after passing the act to enlist healthy slaves, another act was passed '*to repeal the act entitled an act to raise a certain number of healthy male slaves to serve as colonial soldiers to defend and protect the island.*'[18]

Early in 1799 the colonial administration in Dominica was no closer to resolving the issue of the Maroons and the growing discontent among the enslaved. To add to their woes, the question of the abolition of the slave trade was gaining momentum in Britain, which, if successful could ultimately threaten their supply of replacement slaves from Africa. Against this backdrop the authorities attempted to improve the situation of the enslaved in the hope of gaining their continuing fidelity, and ultimately increasing their numbers on the plantations.

In July 1799 the result was an act for the Encouragement, Protection, and Better Government of Slaves. '*Every owner, renter, manager, or overseer shall feed or cause to be fed all such slaves or slave as shall be under his, her or their care with a sufficient quantity of good and wholesome food, and shall give them good and sufficient clothing and shall be provided dry and comfortable lodging for them, and in case of sickness of any of the said slaves or slave, the said owner, renter, manager, overseer, shall provide for the said slave or slaves proper medical assistance and advice, and the said owners shall provide boundary of his, her or their plantation or lot of land, some lodging, wholesome food and medical assistance…*'[19]

The supposed betterment of the enslaved, failed to keep them on the plantation, and as the year progressed, the numbers absconding to join those in the woods only increased. Members in the House of Assembly complained of the growing numbers taking solace in the forests and worse, 'lurking in the woods, and frequently appearing in numbers upon different plantations…'[20] The Maroons appeared to be well organised, had plenty of provision grounds and felt no inclination to returning to the plantations in the hope of improved treatment from their former masters. Frustrated by the failure to control the growing numbers of the enslaved taking to the woods, the discussion now turned to possibly banishing the Maroons from the islands as was done with the black Caribs in St Vincent and the Maroons of Jamaica.[21]

At the same time, the authorities stepped up their patrols in search of the Maroons and continued to offer them pardons in exchange for giving themselves up. Pharcelle, who had surrendered to the authorities more than six years before was constantly called upon to help the 8th West India regiment in their searches. Among those accepting the offer of a pardon was Grubois, one of the leading Maroon chiefs at the time who had been in the forests for over twenty years. He surrendered along with his two wives Grace and Cloe, four children Louis, Little Peggy, Nero, and Jean Pierre; as well as Capola, Kitty, Peggy, Panto, and a pregnant Marie.[22]

For his part, Governor Johnstone reiterated the offer of pardons for the Maroons through a proclamation, while insisting that he was, with the help of the West India regiment, prepared to continue hunting them down. He also considered destroying their extensive provision grounds, being well aware of the over 300 acres under cultivation, plus an untold amount in the farthest reaches of the interior of the island.[23] At the same time, the Legislature once again enacted laws that would severely punish the Maroons, and in particular the chiefs.

Passed on 4 September 1800 was an act '*to provide carriers of ammunition for parties sent into the woods, against the runaway slaves, to enforce affidavits from proprietors of the numbers of slaves runaway and to oblige magistrates to return such affidavits to the Legislature.*'[24] This was quickly followed up by an act on 16 October 1800 '*for the trial and effectual punishment of such runaway slaves as may hereafter be taken, and be known to be chiefs, or leaders of camps, or bands of runaway slaves in the woods.*'[25]

More success for the authorities was to follow later in the year with the capture of two Maroon chiefs Liverpool and Dick. Chief Liverpool had himself being in the forest for over twenty years when he was captured.[26] Another chief Johnson was captured on 11 November and executed[27] under the new stricter regulations to punish chiefs. In addition, Pharcelle had run afoul of the authorities, and was arrested and thrown in jail. With the year 1800 coming to an end, and with four Maroon chiefs secured in jail, and several of their followers either captured or having surrendered, the authorities were beginning to declare victory.

On 19 December 1800, Governor Johnstone wrote to both the Council and House of Assembly, recounting his successful exploits against the Maroons, and expressing confidence that an ultimate victory was at hand. 'By the vigorous and unremitting exertions of the 9th West India Regiment a termination has been put to the runaway war, the camps are in one possession, the provision grounds have been destroyed, four of the runaways Chiefs with a great part of their followers are in confinement, and from the numbers who daily surrender, we may venture to hope that within a very limited period there will not be perhaps a single runaway in the woods.'[28]

At that session of Parliament on 19 December, the Legislature responded by passing one of its most sweeping pieces of legislation against the Maroons, which proffered banishment from Dominica for those who were captured or surrendered. The act was '*for the banishing of sundry runaway slaves, now in confinement and also for the banishment of such runaways of certain descriptions as shall hereafter be taken or surrender themselves and for other purposes.*'[29]

The rational for the act was given as follows: 'Whereas in consequence of the late operations against the runaway slaves who were assembled in the woods of this island, sundry of them have been taken, and others of them have been compelled to surrender, and they are now confined to the common goal, and some of them have become forfeited to this colony, under several acts of the Legislature thereof; and whereas it is expedient to remove the said slaves from this colony as well as to preserve the tranquillity thereof from being again disturbed by them, as by their example to prevent and deter other slaves from the commission of the like offences, be it therefore enacted by the Governor, council and assembly of this Island.'

Top of the list of those to be banished was Pharcelle, who had not exactly behaved according to the terms of his agreement with the authorities. He was accused of deliberately misleading the West India regiment and also harbouring Maroons. 'And whereas the said Pharcell, in consequence thereof, enjoyed his freedom, but, on the late expeditions against the runaway slaves being called upon by his Excellency the Governor to serve as a guide to one of the Parties of His Majesty's black troops employed on that service.

'He so misbehaved whilst on service, that His Excellency, on proof thereof, by affidavit in writing made by the officer commanding the party, thought proper to commit the said Pharcell, to the common goal. And by message to both houses hath recommended that he should be sent off of the island as a dangerous person. And whereas it has been proved to the satisfaction of both houses, that the said Pharcell have also misbehaved in receiving and harbouring runaway slaves since the enjoyment of his freedom.'[30]

Clause 3 of the said act reads: '*be it therefore and it is hereby enacted and ordained by authority aforesaid, that his Excellency the Governor may, and he is hereby authorized and empowered to send off the said Pharcell, from this island at the public expense, in such manner as his Excellency may think proper, and if the said Pharcell shall at any time afterwards, return to this island, he shall be taken up, and deemed as a runaway slave and be treated accordingly.*'[31]

With the authorities satisfied that they had dealt a

destructive blow to the Maroon movement, they now turned their attention to persons whom they considered to be sympathetic to the Maroon cause. One such individual was Reverend Charles Peters, who through his pulpit preached incessantly against the horrors of slavery and appeared to side with the Maroons. Word had also reached Dominica that in 1797 Reverend Peters had travelled to London where he met with abolitionist William Wilberforce. Worse, he was accused by the white planters of being sympathetic to the French republican cause.

On 15 April 1800, John Matson, acting on behalf of Governor Johnstone, addressed a special session of the Privy Council, raising concerns about 'the influence that Reverend Charles Peters may have had in encouraging the agitated state of Maroon revolt in Dominica.' He stated to the Council that 'information had been communicated to him by sundry respectable inhabitants in the Island, that two Sermons had been preached on Good Friday and Easter Sunday last, by the Rev. Mr. Peters, of a nature and tendency the most alarming and dangerous, and such as to threaten the subversion and destruction of the Colony.' The Board was informed also, that the public mind had become agitated; and that from the dangerous tendency such discourses might have (if suffered to be continued) on the minds of the Negroes and other parts of the inhabitants of the Colony, great mischief was to be apprehended.'[32]

Reverend Peters was then summoned before the Council, whereupon he immediately tendered his resignation as rector of the Saint George's Church in Dominica, and returned to London. The move to summon Reverend Charles before the Council was widely welcomed by the white planters, who continually frowned upon his support for the Maroons, and never really trusted him. An article appearing in the *Dominica Journal or Weekly Intelligencer* noted 'of the number of persons who visit Europe, is the Rev. Mr. Charles Peters, late Rector of the Parish Church of St George, but who lately, very prudently, gave in his resignation, in order to avoid the disgrace, which his conduct had so justly incurred, of being displaced by the Legislature. We shall not (for obvious reasons) touch upon the points in his doctrine which gave offence: it is, however, to be hoped the higher powers will forward a relation of the conduct of this self-sufficient reformer, which will reach the source of his ordination; as it is highly proper that this diminutive wolf in sheep's clothing should exchange his gown for the party-coloured trappings of the French republicans.'[33]

The essence of the first sermon, which so riled the white planter class related to a quote from Colossians, Chap. IV verse 1, 'masters, give unto your servants that which is just and equal, knowing that ye also have a Master in heaven.' Reverend Peters then insisted that 'one of the first and most indispensable duties required of every Colonial proprietor or manager of slaves, is to adopt the most judicious and equitable regulations, for the purpose of providing them with the means of a comfortable subsistence.'[34]

Reverend Peters went on to describe 'comfortable subsistence' as 'a proportion of proper clothing and wholesome food as is calculated to preserve the labouring negroes in a state of health and strength, and as will enable them to satisfy the wants of their growing offspring. An allowance sufficient for these purposes is the least that can possibly be granted them, without the most palpable inhumanity and injustice; since, if less than this were generally given to the labouring classes of mankind, it is evident to reason, that they must gradually decrease in number, and that the earth would shortly be depopulated.'[35]

'If there be any who imagine that the Almighty Being will not require the innocent blood (however slowly spilt) of one nation, as much as of another; if, in a word, there be any who conceive that they are permitted to exercise toward that portion of their fellow-creatures who are here entirely subject to their dominion (and therefore peculiarly entitled to their benevolent protection), any other discipline whatever, than such as they could not reasonably deem injurious to their own brothers, or their own children, if placed by Divine Providence in similar circumstances; to such, here I put a period to this discourse. I esteem it my duty to declare, that while they retain these sentiments, it is impossible for me not to consider them as altogether unprepared for joining in that most solemn rite of our religion which we are now about to celebrate,' Reverend Peters concluded.

In his second sermon Reverend Peters continued to build on the theme of the Master being held accountable for the well-being of their slaves, even directly accusing them of criminality in their treatment. 'With respect to the criminality of those proprietors of slaves, whose cruel and short-sighted avarice either exacts of their negroes the regular performance of an immoderate task, or withholds from them a sufficient supply of nutritious food, I have already spoken ; and with regard to the flagrant guilt of inflicting on them, unduly, frequent and vigorous punishments, I shall take occasion to express my sentiments in a subsequent discourse; at present. Therefore, it remains for me only to inquire, how far Colonial masters are justified by the laws of natural and revealed religion, in requiring the daily exertions of their slaves, under circumstances known to be most unfavourable to the duration of human life.'[36]

By the beginning of 1801, the slave population in Dominica had risen to well over 19 000. The number of enslaved would continue to rise until the trade was abolished by the British Parliament in 1807. By the time of abolition, some 434 vessels[37] had already transported over 100 000 slaves into Dominica,[38] with the majority of them coming from Guinea, The Gambia, Senegal, Ghana, Nigeria and elsewhere in West Africa.

Meanwhile, with the authorities recording great success against the Maroon population, the 8th and 9th West India Regiments were garrisoned at Prince Rupert Bay in Portsmouth, to the North of the capital Roseau, and ordered to drain the huge swamp in that area. For years, the swamp had proved to be a very unhealthy place for the inhabitants of Portsmouth, and was particularly severe on the white population.[39] In 1800, the second battalion of the 68th regiment comprised of mainly whites was tasked with draining the swamp. In the process, many of them died, from an unhealthy situation 'that the soldiers could not bear.'[40]

The West India regiments had been ably strengthened with an influx of new recruits directly from Africa in 1798. The relatively new arrivals found the work of draining the swamps to be extremely tedious and undesirable and on 19 April 1802, launched an open mutiny and rebellion against their white officers. The rebellion would go on to last for four days before the authorities were able to restore order. Following is a detailed account in *The Edinburgh Weekly Journal* of the rebellion as it unfolded that day.

'On Friday the 9th instant in the evening, an insurrection took place in the 8th West India Regiment stationed at Prince Rupert's Dominica. The mutiny broke out first at Fort Shirley, where the mutineers commenced a musketry fire in all directions. Major John Gordon who was in a house adjoining the front with Lieutenant Mackie immediately rushed out and endeavoured to form the guard during which they were fired upon and Lieutenant Mackie was killed. Captain Cameron and Ensign Wasteneys the Commissary and the Sergeant in the quarters master General department were also killed.

'They at the same time also desperately wounded the clerk of the cheque, Captain Cameron who was shot by his own servant. Wasteneys a very young man was seized, his hands tied, and dragged by the feet from the outer to the inner Cabrit, where they tied him to a tree and after whipping him, sticking several bayonets in his body, and keeping him three hours in that situation, shot him, cutting off his ears, and otherwise mutilated him.

'Some of the officers with the ordnance storekeeper made their escape through a sally port which leads from the lines to the sea they had a guard to pass, and on their appearing, the sentry ordered them to stop as "no white men were to pass that way;" on which the ordnance storekeeper drew his sword and going up to the sentry threatened him with instant death if he refused to let him pass; on which he complied. They repeatedly called out for Major Gordon, but after a fruitless attempt to stop the mutiny, he had escaped. Captain Barr and Lieutenants Cameron and Rivington fell into their hands. They confined them but treated them with respect.

'The detachment of royal artillery stationed there made their escape. The surgeon and his wife were in bed when the mutiny broke out, but after two shots had been fired through their room, made their escape, and by the greatest exertions in descending the precipice through brambles and brushwood, reached a rock from which they were taken off at daylight by a boat from *The Magnificent* almost dead with apprehension, fatigue and the lacerations they had experienced in their descent. The other ladies three or four fell into the hands of the mutineers.

'The mutineers were entirely composed of Africans the Creoles to a man had nothing to do with it, several of whom made their escape at the moment the insurrection broke out and sought the shelter on board the men of war by swimming and by such canoes which they could find. In the interval between Friday night and Monday morning they offered to negotiate with Captain Gifford of *The Magnificent* who refused to have anything to do with them.

'On Monday morning General Johnstone arrived with the Royal's the 68th regiment and some militia, the marines were also landed from the men of wars. After Lieutenant Cameron had been sent by them with several flags of truce, they agreed to come to their parade (between the two Cabrits). General Johnstone in the meantime passed the causeway and continuing his march, drew up his force in two lines opposite the mutineers; (the first line consisting of 90 of the Royals and two companies of the 68th) within twenty yards of them.

'The mutineers when on the point of proceeding to the parade to meet General Johnstone and the troops, liberated Captain Barr, and offering him his sword insisted on him taking the command of them, and marching them down, both of which he declined; on which they threatened to shoot him if he did not comply; he with the other officers then prisoners, accordingly marched them down and drew them up on the parade, where they received General Johnstone with presented arms and drums beating. General Johnstone instantly formed and then ordered Captain Barr to make them ground their arms, which all but some of the grenadiers obeyed.

'He then ordered them to advance three spaces in front of their arms, on which several cried "no, no" and were in the act of resuming their arms when some person called "Fire!" which was instantly obeyed and several of the mutineers fell. Their grenadiers immediately returned the fire and the whole gave way and fled in different directions. Many of them kept the road (which forms an angle), to the outer Cabrit but the troops pushed straight up the hill, reached the summit before them, and by that means cut them off.

'After this they scattered in every direction closely followed by their pursuers. Some of them on their arrival, at the hospital, are said to have bayoneted some of the sick. Some were taken, and when brought in, ordered to be bayoneted, which was instantly done. Others retreating over the state of the outer Cabrit were shot. A few are supposed to be still concealed in the bushes and some are known to have got into the country.

'The mutineers had manned the several works commanding the approach to the post and when the firing commenced, fired grape from the inner Cabrit upon the troops who had past the post and were drawn up between it and the outer Cabrit, by which and the fire of the small arms, two or three of the troops were killed and near 20 wounded; two of the militia were also killed.

'The number of mutineers killed has not been ascertained with accuracy owing to several having been shot on the face of the Cabrit leading to the sea; about 60 were buried in one hole, it is supposed that more than 100 were killed; and among the prisoners are 40 wounded, some of them desperately. The corps consisted of nearly 500, of which there are said to be in close confinement or prisoners at large on the Upper Cabrit about 370 (including the 40 wounded); of whom it is proposed to try about 15.

'The causes assigned by the mutineers are various---but their having being obliged to work at the draining of the swamp for the two preceding days, seem to have been the principal: it is a work that will require a long time to complete. The mutineers buried the murdered officers with military honours—the whole corps attended; they liberated the three officers whom they held in confinement, for this purpose also. The firing party was selected and was composed of the worse characters among them. The King's colours were kept flying during the whole time the mutiny lasted—the mutineers constantly declared their readiness to fight for King George; and when General Johnstone and the troops marched in, the King's colours were flying in Fort Shirley, with the flag of truce above them.

'Previous to the fire commencing between the troops and the mutineers, General Johnstone, who had been in front retired between the first and second lines and desired the men to be ready. Some of the troops asked if they were to fire. The officers who had been their prisoners ran stopping into the line of the troops. This and the other circumstances mentioned appear to have produced an agitation on both sides.

'The mutineers who appear to have acted with great confidence toward the General, until that moment, resumed their arms, and the first shot served as a signal to both parties to fire. Probably a little address at that moment might have prevented the bloody scene that followed. The account of eyewitnesses vary with respect to the side on which the firing commenced, as well as to the number of the mutineers killed some putting it at 100, while others suppose it to have been nearly double that number possibly the medium between the two may be nearest the truth. One thing is certain it was not a negro insurrection as has been reported both in France and England on the pretended authority of private letters, the mutineers were not joined by a single slave.'[41]

Later, an account was given in *The Caledonian Mercury* of those killed and wounded. 'The 68th regiment, 3 men killed, 15 wounded; militia 1 man killed 3 wounded; the loss of the 8th West India Regiment is stated to be at least 100 killed and wounded.'[42] Following the mutiny there was a collective sigh of relief that it had not spread beyond the members of the regiment. *The Times of London* noted that: 'while we lament the brutality and cruelty to which the mutiny led, it must be a subject of sincere satisfaction that the insurrection has been so speedily quelled, and that the negroes attached to the different plantations have evinced so exemplary a spirit of obedience and fidelity.' [43]

Blame for the revolt was immediately levelled at occurrences in St Dominique with *The Caledonian Mercury* declaring 'the state of our West Indian possessions has become a matter of much interest of late. The spirit of revolt which seems to spread among the natives, no doubt, took its rise in the French islands and the resistance made by Toussaint cannot fail of fostering it, and encouraging the slaves in their rebellious spirit. We are sorry to observe the melancholy effects which it has produced in the island of Dominica.'[44] It was also widely speculated that the mutiny 'may have originated from the apprehension of being disbanded, and returned to a state of labour.'[45]

On 26 April 1802, courts martial were opened against a number of the members of the regiment who had been captured. It was revealed at that time that several of those who escaped to the woods had gone on to join the safe havens of the Maroons. Among those 'involved were Manby, Lively, Genus, Cuffy, and Congo Jack.'[46] Following the trials, an unknown number were summarily executed and others banished from the island.

Two months after the 8th West India regiment mutiny, Governor Johnstone was recalled to London. He would never return to Dominica. Johnstone was replaced in a temporary capacity by General Fullerton until his permanent replacement Governor George Prevost was installed on 25 December 1802, after being appointed on 27 September 1802 by His Majesty King George III. Johnstone for his part instituted proceedings against some of the regiment officers stationed at the Cabrits during the mutiny, including Major Gordon whom he court-martialled on his return to London.

During the trial, Johnstone regretted the impact the mutiny had on his own career while praising his efforts, noting 'by that mutiny and by it alone, I have been deprived of my regiment, I have been deprived of my government, I have been deprived of my rank of Brigadier General, which I then held and which would now have entitled me to hold the office of Commander of the Forces, which has devolved to a junior officer…. And after having attained the high situations mentioned, I now stand in the reduced state of a half pay Colonel.'[47] Ultimately, the court found Major Gordon not guilty, a verdict that was later ratified by the King.

By early 1803 the number of Maroons was still steadily on the increase as they consolidated their position in the forests, having become greatly emboldened by the large number of former 8th and 9th West India regiment members who joined their ranks. However, the Legislature at the same time, appeared to be more concerned about threats from possible invasion by the French, rather than any internal problems on the part of the Maroons. On 11 February, the Legislature passed an act '*to prevent the return to this island of persons who were banished therefrom by sentences of general courts martial held in the year one thousand seven hundred and ninety-five for the trial of sundry persons charged with high treason, and to prevent aliens, as well whites as free persons of colour possessing sentiments inimical to His Majesty's government, from introducing and establishing themselves in this colony, and for other purposes*.'[48]

The act went on to state that some of those previously banished had returned to the island and that others were planning to do so, 'to the danger of the tranquillity of the same.' It was therefore made clear through the act that any of those previously court martialled who were found on the island were to be declared as felons and put to death as such without the benefit of clergy. In addition, those previously court martialled and sentenced to be banished, and who were still on the island, were 'rendered incapable of acquiring any lands, tenements, slaves or hereditaments in this island or any manner of trust or interest therein, by grant, devise, descent, purchase, or otherwise.'[49] In conclusion, the act listed the full names of all the 95 persons who were court-martialled and ordered to be banished for their part in the attempted takeover of Dominica in July 1795. Governor

Prevost for his part, felt the need to also send a forceful message to the Maroons, who were alleged co-conspirators in the July 1795 uprising. In April 1803 he ordered that his West India regiment attack their forest hideouts. Three separate detachments of the militias fanned out across the island with orders to either kill or capture every single Maroon that they caught site of. The 9th West India Regiment 'discovered six or eight Huts which had been previously abandoned.' At the same time, the 8th West India Regiment through intelligence picked up from a captured Maroon was informed that there were 22 huts in the heights above the Batary River.

The regiment immediately set out to attack the huts, which were surrounded and fired upon. However, the Maroons were aware of their approach and successfully escaped before their huts were burned to the ground. As the regiment rested in a deep ravine the following day, they were set upon by the Maroons, who severely wounded the lieutenant of the detachment. Unable to mount a counter attack because of their position, the regiment could only hunker down as the Maroons attacked then retreated to the safety of the forest.[50] This proved to be the only major clash between the Maroons and the authorities during the year 1803.

By 1804 the authorities were reporting an estimate of only 152 male and 58 female runaway slaves in the woods. The estimate was however based on census records from the planters' reports of the number of slaves who had absconded and would not have covered the large numbers who had escaped from their landing in the island, and those from the West India Regiment. In the years ahead the true strength of the Maroons and their large numbers would be made clearer, as an increasing number of slaves, emboldened by rumours of the ending of the slave trade, made their way to the relative safety of the forests.

One year later, the Maroons were the furthest thing from the minds of the authorities as they again faced the threat of invasion from the French, and the complete destruction of the town of Roseau from fire. A powerful French armament under the command of General Missiesse made a daring attempt to retake the towns of Roseau and Portsmouth on 22 February 1805. A letter appearing 'from a gentleman in St Pierre' in *The Tennessee Gazette* gave a glimpse into how serious the threat was. 'A French fleet from Rochefort consisting of 5 sail of the line 3 frigates, 2 brigs, with 3500 troops arrived here [Martinique] the 19th of February and sailed the next day for Dominica. They effected a landing at Dominica and burnt all the houses except four in the town of Roseau; the merchants did not save their books or papers.

'The French met with opposition and found it impracticable to take the island. They evacuated it on the 27th February and sailed for Guadeloupe with 8 or 9 sail of British merchant ships and several small vessels, which they fell in with and captured at Dominica. The merchants and inhabitants of Dominica has lost their all, and must be in a very distressing situation as they had no intelligence of the arrival of the above fleet in the West Indies, until they made their appearance off the town. An embargo was immediately laid upon all vessels in the island of Martinique on the arrival of the French fleet, which lasted for six days.'[51]

'Another account in *The Lancaster Gazette* captured the strength of the French fleet and just what the British were up against. It consisted of *Le Majestaux* with 100 guns, *Le Magnamine* 84 guns, *l'Union* 74, *Le Mappe* 74, *Le Leone* 74, three frigates of 44 guns each, two brigs of 18 guns each, two schooners of 10 guns each with supposedly 5000 troops on board under the command of General Le Grange. About 1200 troops effected a landing at Pointe Michel, and were opposed by 200 men, including a company of the town militia, who were obliged to retire, the enemy having effected a landing at Morne Daniel and advancing on the rear.

'These handful of brave fellows, according to the enemy's returns, killed 373 men, and wounded 600. The loss on our side was ten killed and about 50 wounded. Several merchants had their stores plundered by the French soldiers; but every exertion was made by the French officers to prevent such depredations. General George Prevost, the governor of

Dominica, retired to the principal fortress, Prince Rupert's, with a resolution to dispute every inch of ground with the enemy, who sent him a summons to surrender, but received a very spirited answer. On the 26th the troops reembarked, quitted Roseau on the 27th and arrived at Pointe-a-Pitre Guadeloupe on the 1st.'[52]

In the days ahead, more detailed reports would emerge of the actual fighting and the spirited defence of the island put up by Governor Prevost. One such report was contained in a letter written by Governor Prevost himself and conveyed to the British authorities by Lieutenant General Sir William Myers Bart, who was commanding the British Windward and Leeward Islands defences at the time. 'About half an hour before the dawn of the day on the 22nd February, an alarm was fired at Scottshead, and soon after a cluster of ships was discovered off Roseau. As our light increased, I made out five large ships, three frigates, two brigs, and several small craft, under British colours, and a ship of three decks carrying a flag at the mizzen. The frigates ranging too close to Fort Young, I ordered them to be fired on, and soon after 19 large barges full of troops appeared coming from under the lee of the other ships, attended and protected by an armed schooner full of men, and seven other boats carrying carronades.

'The English flag was lowered and that of France hoisted. A landing was immediately attempted on my left flank, between the town of Roseau and the port of Cachacou [Scottshead]. The light infantry of the first West India Regiment were the first on the march to support Captain's Senant company of militia, which, throughout the day, behaved with great gallantry. It was immediately supported by the Grenadiers of the 46th regiment. The first boats were beat off, but the schooner and one of the brigs coming close in shore to cover the landing, compelled our troops to occupy a better position; a defile leading to the town.

'At this moment, I brought up the grenadiers of the St George's regiment of the militia, and soon after the remainder of the 46th and gave over to Major Nunn these brave troops with orders not to yield to the enemy one inch of ground: two field pieces (an amusette and a six pounder) were brought into action for their support, under the command of Sergeant Creed of the 46th regiment manned by additional gunners and sailors. These guns and a 24 pounder from Melville Battery, shook the French advancing column by the execution they did.

'I sent two companies of the St Georges militia under the command of Lieutenant Colonel Constable, and a company of the 46th to prevent the enemy from getting into the rear of the position occupied by major Nunn. On my return I found the *Majestaux* of 120 guns laying opposite to Fort Young, pouring into the town and batteries to her broadside, followed by the other 74's and frigates doing the same. Some artillery, several captains of merchantmen, with their sailors, and the artillery militia, manned with five 24 pounders and three eighteens, at the fort, and five twenty-fours at Melville's battery and returned an uninterrupted fire. From the first post, red hot shots were thrown. At around noon, Major Nunn, most unfortunately for His Majesty's service, whilst faithfully executing the orders I had given, was wounded, I fear mortally.

'This did not discourage the brave fellows. Captain O'Connell of the 1st West India regiment, received a command, and a wound, almost at the same time; however the last circumstance could not induce him to give up the honour of the first, and he continued in the field animating his men, and resisting the repeated charges of the enemy until about one o'clock, when he obliged the French to retire from their advanced position with great slaughter. It is impossible for me to do justice to the merit of that officer. You will, I doubt not, favourably report his conduct to his Majesty, and at the same time that of Captain James who commanded the 46th, and captain Archibald Campbell, who commanded the grenadiers of the 46th.

'Foiled and beat off on the left, the right flank was attempted, and a considerable force was landed near Morne Daniel. The regulars not exceeding two hundred, employed on the left in opposing the advance of their columns consisting upwards of two thousand men, could afford me no reinforcements. I had only the right wing of St George's regiment of militia to oppose them, of about one hundred men. They attacked with spirit but unfortunately the frigates stood in so close to the shore to protect this disembarkation, that after receiving a destructive fire, they fell back and occupied the heights of Woodbridge estate.

'Then it was, that a column of the enemy marched up to Morne Daniel, and stormed the redoubt, defended by a small detachment, which, after an obstinate resistance they carried. On my left Captain O'Connell was gaining ground, notwithstanding a fresh supply of troops and several field pieces, which had been brought on shore by the enemy. I now observed a large column climbing the mountains to get in his rear. The town, which for some time had been in flames, was only protected by a light howitzer and a six pounder to the right, supported by part of the light company of the St George's regiment.

'The enemy's large ships in the Woodbridge Bay out of the reach of my guns, my right flank gained my retreat to Prince Rupert's almost cut off, I determined on one attempt to keep the sovereignty of the island, which the excellent troops I had warranted. I ordered the militia to remain at their posts, except such as were inclined to encounter more hardships and severe service; and Captain O'Connell with the 46th under the command of Captain James and the light company of the 1st West India regiment were directed to make a forced march to Prince Rupert's.

'I then allowed the President to enter into terms for the town of Roseau; and demanded from the French General that private property should be respected, and that no wanton or disgraceful pillage should be allowed. This done, only attended by Brigade Major Prevost and Deputy Quarter Master General Hopley of the militia forces, I crossed the island, and in twenty-four hours, with the aid of the inhabitants and the exertions of the Caribs got to this garrison on the 23rd. After four days continued march through the most difficult country, I might almost say, existing Capt. O'Connell joined me at Prince Rupert's, wounded himself, and bringing in his wounded, with a few of the Royal artillery and the precious remains of the 46th regiment and the 1st West India light company.

'I had no sooner got to the Fort than I ordered cattle to be drove in, and took measures for getting a store of water from the river in the Bay. I found my signals to Lieutenant Colonel Broughton, from Roseau, made soon after the enemy had landed, had been received, and that in consequence, he had made the most judicious arrangements his garrison would allow of, for the defence of this important post. On the 25th I received the letter of summons I have now the honour to transmit, from General of division La Grange, and, without delay, sent the reply you will find accompanying it.

'On the 27th the enemy's cruizers hovered about the head; however, the Centaur's tender (*Vigilante*), came in and was saved by our guns. I landed Mr. Henderson, her commander, and his crew, to assist in the defence we were prepared to make. As far as can be collected, the enemy had about four thousand men on board, and the whole of their force was compelled to disembark before they gained an inch of ground. I entrust this despatch to Captain O'Connell, to whom I beg to refer you; his services entitle him to consideration. I am much indebted to the zeal and discernment of Fort Adjutant Gualy, who was very accessary to the due execution of my orders.

'I cannot pass unnoticed the very soldier-like conduct of Lieutenant Wallis, of the 46th regiment, to whom I had entrusted the post of Cachacou or Scottshead, perceiving our retreat, he spiked his guns, and immediately commenced his march to join me at Prince Rupert's with his detachment: --- nor that of Lieutenant Shaw, of the same regiment, who acted as an officer of artillery, and behaved with uncommon coolness and judgement, whilst on the battery, and great presence of mind in securing the retreat of the additional gunners belonging to the 46th regiment.

'On the 27th after levying a contribution on Roseau, the enemy re-embarked; and hovered that day and the next about this post. This morning the French fleet is seen off the South end of Guadeloupe, under early sail. Our loss, you will perceive by the returns, I have the honour to transmit, was inconsiderable, when compared with that acknowledged by the enemy, which included several officers of rank, and about three hundred others.' [53]

Much was made about the heroism of Prevost in defending the island. In another despatch from Myers to Earl Camden, Principal Secretary of State, he glorified the exploits of the governor and those who defended the island. 'My Lord, I have the honour to enclose to your Lordship, copy of a despatch from Brigadier General Prevost, dated Dominica 1st March 1805. The details contained therein are so highly reputable to the Brigadier General and the small portion of troops employed against so numerous an enemy, that I have great satisfaction in recommending their gallant exertions may be laid before his Majesty. The zeal and talent manifested by the Brigadier General upon this occasion, it is my duty to present, for his royal consideration; and at the same time I beg to be permitted to express the high sense I entertain of the distinguished bravery of His Majesty's troops and the militia of the colony employed upon that service.

'The vigorous resistance which the enemy have experienced, and the loss which they have sustained in this attack, must evince to them, that however inferior our numbers were on this occasion, British troops are not to be approached with impunity, and had not the town of Roseau been accidently destroyed by fire, we should have little to regret and much to exult in. Your Lordship will perceive by the returns, that our loss in men, compared to that of the enemy, is but trifling , but I have to lament that of Major Nunn of the 1st West India regiment, whose wounds is reported to be of a dangerous kind, he is an excellent man and a meritorious officer.' [54]

In London, the efforts of Governor Prevost in saving the country from a superior force did not go unnoticed. In a meeting of the Association of West India Planters and Merchants held on 22 May 1805, they 'resolved unanimously that the thanks of this meeting be given to His Excellency Brigadier General Prevost, governor of the island of Dominica, for the distinguished gallantry and high military talents he displayed on the 22d of

February 1805, in the defence and effectual protection of that colony against a numerous, powerful and unexpected force from France.

'Resolved unanimously that the thanks of this meeting be given to the field officers, captains, and other commissioned officers of the Royal Artillery, the 46th regiment, the 1st West India Regiment and also to the officers of the colonial militia for the gallant conduct they respectively exemplified and the zealous cooperation they afforded on the same occasion, and that His Excellency the governor be requested to communicate the same.

'Resolved unanimously that this meeting impressed with the highest sense of the important service rendered to all the West India colonies by the able resistance made by General Prevost to the landing of the enemy on the 22d of February 1805 do require that he will accept from the general body of West India Planters and Merchants a piece of plate of the value of three hundred Guineas with an inscription expressive of the sense of this resolution. Resolved unanimously that His Excellency General Prevost be requested, in a letter from the Chairman to signify to the non-commissioned officers and privates of His Majesty's regular and militia forces at Dominica, the high sense this meeting entertains of their services, in resisting the French force on the 22d of February 1805.'[55]

By late 1805, Governor Prevost[56] had made way for Lieutenant Governor George Metcalf who would eventually act in the position for three years. The new governor immediately set to work pursuing the Maroons. He organised 'several excursions against the Runaway Negroes by three detachments from the 8th West India Regiment and five Parties from the inhabitants of the Parishes of St. Paul, St. Andrew, St. Patrick, St. David, and St. Joseph.' [57] Despite his very best efforts, Metcalfe at the end was extremely disappointed at the outcome noting that 'the expedition had not been very brilliant, having taken only four Negroes and killed one.'[58] They however registered more success in destroying some camps and provision grounds.

One year after the attempted invasion of Dominica and the burning of the town of Roseau, the island suffered another calamity. This time a violent hurricane on 9 September 1806 reportedly killed 200 persons in the town of Roseau, flood waters destroyed about two-thirds of the town, eleven of twelve vessels in the port were destroyed, and the barracks and hospital at Morne Bruce completely obliterated, killing several soldiers. In addition, the storm destroyed all the houses on the plantations and devastated the crops.[59] Following the hurricane many more slaves deserted the plantations and joined the Maroons in the forests. Their growing size continued to pose serious problems for the authorities through successive governments. Metcalfe was eventually replaced by Edward Barnes in 1808, then James Montgomerie acted for a brief period between 1808 and 1809. Edward Barnes then returned in 1809 and would remain as governor until 1812.

Meanwhile, the number of Maroons in Dominica at around 1810 was estimated to be eight hundred strong and camps had been established behind Woodford Hill, Hampstead, Rosalie, Pointe Mulatre, River Claire, Morne Anglais, and in the upper Layou area as well as the other earlier sites behind Colihaut and Dublanc. Key Maroon leaders at this period were Elephant, Soleil, Gros Bois, Battre Bois, Hill, Nicholas, Diano, Noel, Robin, Quashie, Apollo, Jean Zombie, Lewis, Moco, Nico, and Jacko. Census results indicated a white population of some 1,325, free people of colour 2,988, and enslaved blacks 21, 728.

In Jamaica, Grenada and St. Vincent the colonial authorities had comprehensively defeated the Maroon populations. However, in Dominica, it was a distinctly different situation. George Beckwith, Governor of Barbados, wrote to governor Barnes in September 1810 to inform him that: 'Dominica was the only British colony in which The Kings Troops were still employed in the pursuit of Runaway Negroes in the Woods.[60] Far from being defeated, the Maroons of Dominica were consolidating and preparing to engage their former masters and the colonial government in a bloody showdown.

Governor Barnes for his part was well aware of the growing strength of the Maroons, a point he made clearly in a letter to Lord Henry Bathurst, Great Britain's Secretary of State for War and the Colonies. 'Bearing constantly in mind the occurrences which took place in Jamaica and St Vincent some years ago, as well as the more dreadful events of St. Domingo. I considered it as primary object of my duty to use every exertion to suppress the Maroons of this island, but in the course of time they should become as formidable as those of Jamaica were, or as the Caribs of St. Vincent or the Negroes generally in French St. Domingo. I sent some parties of troops into the woods with an intention to continue there until the service was effectually completed.'[61]

Just a month before his letter to Bathurst, the Governor had written to the President and Board of Council expressing his frustration with the 'Kings Troops' inability to apprehend or kill the Maroons, notwithstanding their discovery of many settlements. 'The Forty-Sixth Regiment discovered another large settlement of twenty one huts...and were almost daily discovering new settlements…they have failed to take any prisoners.'[62] Governor Barnes could not have foreseen how drastically the situation would change with the arrival of Governor Robert Ainslie, and how his actions towards the Maroons would reverberate throughout the British colonial empire, setting in motion an irreversible march toward eventually abolition of the slavery.

11

Maroon Trials of 1813 and 1814

Governor Ainslie

On 1 June 1812, His Royal Highness the Prince Regent, on behalf of His Majesty King George III, appointed George Robert Ainslie as Governor and Commander in Chief of Dominica. A little over ten months after his appointment, Governor Ainslie arrived in Dominica on 17 April 1813, from Grenada where he served for one year as that country's Lieutenant Governor. He would replace John Corlet who was acting Governor after Edward Barnes left a year earlier.

Governor Ainslie's short stint in Grenada had been mired in controversy. On leaving that island, *The Examiner* noted that: 'his habits were offensive to the respectable inhabitants, particularly the married portion of them, who carefully avoided the government house in which its neglected occupier used...Instead of being followed to the shore by a grateful and applauding multitude, as many of his predecessors had been, he was merely accompanied and guarded, as it were, by a few menials and satellites, the people looking on with high satisfaction at his departure, and expressing their contempt of him by repeated hissings.'[1]

Ainslie's arrival in Dominica coincided with the ascendency of the Maroons. They had over the years successfully increased in numbers and strength. Several new leaders had emerged, replacing those killed, standing alongside those like Jacko who had survived the ravages of previous governors. It had been over 27 years since Jacko had stood resolutely with Balla in popularizing the resistance movement, and in carrying out the audacious attack on the Rosalie estate. On Balla's death he had joined forces with Pharcelle and Pangloss, until they too had been neutralized by the authorities. Throughout that period, Jacko had successfully evaded capture and had become the Chief of Chiefs, taking on the vaunted position that Balla had enjoyed so many years ago.

By 1813 the Maroons had seen the largest increase in their numbers since 1763. However, unlike the turbulent times of the late 1780s they appeared more willing to live their lives peacefully in the forest. They however kept in constant contact with the slaves on the estates, all the time encouraging them to leave, but also depending on them to provide support. However, they did not actively participate in the destruction of the estates as they did during the 1780s. Years had passed since the heyday of the French revolution and its impact on their resistance movement. Now resistance was not as violent, it was more passive. While maintaining the constant refrain of freedom from slavery they were prepared to approach it in a less confrontational matter.

For Ainslie on the other hand, he could not conceive of the notion that the slaves would ultimately free themselves and thus provide an impetus for the other slaves on the more populous colonies of Jamaica and Barbados. The governor was also aware of the sentiments being played out in the British public and growing attempts to abolish slavery all together. Getting the upper hand on the Maroons and restoring the belligerent colony to a steady calm was the only way forward. And to do this, the Maroons would need to be completely annihilated. More importantly, in the absence of the slave trade it was vitally important that the planters held on to the slaves that they currently owned. Without a constant supply of new slaves the cost of losing those already at hand was infinitely higher.

Jacko meanwhile had continued to groom and work with Chiefs such as Quashie, Elephant, Apollo, Noel Louis, George Moco, and Gabriel. These chiefs had proven very effective in their campaign to lure an increasing number of slaves away from the plantations, and to the relative safety of the forests; much to the chagrin of the authorities and planters. Jacko was a marked man and would face the fury and resentment of Governor Ainslie. Much like Governor Stewart before him, Ainslie immediately set his sights on trying to destroy the leadership of the Maroons. However, unlike Stewart, Ainslie was prepared to go to any lengths targeting men, boys, women and children in his callous and brazen quest to gain the upper hand over the Maroons and to stifle a burgeoning revolution.

Determined to reverse the growing influence of the Maroon population, Governor Ainslie wasted no time in attempting to assert his authority. Within one month of his arrival in Dominica, he issued the first of several proclamations, with each successive one more brazen and callous than the one before. On 10 May 1813 he issued the following proclamation:

> *'Whereas several negroes have under different pretenses absented themselves from their masters' service and whereas if a free and unconditional pardon were offered to such runaway slaves that might return to their duty I do therefore by this my proclamation offer a free and unconditional pardon to all such runaways who return to their duty and deliver themselves up to the magistrates of this colony or surrender themselves up to Governor House in the town of Roseau on or before the 4th day of June next, where their grievances will meet with every proper consideration. And I do further declare that all such runaways that shall be taken after the 4th day of June shall be treated with the utmost vigour of military execution; their places of refuge and harbours destroyed, their provision grounds laid waste and the punishment of death inflicted on those who are found in arms.'*[2]

After barely three weeks and before the expiration of the June 4th date for the amnesty, Ainslie reissued the May proclamation on 1 June 1813. It contained the same offers and threats as before but extended the date of the amnesty to 1 July 1813. Ainslie claimed that the change was necessary in order to ensure that his proclamation reached the ear of every Maroon in every camp on the island. Although just how this would be accomplished was uncertain. The Governor also attempted to use former Maroons or trusted slaves to take the message to those in the forests.

In one such case, in May 1813, he sent a former slave, as an ambassador, into the camp of one of the more feared leaders, Quashie. He intended to talk to them and induce them to return peaceably to their owners. However, showing his disdain for the traitor, Quashie immediately had him captured, and set up a mock trial before a Negro Chief Justice name Fabien. He was condemned to death and subsequently shot. A short time later, Fabien was taken prisoner by a party of Rangers and brought to the town of Roseau, where he was tried, and hanged at the Roseau market. Fabien was found guilty for having sentenced the slave to be shot. On the morning after his execution the following verses appeared stuck on the gallows, and elsewhere in the town of Roseau:[3]

In this town so devoted to faction and strife;
A negro Chief Justice was tried for his life;
Of his fate should a stranger among us inquire;
On the gallows the wretch was allowed to expire;
But what had he done to incur the disgrace;
Was the heart of old Fabien as black as his face?
Oh no, my good Sir for a sentence he died;
That be passed, in the woods, on an Envoy he tried;
Perhaps by the laws of a Chief he obeyed;
He was forced to abide and his judgment was sway'd;
Perhaps he might think that the man came as a spy;
And that his offence he might legally try;
If he erred from the head in condemning the slave;
'Tis hard that his justice should sleep in the grave;

But another Chief Justice long time I have ey'd;
Who, instead of the Black, in his place should have died;
Much whiter, I own, to the view, is his skin;
And no blackness without but all the blackness within;
A Traitor to God, to the laws and his King;
Who justly deserves on this gallows to swing.

Following the execution of Fabien, Ainslie set a bounty of one thousand pounds on the head of Quashie, who immediately announced that he was doubling the bounty for the head of Ainslie.[4] Two months later in July, Ainslie would begin his formal trials of the Maroons who at that time were being hounded and searched for by the rangers deep in the Dominican forests.

Three months to the day since his arrival in Dominica, on 17 July 1813, trials for the Maroons captured during the relentless raids by the Loyal Dominica Rangers started. The court of special sessions, arranged for that purpose, comprised of three justices of the peace: John Gordon, Charles Bertrand, and William Anderson Esquires; Attorney General Webb Glanville Esq.; Acting Provost Marshall, Edward Beech; and Acting Clerk, Thomas Hays.

The accused that day included a mix of Maroons and slaves; Guillaume, a negro slave, found guilty of striking a white overseer with a cutlass, which resulted in a cut to the nose; Caliste and Angelle found guilty of harbouring runaway slaves after being charged with having had intercourse and correspondence with runaway negroes; Dundas found guilty of running away for almost a year and also stabbing the driver on the estate with a bayonet; and Toussaint remanded to jail for further evidence after being charged with practicing witchcraft.[5]

Two days later the court returned with the sentences. Caliste and Guillaume were sentenced *to be hung by the neck until dead*, while Angelle and Dundas were sentenced to be banished from Dominica. Caliste would later die in jail before his sentence was executed. Just four days after the sentences were read, a terrible hurricane slammed into the island on 23 July. No deaths were recorded but there was substantial property damage, which delayed additional trials until 13 August 1813. At that trial, Chance, Johnson, Quashee, Etienne and Buoy were brought before the court of sessions. This time the Justices of the Peace were Archibald Gloster,[6] George Garraway and James Johnson Esquires; along with Attorney General Webb Glanville Esq.; Acting Provost Marshall, Edward Beech; and Acting Clerk, Thomas Hays. Quashee and Chance were accused of attempting to run away from Canefield Estate and were given 25 and 39 lashes respectively in the market place, while Johnson was sentenced to goal for an indefinite period.

Buoy was found guilty for having escaped from his master's estate and for being a runaway for six months. He was sentenced *to be hung by the neck until he be dead.* Surprisingly, Etienne was found not guilty for providing salt and other provisions to the Maroons.

In a little over one month, on 28 September, the trials resumed with Frank, Billy, Salestine, Sampson, Charles, Jack, Johnson, Cuffy, Toby, Joacinthe, and Harry brought before the special court of sessions. All eleven were charged with being runaways and absenting themselves from their master's plantations. In the interim, another devastating hurricane had ploughed into the Island on 25 August. For this session, Glanville, Hays and Beech were joined by three new Justices of the Peace: William Bremner, Robert Reid, William Anderson and Alexander Fraser Esquires.

Following a quick hearing, John, Cuffy, Charles and Salestine were all found guilty and ordered to be kept in goal until they could be banished from the island. Sampson, Toby, Joacinthe and Billy were sentenced to goal for an indefinite period; Jack and Johnson were ordered to return for the next court session, as more evidence needed to be collected; and Frank was discharged for lack of evidence.

It was not too long, before Ainslie upped the ante against the Maroons. Recognising that his previous two proclamations were largely ignored, Ainslie decided to issue yet another on 3 October 1813. This proclamation however would be different. Ainslie now threatened to indiscriminately bayonet all the runaways who were apprehended irrespective of sex or age. In essence, that proclamation amounted to a kill on sight order, even for women and children.

> *'Whereas detachments of his Majesty's troops have been sent into the Woods, and have discovered the tracks of the runaway camps and whereas I am desirous of affording the misguided slaves who have absented themselves from the employ of their owners, an opportunity, before I proceed to extremities, of returning to their duty; I do by this my proclamation promise a full and unconditional pardon to all runaway slaves who shall surrender themselves at the Government House in the town of Roseau, on or before the twenty-fourth day of this month of October: And I do further declare that, the utmost rigour of military execution shall be put into force against all those runaway slaves that may be apprehended, after that period, neither age nor sex spared, all indiscriminately shall be put to the bayonet. Given under my hand and seal at arms, this third day of October, one thousand eight hundred and thirteen and in the fifty-third year of his majesty's reign.'*

A few days after the issuance of the proclamation, on 13 October the three Maroons from the 28 September court of special sessions were brought in for sentencing along with three additional slaves. Billy was found guilty for being a runaway from the La Rocque estate for over seven years and ordered held in goal until he could be banished from the island. Similar sentences were imposed on Sampson, Harry, and Toby, who were all found guilty of being runaways. Meanwhile, Jack and Joacinthe were found not guilty and discharged.

Towards the end of the year, the Rangers had significantly stepped up their search for the Maroons and were said to be bringing in up to 20 of them a week; either through capture or surrender. However, these were mainly women and children being captured. The more seasoned Maroon leaders and a significant number of men proved way more elusive. In the meantime, the trials continued, with the fourth session taking place on 12 November.

This time the court of special sessions was presided over by David Rand who was serving as the acting Attorney General, and joined by Benjamin Lucas, Robert Reid and John Gordon Esquires; all justices of the peace along with Beech and Hayes. Facing the court this time were six men all charged for the crime of being runaways: Billy, Toby, Jean Pierre, Charles, Calais, Francois, and Charles. After their charges were read to them, they were all ordered to goal until further evidence could be gathered in their cases.

Two weeks later on 25 November, Jean Pierre, Etienne, Mingo, Magdelane and Johnson were brought before the court of special sessions to face charges of being runaways from various estates. Serving as Justices of the Peace were James Clark, John Gordon, and George Garraway Esquires. All the Maroons on trial, with the exception of Etienne, were found guilty and sentenced to goal until they could be banished from the island. Etienne was ordered back to goal until further evidence was found, at which time he would be returned to court.

The final court of special sessions for the year 1813 was held on 9 December, presided over by David Rand, acting Attorney General, and joined by Archibald Gloster, Robert Reid and Robert Garraway Esquires; all justices of the peace along with Beech and Hayes. This time Etienne was charged with having held intercourse and correspondence with the runaways, and found guilty. He was ordered held in goal until he could be banished from the island. Another Maroon, Tim, faced the same charge but was found not guilty. Caliste and Laws were found not guilty on charges of being runaways. In the case of Laws, the court was induced to order his dismissal 'based on his miserable and wretched appearance.' Finally, Simeon who was charged with having sold, given, or battered firearms, cutlasses and rum to the runaways, was found 'not guilty' and discharged.

By the end of 1813, Ainslie and his Attorney General had succeeded in bringing 30 of the Maroons to trial, with 27 convictions. On the other hand, the number of runaways was steadily on the rise, as slaves increasingly deserted the plantations, spurred on by dreams of enduring freedom in the vast mountains of Dominica. William Bremner who served as a justice of the peace during the trials, remarked on the 'insolence, depredations and outrages of the runaways', which he said increased daily even as their numbers continued to rise. To compound matters, rumors persisted that the Maroons were planning a large-scale attack on the town of Roseau. Bremner notes that the threat was considered credible and taken very seriously, because of the large numbers of Maroons.[7]

Further, the whole garrison at Morne Bruce and the entire militia were called out by the Governor to defend Roseau, and 'guns planted at every avenue of the town to oppose them.' Even when it was determined that the rumour was unfounded the fear among the planters continued. A situation reminiscent of the trepidation and panic that pervaded the town twenty-six years earlier, when Balla was rumored to be on his way to attack Roseau. And like that time in 1785, white women and children made their way hurriedly to boats anchored at sea, in order to make good their escape. Ainslie could not countenance that his strategy at breaking the back of the resistance had failed, he would now escalate the violence against the Maroons to unprecedented levels.

On 16 January 1814, Ainslie declared martial law, with the suspension of civilian liberties, and rapid trials for the Maroons who were either captured or had surrendered peacefully. At the same time, the court sessions were moved from the original court house in Roseau, which had suffered some hurricane damage, to a building adjacent to the market square, where executions took place. Another key part of Ainslie's strategy at extermination of the Maroons was the strengthening of the Loyal Dominica Rangers. This group consisted of trusty slaves recruited through their owners, and was led by Captain Sevarin, a former army lieutenant who was assisted by Sergeant Nash a free black from St Vincent. The rangers were fed, paid and clothed in new uniforms. Importantly, they were offered their freedom if they succeeded in capturing a

Maroon Chief. The ultimate triumph of Ainslie's self-declared war against the Maroons, would owe its success to these slaves. Familiar with the forests, they were prepared to betray the Maroons for a few joes, and a promise of freedom.

The same day that Ainslie declared martial law, he wrote the first of several letters to Lord Bathurst.

> *'I do myself the honour to acquaint your Lordship that I have judged proper to put this colony under martial law for one month from the 16th Instant. The runaway slaves who have been for 30 years established in the almost inaccessible mountains of Dominica, having become very troublesome from the depredations they were committing. I adopted this measure at the same time that I sent out parties from the Militia aided by a small force of Black troops. Some camps have been destroyed, a good number of the runaways have returned to their masters and I have little doubt, that at the expiration of the existence of martial law when, a colonial corps of Rangers now in training is to be posted to the principal camp, the colony will be comparatively freed from this evil.'*[8]

Trials of the Maroons under martial law, began immediately, on 15 January. Unlike the court of special sessions, a lone Judge Advocate, WW Granville, presided over the hearings. There was no legal representation for the Maroons, but they were expected to defend themselves against the testimony of the rangers, militia, owners, overseers, drivers, slaves and captured Maroons. The trials would run from January until May 1814, with the cases of 44 Maroons and slaves heard. Charges ranged from being runaways to assisting Maroons with the supply of guns, ammunition, salt, provisions and other necessities. By the time the trials were over, twelve Maroons including six women were sentenced to death by hanging. Of the twelve, ten would serve the ultimate punishment, with one woman, Rebecca being pardoned at the gallows, and Hester defied the gallows when she died in jail while pregnant. The remaining 14 men and 18 women were all either flogged or banished from the island after serving time in chain gangs.

The first to be tried on 15 January was Jean Pierre, accused of attempting to return to the camp of the runaways with a bag of wild yams. After a day's adjournment he returned to court only to be 'sentenced to be hanged at such time and place that the Governor shall appoint.' Next was Peter, who was charged with starting a mutiny of twenty slaves on the Hillsborough Estate, and that he furnished them with provisions while being a runaway. After his capture, Peter promised to take the authorities to the Maroon camp, but failed to do so, instead he kept them for over two days wandering in the forest.

On 16 January the court found Peter guilty as charged and he was sentenced 'to be hanged at such time and place as the Governor shall appoint.' The court also added that he was a fit and proper person to take the authorities to the Maroon camps at Layou. 'And he having professed a willingness to act as such, recommend to the Governor to employ him in that capacity, provided that he shall faithfully act as such, and that he be afterwards banished from the island for life.' [9] Immediately on receiving the court's verdict, Governor Ainslie wrote: 'I approve and order the sentence to be carried with effect tomorrow, at the usual hour, the head to be cut off and put on a pike in the market place, the body to be hung in chains at the Hillsborough Estate.'[10]

That same day, Hector was tried for being a runaway, he was found guilty and sentenced to flogging with 39 lashes of the whip. Ainslie then unilaterally increased the number to 100 lashes, which was duly carried out. Rachel, the first woman to be so tried was the wife of Jean Pierre who had just the day earlier being sentenced to death. She was tried on the charge of being a runaway, found guilty, and as punishment sentenced to receive fifty lashes of the whip. In addition, she was ordered to be worked for three months in the galley gang.

Closing out the second day of the trial was that of Sarah, Hetty, Placet, Daniel and Dick. They were all accused of being part of the twenty slaves enticed to mutiny by Peter on the Hillsborough Estate. Found guilty, the men Daniel and Dick were sentenced to receive 100 lashes of the whip while the women, Hetty, Placet, and Sarah the accused ring leader, were all sentenced to receive 50 lashes each. The orders of the court were duly signed by Ainslie and he gave instructions to have the sentences 'to be carried into execution tomorrow between the hours of ten and twelve.'[11]

More trials were to follow on 28 January and 26 February respectively. Facing trial for being runaways were Joseph, Pierre, Charles, Augustin, and Victor. Pierre and Charles were found guilty and sentenced to receive 100 lashes each in the public square and to work in the galley gang for six months. Joseph was found not guilty and the court ruled that Augustin was an idiot, and not deemed a fit object for trial, he was ordered discharged. Victor however would suffer a more severe punishment after being charged with providing gunpowder, saltfish and tobacco to the Maroons. He was immediately sentenced by the court to be hung by the neck. Ainslie quickly accepted the verdict and wrote: 'I order and approve the order to be carried into effect at the usual hour tomorrow being Sunday the 27th instant; after hanging till two hours the head to be stuck on a pole, the body again suspended by the arms till 5 o'clock when it must be burned on the beach.'[12]

At the beginning of February, the relentless raids by the 'trusty slaves' was yielding fruit as several more of the Maroons, particularly those belonging to the camp of Elephant were rounded up. The feared leader Elephant was shot by the owner of the Edenbro estate, on 7 February as he attempted to entice a number of slaves to take to the forests. He survived and was then hung, before his head was stuck on a pole.

It was already clear to the authorities, however, by late February, that not even the declaration of martial law, and the ongoing trials was serving as much of a deterrent. The number of slaves abandoning the estates were growing and far exceeded those caught or returning voluntarily. Driven by a deep sense of frustration and growing desperation, Ainslie made his fourth proclamation on 25 February 1814. This time it would even be more shocking than the one in October. He again reiterated his plan to grant a full pardon to those who surrendered, but this time he ordered the rangers to take no prisoners, but to '*put to death men, women and children.*' One British newspaper, *The Liverpool Mercury* was so appalled that it issued the following apology to the British public: 'We give the following proclamation, which is abhorrent to our feelings as Englishmen and as friends of humanity. We are unable to imagine circumstances sufficiently dreadful to authorize such orders.

> *By his Excellency George Robert Ainslie Governor and Commander in Chief in and over the Island of Dominica, Chancellor, Vice Admiral, and Ordinary of the same.*
>
> *Whereas the Camp of Jacko, Noel, Mucho, Appollo, Diano and Sambo, in the Layou district and those of the Elephant and six others, in the quarter of Couliabonne, and on the river Claire have been utterly destroyed, the Chief Elephant hanged and his head stuck up in Roseau, and the Dominica Rangers stationed permanently in the woods for the purpose of harassing and pursuing to death such runaways as still keep out willingly, however, to show mercy to those whom ignorance of my intentions prevent returning to their masters, I by this my proclamation, do declare that I will fully pardon all those who surrender themselves either to the commissioners of parishes, to their masters, or who appear at Government House Roseau before Monday the 21st of March, with the exception of the Chief of the Camp, and such as have committed murder.*
>
> *And I do hereby offer besides a full pardon twenty joes reward to any runaway or runaways for every Chief they bring to me, and three joes for each murderer. And I do hereby declare to the Maroons who are still in the woods that the Rangers have orders to take no prisoners, but to put to death men, women, and children, without exception.*

Given under my hand and seal at arms at Government House, Roseau this twenty-fifth day of February one thousand eight hundred and fourteen and fifty-fourth year of his Majesty's reign.[13]

A day after issuing this proclamation, Ainslie wrote to Bathurst requesting additional arms to assist in his fight against the Maroons. 'I beg leave to call Your Lordship's attention, once more, to the state of the militia of this colony, where important services against the runaway Negroes, are much impeded, by the state of their arms and accoutrements. I need not state, the total inability of the colony in its present distressed situation to supply the deficiency. I begin to remark that the lighter the arms are, the better for the woods service, which is almost as fatiguing as that of the Chasseral mountain in Switzerland, the places of retreat of the Maroons, being in a country, broken in the most singular manner and composed of wooded precipices; *fusils* are the only arms calculated for this country. Total required: 300 each of musquets, ramrods, bayonets, slings, pouches, belts, bayonet belts, scabbards.'[14]

Growing increasingly confident of the success of his barbaric plan, Ainslie addressed both the Board of Council and House of Assembly, the colony's two legislative bodies, on 2 March 1814:

'The operations carried out against the Maroons since martial law was proclaimed have been successful, 14 settlements burnt, the provision grounds (which at one place alone presented to the eye an extent of four miles of the finest plants) given up to public use, or entirely destroyed, the alternative alone remaining to the runaways of perishing from hunger in the woods or taking advantage of my proclamation to give themselves up. Already about 50 of these misguided wretches have returned to their masters and a considerable number have paid the forfeit of their lives exclusive of those who have perished through want which must have been great when we reflect upon the large number of men, women and children deprived of every means of subsistence except wild vegetables.

It is my intention not to relax in the least in pursuing the system of harassing the Maroons, and I hope, in very few weeks will accomplish our object, which circumstances not to be controlled by me, have hitherto prevented in the extirpation of an evil of great and increasing magnitude, and consequently security of property restored to the colonists.

I intend that the Ranger Corps shall remain permanently in the woods for the purpose of having parties on the alert in search of the fugitives. Twelve volunteers of people of colour have been added to that useful corps, who, I may readily promise will settle on allotments of Maroon lands, which I promise to give them, and thus open the communication between Layou and the Windward side of the island towards Pagua and Castle Bruce.[15]

In response, the Board of Council felt compelled to send a congratulatory message to Governor Ainslie, on 7 March, which contained the following passage:

> 'The success, which has attended the late exertions against the runaway slaves is a matter of congratulations to all who are interested in the safety and prosperity of the colony. Neither our properties, nor even our lives could be considered in any tolerable state of security, while such lawless bands were permitted to possess, unmolested, the woods and fastnesses of the country. And we experience much gratification from the expectation signified by your excellency, that a few weeks more will be sufficient to put an end to this warfare.'[16]

A series of newspaper reports coming out from Dominica in March 1814, seemed to support the assertions of Ainslie that he was gaining the upper hand on the Maroons and that it was only a matter of time before victory was declared. *The Caledonian Mercury* printed this exert from 12 March: 'The perseverance of those employed under his Excellency's directions in harassing the runaway slaves, continues to be crowned with almost daily success. Yesterday the head of a runaway negro belonging to Betsy Wallace, was sent in by the

Royal Rangers, from Layou. He was shot while pillaging the provisions in the camp called Noel. One of his comrades who is said to have been runaway 17 years was detained and taken for a guide, another escaped been taken but is supposed to have fallen down a precipice.'[17]

Another extract from the same paper dated 19 March read as follows. 'The operations against the Maroons continue to be crowned with almost daily success, and hold the prospects of a speedy termination to their nefarious practices. On Saturday last five women and four children were sent in; two of the women were put on trial, convicted of being notorious offenders, and received sentence of death. One of them Francoise, belonging to Madame Eynard was executed pursuant to her sentence on Sunday last, but the other Esther [Hester], belonging to Mr Menier, being pregnant was respited during his Excellency's pleasure.

'On Wednesday a deserter from the 60th regiment named John Elvin, who has been long absent with the runaways, surrendered himself. And yesterday, Hypolite a black deserter from the 4th West India Regiment, and a number of runaway slaves gave themselves up. The private camp of the Chief Louis Mocho, has been discovered and destroyed. A great quantity of baggage, poultry, stock, furniture etc. carried away by volunteer Vidal, with a party of the rangers. Hypolite and Somers, another deserter from the same regiment were shot in Church Savannah at New Town on 2 May as punishment for deserting and taking refuge in the woods amongst the Maroons.[18]

The Morning Post provided additional detail under the headline '*The Maroon War*.' 'The exertions used to suppress the Maroons continue with unabated vigour, and continued success: 21 runaways were sent into town on Thursday, they belonged to Quashey's private camp, which was taken and destroyed by a detachment of the Dominica Rangers under volunteer Vidal. On this camp was found 24 houses or larger huts, four loaded muskets and some powder, a great deal of clothing, a few dollars and a considerable number of poultry, which of course became the property of the Colonial Rangers.

'The same night intelligence was received from Captain Savarin of the capture of George Mocho's camp near the Trois Piton, the Chief and two others were killed their heads cut off and stuck up at Portsmouth. The party was in pursuit of the remaining fugitives. A woman and two children were also taken and sent to town on Thursday. Scarcely a day passes that maroon women and children and runaway slaves are not brought in for trial and punishment. Many of the former declare they were born in the woods and never saw a white man until the moment of their apprehension. During the last five weeks a great number of females have been tried by military commissions, condemned executed and their heads cut off.

'It has been discovered that to guard against surprise they surround their camps with deep pits into which stakes with pointed tops are driven. They also drive sharp pieces of wood and bone into the footpaths. If, on the first alarm of their scouts the Rangers cannot bring down the fugitives they dare not pursue until the road be explored, lest they should fall into the pit and be staked alive, or crippled by treading on the footpaths. In the meanwhile, the Maroons to whom certain bye-paths are always known, escape with their families.[19]

Meanwhile, all through March, April and May the court martials' would continue as Ainslie extended the period of martial law. Ainslie however, moved the court days to Sunday, the traditional market day, when the town of Roseau would be crowded with persons. On 6 March, Joe appeared before Judge Advocate Granville on a charge of supplying the Maroons with saltfish and provisions. After a quick trial where former Maroons were brought in to testify against him, Joe was found guilty and sentenced to be hanged in the market place in Roseau.

A short while later, Gabriel was found guilty of causing bodily harm to another negro, and robbing the Negro ground; he was sentenced to 100 lashes. However, Ainslie objected and told the court that he really should be charged as a runaway. The court duly compiled and Gabriel was found guilty a second time, and sentenced to six months working in the galley in addition to the 100 lashes of the whip.

On 13 March an unprecedented six women were brought before the court. Jenny, Betty, Perine, Francoise, Registe and Hester with her two children, who were all charged with being runaways. Members of the Loyal Dominican Rangers gave testimony of their capture, and worked at ensuring their convictions. Hester, who was pregnant at the time was found guilty and sentenced to goal until she had delivered, then she would be hanged. Francoise was also sentenced to be hanged[20] while Perine was sentenced to 50 lashes and attached to a chain gang for six months. Jenny and Betty were allowed to go free on account of their poor state of health, while Registe and Hester's two children were acquitted. Ainslie thereupon approved and ordered the execution of Francoise to take place immediately, with the head struck off after hanging two hours, placed on a pike, and the body burnt at 4 P.M.

Three additional women; Flora, Adelaide and Caroline would come up for trial on 27 March. Charged with being runaways for varying periods, they were all found guilty. Adelaide was sentenced to be hung, and Flora and Caroline were ordered to work in the chain gang for six months, before both being banished from Dominica. Ainslie then ordered the immediate execution of Adelaide. At 4 o'clock on Sunday 27 March her headless body was burned on the beach.

The following Sunday, 3 April, three additional women all belonging to Jacko's camp, Zabeth, Ebo and Rebecca appeared before Judge Advocate Granville, and under the accusatory complaints of members of the Dominica Rangers. Vielle (old) Ebo, was accused of practicing witchcraft and being a runaway for over 10 years. The raid in which she was captured in the mountains above Portsmouth resulted in one Maroon being shot to death and seven others held. Ebo was too old to attempt to escape. Her age however, did not spare her from the gallows. She along with Zabeth and Rebecca were all found guilty of being runaways, and were all sentenced to be hanged, at such time and place that the Governor may appoint. Ainslie gladly signed the warrants for their execution, with immediate effect. That same afternoon, three women who simply yearned for freedom from slavery, slipped into the great beyond, at the end of a hangman's noose, at the Roseau Market.

One week later, this time on Saturday 9 April, Andrew, faced the courts on a charge of providing intercourse with the runaways, while, Julien, Jane and Selimene, were all charged as runaways. Andrew was found guilty and ordered banished from the Island, after being worked in chains. The other three were all found guilty and ordered to receive 39 lashes, and worked in a chain gang until they could be banished from the colony. The Loyal Dominica Rangers were recording victories both at the court and on the field. On 20 and 30 April, they reported the killing of Chiefs George Moco and Gabriel respectively.

The trials continued on 3 May with court appearances for Michel, Louisonne, Eugenie, Flora, Madge, Sandrine, Lisette and Angelique, all charged with the crime of being runaways. The lone male Michel, was found guilty, sentenced to be hanged and that 'his head be struck off and put upon Hertford Bay.'[21] The six women were all found guilty and sentenced to be worked in chains, and remain in jail until they could be banished from the island. Madge was singled out for additional punishment of 39 lashes, given that she was a new negro slave.

Sunday 22 May would witness the final session of the court martials, with Quashie, Mills, Beauty, and Eualie appearing before Judge Advocate WW Granville. Beauty, the wife of Maroon Chief Apollo was charged along with Quashie and Mills from the Woodfordhill Estate, with providing intercourse to the runaways; while Eualie was charged with being a runaway. The sentences were no less severe than those before. Quashie was sentenced to hang and his head cut off and fixed upon a pike at the Woodfordhill Estate. This particular punishment would catch the attention of Bathurst, and become a subject of complaint when reprimanding Ainslie. Mills and Beauty were sentenced to receive 100 lashes of the whip, and worked in chains until they could be banished from the island. Eualie was sentenced to 39 lashes of the whip, and worked in chains for six months before banishment.

At the same time of the trials, an undisclosed number of

Maroons, including two chiefs were killed by the rangers in the forests. The reign of terror against the Maroons, was however far from over. Troubling questions were raised about the conduct of Ainslie within the local establishment, but never publicly. For the most part, the planters and other white inhabitants were extremely pleased with the onslaught against the Maroons. However, several months after Ainslie's departure for England, William Bremner a white doctor, and attorney for several estate owners; as well as Benjamin Lucas questioned the legality of the court martial.

Bremner noted that: 'the trial was for the most part short and summary, and the sentence when agreed on by the court, was in the usual manner carried immediately to the Governor for his approbation. When the culprit was found guilty and condemned to death, the execution was as summary as the trial, for generally the sentence was carried into effect in a couple of hours, always in the course of a day, and in one instance the culprit was carried from the place of trial directly to the gallows, a distance not exceeding 100 yards.... Such a mode of trial and punishment was certainly calculated to inspire terror, but I entertain very strong doubts of its legality.'[22]

For his part Lucas was somewhat more guarded when writing to Bathurst about Ainslie's conduct. 'Whether slaves are amenable to such a court; whether that court was legally formed; whether they exceeded their powers, and whether the addition to the sentences of the court ordered by the Governor were proper, and legal or not, are matters for your Lordship's consideration, on which I do not presume to offer an opinion.'[23]

Doubts were also been raised as early as May, in the papers about how far Ainslie was prepared to go with his campaign of extermination. *The London Observer*, after receiving the Dominica papers from May, made the following observation. 'The war against the Maroons was continued with unabated vigour; but not quite in that spirit of extermination which the late sanguinary proclamation[24] had led us to apprehend. More camps had been discovered among the woods, in the interior of the Island; such of their male inmates as were not fortunate enough to escape were shot.

'The women and children appear to have been exempt from this severity as we find in the papers, now before us, repeated mention of females with their infant offspring having been brought into Roseau and committed for summary trial. After execution the heads of the offenders are struck off and exhibited on poles in different plantations. If we may credit the journals there is every prospect of tranquility being restored to the colonists and the inhabitants of Dominica by the utter extinction in a few weeks of the Maroon name and power.'[25]

That same paper also went on to herald the exemplary work of the ranger corps, while attempting to demonstrate that the Maroons were likely on the verge of defeat. 'Yesterday another instance of the vigilance and activity of the ranger corps was exemplified by the arrival of seven runaways sent in by them, belonging to the camp of Jacko, surprised near Lasoie Quarter consisting of one man, three women and three children (two boys and one girl), all property of Mr. Marceau, there were two other men in company, one of whom, the property of the same master was shot, his head was afterwards taken off, carried to Colihaut, and placed upon a pole on his master's estate.

'The other, the property of Mr. Duboc at Bioche was wounded and is retained as a guide; the party which took them was commanded by Sergeant Major Nash. It now appears evident that the effective and vigorous measures adopted have driven these misguided wretches the Maroons to the utmost shifts to obtain subsistence, and those whose obstinacy will not suffer them to surrender themselves, send out small foraging parties who are continually surprised and taken without much resistance.'[26]

In June 1814, Ainslie dispensed of the martial law trials and reverted to the court of special sessions. As before, a number of slaves and runaways were tried in three separate sessions, which lasted until August 1814. During the three-month period, fifteen defendants came up for trial, one was executed and the others given varied sentences. It all started on 1 June with the trials of Francois, Joseph, Scotland, Peter, Fox and Peggy; in the court presided over by Justices of the Peace, Benjamin Lucas, William Anderson and Archibald Gloster; attorney general, WW Glanville, acting clerk Joseph Court, and Joseph Laing and Thomas Beech, acting Provost Marshall and interpreter respectively.

The six slaves, all belonging to the Hillsborough estate, were charged with providing intercourse to the runaways. After a quick trial they were found not guilty for lack of evidence. On 8 July the second session was held with only one slave, Charles, charged with the sale and barter of salt, provisions and gunpowder, as well as with providing intercourse with the runaways. Charles was found not guilty and released. One other session would follow for the month on 23 July. Charged with absenting themselves from their owners employment for more than six months were Martin, Isidore, Condo and Marie. The four were subsequently found guilty, sentenced to receive 39 lashes each, then to be banished from the colony.

Ainslie claimed a major breakthrough in the war against the Maroons on 12 July, when the Chief of Chiefs, Jacko, who had remained free, in the mountains of Dominica, for over 46 years, was shot to death. *The Caledonian Mercury* recalled the event like this. 'On the 12th July the camp of Jacko, one of the chiefs was surprised, while many of its inmates were absent, seeking for wild yams, and other vegetable stores, to enable them to make their retreat to another quarter. Jacko made a desperate resistance he killed two rangers, wounded a third, and was shot through the head while in the act of leveling a musket at a fourth. He had been resident in the woods upwards of 40 years and was considered as head chief of all the runaway camps on the island. His male adherents fought their way and escaped on bye paths, which the rangers could not follow.'[27] Another newspaper *The Morning Post* said simply: '*Jacko Chief of the Runaways was lately killed at Dominica.*'[28]

Chief Jacko, who had conducted raids with Balla, Pharcelle, Mabouyah, Congoree and others in the 1780's and 1790's, had made his base in the heights of the Layou flats, close to Belles, on a ridge surrounded on three sides by the Layou river. He had survived 14 Governors,[29] the West India Regiment, Loyal Dominica Rangers, trusty slaves, and others, through wit, guile, and an enduring fortitude. He was finally dead, killed by ranger John LeVilloux. His death proved to be a major blow for the Maroons and signaled the beginning of the end to their ascendency in Dominica.

Just days later, a triumphant Ainslie wrote to Bathurst, exulting the Maroon Chief's death, while failing to mention that Jacko had killed two of his men. 'Jacko the Supreme Chief who titled himself 'governor of the woods,' he was shot in the act of levelling at the Sergeant Major of the Colonial Rangers. He possessed great influence over the other camps, who acknowledge his supreme power, and I think his death's a great circumstance. I mean to shed no more blood, except that of a chief named Noel, the wanton murderer of a white man a Mr. McFarlene who was put to death by him while sheltering in his house. It may appear worthy of remark that since I commenced operations against the Maroons in January last, I can hear of no instance of a single Negro deserting from his master. *NB: Jacko had been in the woods for 46 years in hostility to His Majesty's government.*[30]

Ainslie also expressed his hope that it was just a matter of time before the Maroons were completely conquered. 'I have not found it necessary to inflict the most trifling punishment on the prisoners, my object is nearly accomplished, and I trust that the capture of the Chief Apollo an event, at no great distance, who only escaped by a wonderful exertion of strength, in a struggle latterly, when his wife and others seemed taken, will complete the tranquilisation of the interior.'[31]

The final trials overseen by Ainslie took place on 25 August 1814 with the appearance of Lafleur, Belinda, Charlie and Cuffy before the courts. Lafleur, Belinda and Cuffy were all charged with absenting themselves from their masters' estates. Cuffy was remanded in jail until more evidence could be found while Lafleur and Belinda were found guilty. They were both sentenced to work in the chain gangs until banished from the island. Charlie was charged with having sold, bartered or given salt, gunpowder, firearms or provisions to the runaways. He was found guilty and sentenced '*to be hung by the neck until he be dead.*'

As had been done 28 years before on the death of the great leader Balla, the rangers intensified their search for other Maroon leaders and their followers. A report appearing in the Dominica Chronicle of 17 August 1814 reads as follows: 'Maroon War. We are happy to say that yesterday morning, five runaways (men) part of Jacko's people surrendered, and in the evening 16 came in from Quashey's camp and a few days ago, 11 more including Quashey the chief were taken by Sergeant Gardier and his rangers. We have authority also for inserting the undermentioned list of Maroons killed and pardoned, since the commencement of the operations against them:

Executed.................................. ...	8
Sentenced to be executed but pardoned by his Excellency the governor.....................	2
Died in Goal	1
Killed in action with the Colonial Rangers	13
Pardoned	304
Flogged....................................	18
Worked in chains and banished	24
In goal for trial	6
Surrendered to their masters of whom no regular account has been kept, at least,.	100
TOTAL	376

N.B of this number, 54 has been taken within the last fortnight.

No treaty or compact was made they delivered themselves up without stipulation or condition. The surviving chiefs were pardoned, and the slaves upon title and identity shewn by their owners, returned to the plantations. It was difficult but not impossible to ascertain with precision, the rights of individuals in these people their reduction only restored them to the dominion of their proprietors.[32]

Following the death of Jacko and the many trials, both at the court martial and the court of special sessions, the Maroons appeared dispersed, leaderless, and on the verge of defeat. However, it was not yet over, and those remaining in the forests continued to resist. An unknown planter, whose 4 September letter appeared in several newspapers at the time, noted that 'the runaways and Maroons are almost subdued, yet the island is very far from being tranquil.[33] Great discontent prevails, which is not likely to be removed under the present administration. The Legislature have been dismissed and the tone assumed by the Governor in exercising this act of authority, is worthy of notice. …The ranger corps being formed of drafts of slaves there have been recently several desertions from it. The service is disliked.'[34]

By November 1814 the feeling that the Maroons were not yet defeated remained pervasive within the colony. The general sense of unease persisted, and even the Board of the Council weighed in on the debate. When it was proposed that Ainslie be rewarded with a sword inscribed with the word 'extinction' members of the Council balked, arguing that the Maroons were far from being defeated. In one such exchange on 11 November, the Board commented:

'We willingly acknowledge that much has been done towards the suppression of the renegades. It is nevertheless true that a large proportion of those who have either been taken, or have voluntarily given themselves up, consist of women and children, and that a very small comparative number of adult males have yet been either apprehended or surrendered while therefore two such notoriously desperate characters as Noel and Apollo continue to head a body of runaways in the woods whose numbers it is to be feared are yet considerable and who may reasonably be deposed from their determined resistance to submission to consist of desperadoes like their leaders while such a formidable body still exists and continues to elude all the vigilance and defy all the exertions of the Rangers.

'The Board can never consent to sanction a declaration that those hordes are extinguished or that the colony is yet placed in anything like a state of complete safety from so dangerous an intestine enemy. [35] After a prolonged debate between the Board of the Council and the Assembly, it was agreed that Ainslie would receive his sword, with a panel inscribed as follows: *To His Excellency Major General Ainslie Governor of Dominica. This sword is presented by the two branches of the Legislature/ In testimony of his meritorious conduct of the reduction of the Maroons in the year MDCCCXIV.*

Official British reaction to Ainslie's conduct in Dominica came swiftly. On 10 February 1814, Henry Goulburn, Undersecretary of State for War and the Colonies, wrote to him after reports of the 3 October 1813 proclamation appeared in several British newspapers.[36] To the British press, what was particularly repulsive was the threat from Ainslie to '*put to the bayonet without exception to age or sex*,' all the Maroons who refused his offer of amnesty by 23 October 1813.

Goulburn's letter read: 'I have the honour of enclosing a copy of a paragraph, which has appeared in many of the London newspapers. You must not suppose that I am induced to do it from any belief that the proclamation alluded to in it has been issued, still less that it has been acted upon. The real ground of my troubling you on the subject is the anxiety to have it in my power to meet any observations, which may be made on the subject in the House of Commons by a contradiction from authority and, as a paragraph in a newspaper cannot be made the subject of official correspondence, I have therefore taken the liberty of requesting by a private letter that you would give me any information in your power respecting the transaction to which the paragraph relates.'[37]

Pressure continued to mount on Ainslie and by mid-March 1814, it was becoming increasingly clear that his misdeeds were beginning to catch up with him. Ainslie's unprecedented attacks and destructive action against the Maroons were not as yet well-known just yet, but his imprudence whilst Lieutenant Governor in Grenada had reached the ears of Lord Bathurst. And so it was on 12 March Bathurst wrote to Ainslie the following:

'Sir, A complaint was sometime since made to me, of your having, while administering the government of Grenada, inflicted a severe punishment upon a colored inhabitant of the name of Michell, I thought it my duty immediately to make enquiry into the subject, and to require from the Governor, a full statement of all the circumstances, and the minutes of what passed on the trial, which afterwards took place. I am sorry that I cannot find in them a complete justification of your conduct; for although that part of the charge; which accused you of having maltreated a free inhabitant, is certainly disproved, yet you have not denied, either by your counsel or by evidence that you ordered a slave to be seized, punished and confined, without any specification of his offense.

'As, however, you immediately offered to the injured individual what was at the time accepted by him as a sufficient compensation for the injury sustained, I am led to hope that your violence towards him proceeded from momentary passion, and not from any settled disposition to act violently towards an individual of the class to which he belonged; and I trust that you will sufficiently see the necessity, of guarding, by your future conduct, against the repetition of similar complaints against you, which, if substantiated, would not fail to call for the expression of the severest animadversion.' [38]

In the meantime, on 14 March, Ainslie perhaps spooked by the growing clamour over his harsh treatment of the Maroons and declaration of martial law, wrote to Bathurst in an attempt to justify his actions. The letter also provided some insights into his unfailing hatred for the Maroons. It read: 'People ignorant of the state of Dominica, erroneously believe that the runaways are slaves, who to avoid punishment for some venial or menial offense, from a harsh master, run to the woods for a short time, and then return to their duty, a few unfortunate, persecuted, isolated beings, without concert whose only inheritance is slavery whose conditions demand our pity.

'No misapprehension, Sir, can be greater. They are a banditti under government of chief, sub chiefs and captains inhabiting a country, difficult beyond description having regular outposts/or camps, as they are called in advance of the Grand cantonment where the chief resides, with provision grounds cleared for miles. This 'imperium in imperio [state within a state]' has been established above 30 years.

'It is the practice of these people to increase their number, by enticing from their masters well-disposed Negroes by means of persuasion, in which unfortunately they succeed too well, to the great loss of the planters, of whom a few months ago one advertised his estate for sale in the gazette as 'his slaves had all run to the woods!' Neither are their depredation on property confined to this, they attacked and robbed houses and estates to which the last remaining fugitives belonged, who are their guides, of which the following is a daring instance.

'A short time previous to my arrival, the cellar of a house on the market place of Roseau the chief town, was broken into, during the night by a party of three miscreants, headed by the sub-chief Elephant who had run away from the unfortunate owners of the cellar, and carried off a considerable quantity of Madiera, and salted provisions undisturbed! There are many instances of entire "gangs" of slaves throwing off their allegiance to their masters, retiring to the woods and remaining until an overseer, whom they disliked, because he had ventured to inflict a well-merited punishment, was removed.

'Threats of murder and flames were conveyed to two very respectable proprietors of estates, both captains of Militia, and one, my deputy in his parish, from this same Elephant, whom a few nights after, before he could put his threat in execution, was shot at the head of a party, in broad daylight, attacking for the avowed purpose of murder, the house of a small planter, which, during the absence of the owner, they had plundered of everything two days before. I have been obliged to furnish ammunitions to many of the poorer planters, not to attack but to defend their lives from these outlaws!

'The evil had arrived at the most alarming magnitude, the slave population seem animated by the unquiet spirit, which exploded and founded a black government in St Domingo, the high tone of the French people of colour, had only been lowered, by administering the oath of allegiance to the King, to above 1000 of these (one of my first acts) an organized force (among whom some French deserters) in the interior in opposition to His Majesty's government, plundering and murdering white and peaceable coloured inhabitants, life and property were equally insecure.

'Such was the state of things, when I issued the proclamation, which has given rise to this correspondence, had I hesitated to adopt the most prompt and decided measures, I would have been wretchedly defunct in duty to His Majesty and unworthy of the station, I have the honour to fill. From the moment I was issued with authority, this important object occupied my deepest attention; the season of the year precluding the practicability of certain operations, and wishing to mark my administration by clemency and its commencement, I offered to the Maroons a full pardon, if they returned to their duty.

'I sent a slave, who after surrendering, volunteered his services to the Grand Camp, with many copies of my Proclamation, couched in language the fugitives could understand, this unfortunate man Quashee the Chief tried, and ordered to be shot, which was instantly executed. I set a price on the head of this barbarian, who, I understand, immediately offered 2000 dollars for mine.

'The dry season affording a prospect of success I sent a strong detachment against the Maroons but from the treachery of the guides, or the overwhelming hurricane of the 28th July and almost equally destructive deluge of the 25th August, having totally changed the appearance of the country, they returned without having been able to reach their object. This was the period when the proclamation in question was issued; no instance exists of anyone being put to the bayonet. It was necessary to strike the Maroons with terror and success has justified my idea. Those put to death in the mountains, were shot running away, after invariably firing at their pursuers.

'I transmit every public paper written by me, relative to these transactions, that you may see how invariably mercy has accompanied the steps of justice; numbers are daily pardoned, even sub-chiefs if not guilty of murder, and as the Rangers (a colonial corps of my organising) are vigorously pursuing those who still hold out, in their last retreat, powerfully aided by the desolation of their provision grounds, I trust that [this] country before next June will be completely cleared of those desperate bands of Maroons who for 30 years have set the law at defiance.'[39]

The atrocity complained about by Lord Bathurst against Ainslie in his letter of 12 March, concerning Grenada, paled in significance when compared to the monstrous misdeeds to which he subjected the Maroons of Dominica. Ainslie's letter sent two weeks earlier had not yet reached England, before Lord Bathurst wrote to him on 29 March, concerning his surprise at hearing of the imposition of martial law on Dominica.

'I confess that I learnt with some surprise that you had found it necessary to subject the colony to martial law, and though I'm ready to admit that such a measure may be in some cases necessary, yet I cannot sanction it without a more detailed statement of the causes, which in your opinion justified such a proceeding. The mere fact of the increase of runaway slaves is certainly not an adequate ground for suspending the ordinary course of law, nor do I consider that any advantage can have been derived from this measure either as to the detection or punishment of persons guilty of offices which previously did not exist.'[40]

Less than one month later, Bathurst wrote again to Ainslie, on receiving further information about the atrocities committed, and even before giving him an opportunity to respond to his earlier letter. This time, Bathurst, thoroughly outraged by Ainslie's action, would summon him to England to respond in person to the crimes he committed against the Maroons, and his vile actions while in Grenada. This came in the form of a letter addressed to Governor Ainslie and dated 23 April 1814.

'When I couple this intelligence with what has already reached me of your having issued a proclamation of an outrageous nature (upon which my undersecretary has some time since received information)[41] and of your having proclaimed martial law in the island, I am compelled to give more credit to the subsequent proceedings than I should otherwise have done, and as I look in vain to your correspondence for any information as to the measures, which you might have had in contemplation, I am under the necessity of signifying to you the pleasure of His Royal Highness the Prince Regent that you should take the first opportunity of returning home and giving a personal explanation of the measures, which you have adopted, and of the motives, which has led to their adoption.[42]

In the meantime, not only had Ainslie attracted the attention of the Colonial Secretary, but some members of the House of Commons were also calling for action to be taken against him. On 25 April 1814, Sir Henry Mildmay, at a sitting of the House of Commons asked 'if government had any information respecting a proclamation issued by Governor Ainslie in Dominica, threatening runaway slaves with the destruction of their wives and children.'[43] In response, Mr. Goulburn indicated that the governor had been written to for information on this subject, including a request to send a copy of the proclamation. In addition, he had written to the Governor of Jamaica to ascertain the facts. [44]

Around the middle of June Ainslie received the letter from Bathurst, dated 23 April, instructing him to return to London. He then soon afterwards, on 21 June informed the House of Assembly of his recall to London. The Assembly for the most part appeared sympathetic to Ainslie and publicly gave him their support. They also expressed their sorrow at his recall, and encouraged a speedy return back to the colony. However, that seeming harmony would not last long and on 29 August, Ainslie moved to expel the entire House of Assembly through the following proclamation.

Whereas I judged it necessary to call together the House of Assembly for the dispatch of public business of the colony, and as the majority of that House have, in times of unexpected distress, shown themselves totally negligent of their interests of their constituents, in as much as during the course of thirteen months only two bills have been offered for my sanction, one of which has been rejected, it is my will and pleasure that the House be dissolved, to give the country an opportunity of shewing their sense of the services of their Representatives. And the House is hereby dissolved accordingly.

Given under my hand and seal at arms at Roseau, this 29th Day of August 1814, and 54th year of His Majesty's reign. George Ainslie Governor By His Excellency's Command William Bruce.[45]

By the end of August, four months had elapsed since Bathurst ordered Ainslie to return to London, but he had yet to respond in the affirmative. Bathurst was arguably getting impatient with Ainslie's failure to report. It was becoming clearer to Bathurst that the situation in Dominica, far from improving was getting worse, particularly with news of hurried executions under Ainslie's declared martial law. On 8 September, Bathurst wrote yet another letter to Ainslie requesting that he obey his earlier order requiring his return to England. 'I am persuaded that nothing short of the strong conviction you must have felt that your response at Dominica was at the time indispensably necessary could have induced you to hesitate respecting the course you had to adopt upon the receipt of my dispatch of 23 April last.

'I am satisfied however that the circumstances which gave rise to the instructions contained in that dispatch will render you anxious to avail yourself of the earliest opportunity of returning to this country in obedience thereto, in case you should not already have taken your departure from Dominica, which under every view of the subject is more to be expected.'[46]

Once Ainslie had settled on his plan to travel back to London, he addressed the House of Assembly on 10 October. 'The Governor thinks it right to inform his Honour the President, and the Honourable Board of Council, that he intends returning to England and shall embark on the 8th of November for that purpose. The object of his going is to give further explanation on the subject of the Maroons than can be conveyed in a dispatch. The Honourable Board may rely with confidence, that he will use every effort in his interviews, with the Right Honourable the Secretary of State for the Colonies to promote whatever he thinks will be of benefit to Dominica, and invites the correspondence of the Board during his absence, which he trusts, will not be beyond six months.'[47] Ainslie also congratulated the Parliament on "the Maroons having being subdued with the exception of Noel the assassin of Mr. Macfarlane who continued at the head of some few desperados."[48]

In his address to the newly installed House of Assembly, Ainslie pleaded his case noting: 'Mr. Speaker and Gentlemen, I have directed returns of casualties since the commencement of the Maroon war to be laid before you, and I earnestly recommend a certain provision to be made for those men who have been maimed in freeing the country from bands, who carried desolation and terror wherever they appeared. I congratulate the House on the return to their masters and habits of industry of so many, Maroons, the interior (of which not long since they had entire possession) being almost free from those sanguinary marauders.

'The supreme head, as well as the principal chiefs, have been killed with arms in their hands, and the colony enjoys a security which it has not known for a long series of years. Justice has been appeased by the sacrifice of eight or ten lives at the place of execution, a necessity always to be deplored, but in this instance unavoidable, when we consider that this daring banditti was so formidable at the commencement of the year, as to cause the senior member of his Majesty's Council to seek refuge in town with his family, and ask for a party of regular troops to protect his property, although only half a mile distant. It is still fresh in the recollection of every person, that a short time previous to my assuming the government, a body of twenty armed Maroons entered this town, the capital of the island, and after robbing a house in one of the principal streets to the amount of six hundred dollars in provisions, and retired unmolested. Example was necessary to prevent a recurrence of these scenes.'[49]

Six days later, on 10 October, Ainslie wrote this terse note to Bathurst announcing his expected date of travel to London. 'I have received your Lordship's dispatch of the 8th September and beg to acquaint you that I shall leave this colony for Europe on the 8 November.'[50] In preparation for his travel, Ainslie secured several affidavits from close friends and confidants, which could ostensibly be used in his defense. He was determined to put the best spin on his actions in his defense before the British Parliament.

One such letter came from Captain Savarin, the faithful head of his Loyal Dominican Rangers. 'I do thereby declare and certify on my honour, that I never received order from his Excellency Governor Ainslie to put to death any runaways, either men, women or children as stated in His Excellency's Proclamation. And that I never gave any such order to the officers and men under my command; the contrary was the fact; as on all occasions every humanity consistent with our own safety, when engaged in the mountains with them, has been shown to these poor deluded wretches, as well by his Excellency as myself. That on no occasion was a child ever killed or even hurt . On the contrary there were many instances when children and even women were carried out of the woods on the Rangers' back.[51]

Another letter in support of Governor Ainslie came from the West India Planters and Merchants in London to Earl Bathurst. 'We, the undersigned Proprietors. of Estates, Merchants, and others, interested in the Island of Dominica, now residing in London and its vicinity, consider it incumbent on us to represent to his Majesty's Secretary of State for the Colonies, the sense we entertain of the essential services rendered to the Colony of Dominica, by Major General Ainslie, by whose spirited exertions, in dispersing and crushing a most dangerous horde of runaway negroes, the lives of many white people and others were saved, and much property preserved from total destruction.

'These deluded people had become *so numerous, their*

plans were so well formed, their communication with the estates was so extensive, that there was much cause to apprehend a general massacre of all the white inhabitants and free people of colour, who were not immediately under the protection of the garrison. Such a plan was certainly formed. This dreadful catastrophe, we believe, was averted by the measures adopted by Governor Ainslie. The nature of the case, unknown to the inhabitants of this country, required prompt and decisive measure; and when the number of rebel slaves is considered, the ferocity of their dispositions, and the almost innumerable strong holds they possessed, the number of them which were killed is comparatively small, and the examples made, a still smaller proportion.

'We are convinced that the Proclamation, of which so much has been said, was only issued to induce the fugitives to return to their duty, that the effusion of blood might be prevented; it never was acted on, nor do we believe that any act of cruelty was committed either by order or sanction of Governor Ainslie. The few slaves who were executed, suffered by the laws of the Colony, and the example was most salutary, in preserving the lives of many of his Majesty's loyal subjects, and property to a large amount. We also beg leave to state, that if any censure is passed on Governor Ainslie for his conduct on that occasion, it would encourage similar revolts in that and other colonies, the consequences of which it is unnecessary to point out.'[52]

Just a few months after arriving in London, a special hearing was held in the British Parliament from 2 to 4 June 1815 on the conduct of Governor Ainslie while he was governor in Dominica and Lieutenant governor in Grenada. Member of Parliament Gordon rose to move for a Committee of enquiry into the conduct of the Governor. 'He stated the accusations against him to be a tyrannical exercise of his authority in causing a free man of colour to be flogged in Grenada, without any reason and also when in Dominica of flogging four soldiers without trying them, of having a negro executed and sending his head in a box to a planter and stuck on a pole on his estate, with other circumstances which proved much indiscretions, and that he was unfit for his situation, to which, since his recall he had been re-appointed.'[53]

During the course of the debate, Gordon went on to harshly criticise the Governor's conduct.[54] He began by expressing his regret that in the performance of his duty as a member of Parliament to animadvert upon the conduct of an individual of high rank and who previous to the instances which he had to submit to the consideration of the House had maintained an irreproachable character. But it was due to justice and humanity to call the attention of the House to the conduct of Governor Ainslie at Grenada and Dominica in both of which colonies that officer was accused of acts utterly subversive of those principles.

Gordon went on to state that 'from the papers before the House it appears that at Dominica as the insurrection was said to prevail, occasioned by slaves who were either deserters from the plantation or who always resided in the woods and in consequence of this insurrection, as it was alleged, Governor Ainslie issued a proclamation dated October 3rd 1813 that unless they should come in from the runaway camps and submit by the 24th of that month the troops should be employed against them adding that neither age nor sex would be spared but that all would be put to death.

'Combining this flagitious proclamation with the gross abuse of authority in the case of Michele [from Grenada] the House would see how far such a man as Governor Ainslie was worthy to hold the office assigned to him, or to be invested with the almost absolute power, which belongs to that office. It was, he understood, asserted, that this proclamation was never acted upon, but this was not owing to the disposition of Governor Ainslie, but to the discretion of the Officer who commanded against the Maroons. It was however a fact that in this war 9 slaves were executed, 12 killed in the woods, 42 punished and 592 were brought in prisoners, some of whom had been 35 years in the woods, all these prisoners were restored to their owners as they were called, but how, he would ask could slaves so long absent be identified?[55] Yet upon the allegation of their identity these unfortunate beings were handed over as runaways to men from whom, of course, they could not expect very kind treatment.' [56]

Gordon also took issue with the Legislative Assembly in Dominica which had voted an address of thanks to Governor Ainslie for putting an end to this war. He however urged the House not to judge the character of Ainslie from that proclamation of the Assembly, but rather 'from the Proclamation of the Governor himself, who ordered its dissolution on the express ground of its incapacity and inattention to business. The new Assembly, elected under the auspices of Governor Ainslie, had also, no doubt, thanked him for terminating the war alluded to and it would be for the House to appreciate that testimony in favour of the Governor.' [57]

In concluding his remarks to the House, Gordon cautioned 'that any colonial Governor who was found guilty of abusing the extraordinary power with which he was invested, should be visited with condign punishment in order to restrain other governors to secure the rights of the freemen of colour, of whom the persecuted Michele was one and to protect the slaves from injustice and cruelty.'[58]

Samuel Romilly another member of Parliament was harshly critical of Ainslie observing that based on the documents referred to the only conclusion he could draw is that there was no war on the island of Dominica, but merely the fear of future disturbance. 'It appeared that no less than 700 of these Maroons had been reduced to slavery; from which he suspected, that one great cause of the war proclaimed against them, was to procure slaves that could not be obtained by importation.'[59]

One Member of Parliament who vigorously defended Ainslie, however, was Robert Heron, noting that: 'On the charge which respects the proclamation in Dominica, and the whole conduct of the Maroon War, I have no indiscretion to acknowledge, I have not to deprecate censure, but to claim approbation and applause. The Governor is accused of having issued a violent proclamation against the Maroons; certainly the proclamation was bloody enough, but before any criminality can be attached to it, it must be proved that he acted upon it; words without an overt act constitute no crime. Sir, the measures of the Governor were at once vigorous and effective.

'But I must first inform the House what were these Maroons; they were not like those in Jamaica; the Jamaica Maroons are a body of men originally composed of the Coromantyne Negroes, who fled from the Spaniards at the first conquest of the Island by the British, and establishing themselves in the difficult country in its centre, sometimes recruiting their number by runaway slaves, at other times giving them up, were acknowledged by repeated treaties, and obtained a political existence.

'The Dominica Maroons, on the contrary, more numerous and far more savage, consisted entirely of runaway slaves, never acknowledged by any treaty or truce whatever. It is very difficult for us to conceive that in an island only 29 miles by 12, there should be a territory in the interior ever so strong, that I believe it would occupy more days to traverse its breadth than the distance contains miles; this country the Maroons inhabited, they cultivated some provision grounds, but their chief dependence was on plunder, robbery their subsistence, their occupation murder.

'Their numbers having increased to about eight hundred, by carrying away the slaves from the estates, the moment was arrived when the plantations could not have been cultivated, and the settlement must have been abandoned; all the efforts of former governors had been ineffectual, and attended with great loss, and to such a degree had the daring boldness of the Maroons increased, that they had murdered the messengers Governor Ainslie sent to them with the offer of pardon; had set a price upon his head; and in the open day had attacked the principal in the capital of the Island, and plundered it of provisions and ammunition.

'I cannot agree with the honourable gentleman in thinking the execution of nine persons cruel in the course of such a war; and as to the giving up the slaves to their masters, what was to be done with them? He says, indeed, their masters could not know men who had been thirty-five years in the woods; true, but there were few of these, and they might know their masters. It is a remarkable proof of the humanity exercised towards them, that of six hundred so given up, one instance only occurred of a slave returning to the woods. The honourable gentleman has told us a romantic story of head in a box; however, human blood was really shed, and I cannot treat it lightly.

'Sir; this story contains its own answer and explanation; the two men were condemned to death by a court-martial; after a fair trial, they were fully convicted of supplying the insurgents with provisions and ammunition. Instead of cruelty, the Governor shewed great lenity in putting only one of them to death. When the head was severed from the body, the manner of its disposal does not seem very important; the fact however is, that it was sent to the place where the crime was committed in a box, to be exposed on a pole; this practice was frequent, because it was found beneficial.

'By the means I have described, the Governor succeeded in putting an end to the war, and saved the colony. His great services have been acknowledged by addresses from every rank and every colour, and he possesses a magnificent sword, the unprecedented gift of the Legislature, the testimony of the high sense they entertained of his merit. But the honour, able gentleman is of a different opinion, he says indeed that he does not desire his punishment, but that his object is to prevent his return to the West Indies. Is it then no punishment to see his honourable ambition thus early blighted, his prospects of his rising in his profession terminated, his hopes of serving his country annihilated? Is it nothing that with a broken constitution and a shaken reputation (shaken as it would be, if the House agreed to the proposition of my honourable friend,) he must abandon his family to that poverty, from which his disinterested character and his honourable principles have alone prevented him from emerging.

'I have now, I think, sufficiently proved that his conduct in Dominica was highly meritorious, and that, if he was guilty of an error in Grenada, it cannot be attributed to any base or unworthy motive, and that besides it has been already more than sufficiently expiated. If, Sir, one indiscreet act is to cancel the debt due to patriotic zeal, and essential public services, there will remain but little encouragement for the exertions of future governors. Bring before so rigorous a tribunal the greatest ornaments of humanity, and even they cannot hope to pass without censure. Those whose hearts glow with the purest benevolence, whose minds are expanded by the noblest views, are still not exempted from the human frailty of error.'[60]

A few days later on 7 June, Samuel Romilly rose in the House of Commons to move a motion to the Princess Regent asking that: 'he would cause an account of the 615 persons of colour, stated in the returns of Governor Ainslie, before the House to have been captured in the woods during the Maroon War, subsequent to his proclamation of May, 1813 distinguishing their names, sexes and ages: the means taken to restore them to their former masters, and the manner in which those who could not be so restored had finally been disposed of.'[61] The motion was agreed to.

After the heated exchanges in the British House of Commons, Lord Bathurst was prepared to make his decision on the fate of Governor Ainslie. This he did with a letter to the Governor dated 21 December 1815, informing him that he would not be returning to Dominica. "I have had under my consideration the documents, which I thought it necessary to require from the island of Dominica for the purpose of investigating those parts of your conduct for the explanation of which his Majesty's government originally thought it necessary to require your presense in this country. I have also attentively perused the various papers upon which you have rested your vindication.

'It is with great regret that I acquaint you that the result has been a conviction that it would not be expedient to authorize your return to that colony as governor. For although I am disposed to admit that, during the latter period of your administration, there was great apprehension of danger to the colony from the increased force of the runaway Negroes in the interior, and that measures of greater vigour were necessary for their suppression, yet I can discover no necessity for that repeated recurrence to the exercise of martial law, and that supersession by courts martial of the established tribunals of the colony, which has distinguished that part of your administration.

'As soon as the runaway Negroes became too powerful for the control of civil authority, and so long as they continued in arms to carry our depredations under regular leaders, the proclamation of martial law and the employment of the troops against them were Acts as much of duty as of necessity, and so far your conduct merits the approbation which it has received. But when the object of putting down those insurgents had been attained, and the mass of offenders had been secured, the colony had a right to expect an immediate return to the regular administration of justice. The penalties imposed by the acts of the legislature of Dominica upon runaways were certainly not adequate to the offences, however aggravated by other circumstances.

'The civil courts appointed by those acts for their trial were easily assembled -- they had on former occasions evinced no indisposition to punish with severity where severity was expedient – nor was there on the present occasion any reason to doubt their inclination rigidly to enforce the law. The subjection therefore of the island to martial law, expressly, as it appears, for the purpose of trying such offenders by courts martial can admit of no sense. It was neither required for purposes of examples, nor was it calculated to raise the character of the government, because there was always just ground for apprehension that officers who had been actually engaged in warfare against the prisoners would not bring with them into court feelings the best fitted to make them impartial judges. And as the courts in question were composed entirely of officers belonging to the Dominica Rangers, there was still further reason to fear that to military feelings they might add colonial prejudices.

'In adopting the decision of courts thus constituted, it equally behooved you to have proceeded with extreme caution.

But I cannot observe that nay peculiar care was exercised by you in the examination of their proceedings, or that you evinced any great discretion in the selection of proper objects for punishment. And although his Majesty's government are disposed to acquit you in this as well as in the other instances in which your conduct has been arraigned, of any systematic violence or cruelty, and are willing to acknowledge your zeal and good intention, yet they are nevertheless compelled to admit that you have evinced so little discretion in the exercise of your authority as governor of Dominica that your return there could not be attended with any beneficial consequences.

'I have therefore been under the necessity of submitting to his Royal Highness the Prince Regent the propriety of superseding you in that command. But as his Royal Highness feels that the length and merits of your former services give you a claim to consideration, and that your supersession may give rise to a misconstruction of the real ground on which it has taken place, more specially on the part of your enemies, whose hostility towards you appears to have originated in most unworthy motives, His Royal Highness has been pleased at the same time to signify his gracious intention of conferring upon you the government of Cape Breton, and I have, in consequence, to signify to you the commands of his Royal Highness that you do proceed to that colony at the earliest opportunity, and take upon yourself the administration of the government.'[62]

Ainslie's response was swift and came the next day in a letter addressed to Bathurst. 'I have the honour to acknowledge your Lordship's letter of yesterday announcing his Royal Highness the Prince Regent's command to supersede me in the government of Dominica. As that letter contains the first notice of disapprobation of that part of my conduct, which regards the courts martial constituted for the trial of the runaways, the papers your Lordship had previously under consideration could not contain any vindication of my conduct, respecting these courts; it becomes necessary (and I trust your Lordship will pardon me, for so doing, on account of the serious and to me the ruinous consequences of this premature decision) to lay before your Lordship, my answer to this communication, it appearing, that the constituting of these courts and certain parts of my conduct [could] have influenced your Lordship to form an opinion of want of discretion in the exercise of my government.......[63]

Ainslie ended by saying that 'I trust that the explanation I have now given, added to the unanimous voice of the whole people of Dominica, White, Coloured and Black for my return (with the exception of four or five individuals) as the Saviour of the Island will induce his Royal Highness to reconsider his decision.[64] Notwithstanding Ainslie's impassioned plea to Lord Bathurst, he would never return to Dominica. In 1816 he took up his appointment as Lieutenant Governor of Cape Breton where he remained until 1820, when it became part of Nova Scotia.

By the time Ainslie was removed as governor of Dominica, the damage to the Maroons was nearly complete. They would never recover their numbers nor their fierce resistance to slavery. In any event, Wilberforce and the abolitionist movement was gaining added traction in forever putting an end to slavery. In another eighteen years, abolition and complete and total freedom from the clutches of slavery would be realized in Dominica and the rest of the British West Indian possessions.

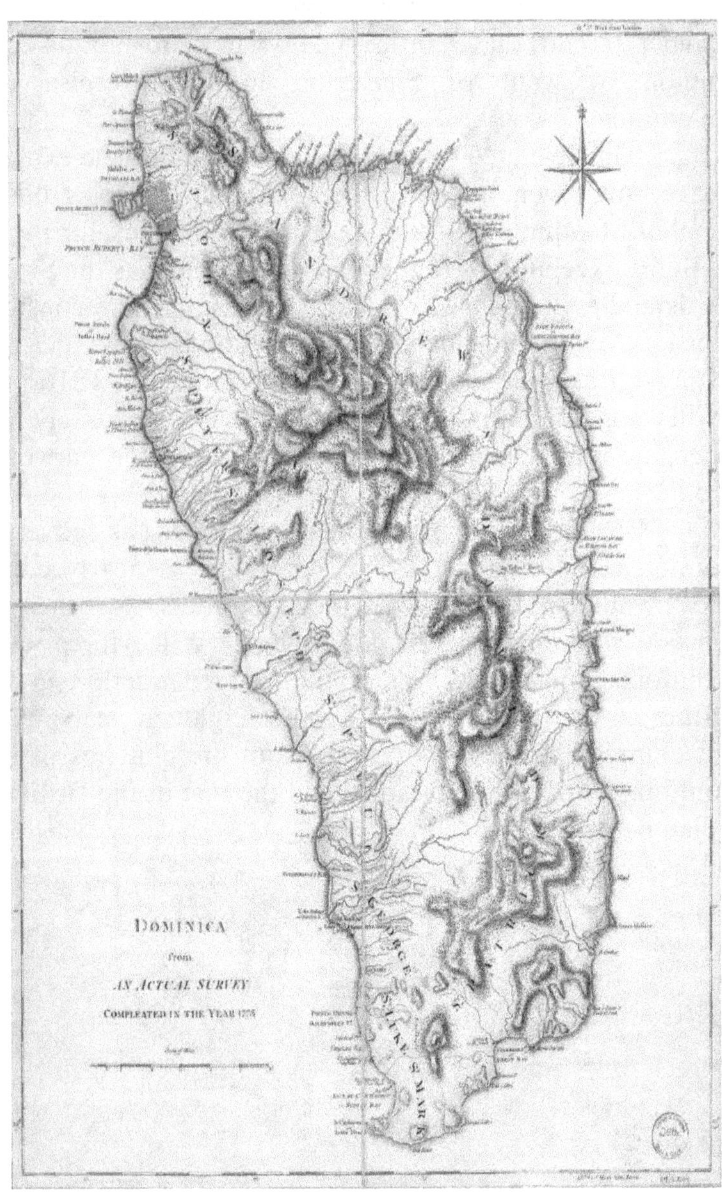

A map of Dominica in 1780.

12

Maroons and the Slave Abolition Debate

The head of a Maroon stuck on a pole in Dominica in 1814.

Sometime in 1816, Archibald Gloster, Chief Justice of Dominica described the Maroons as such: 'these sable bands were property --- They were rebel slaves from sugar and coffee plantations, who commenced savage hostilities against the white inhabitants, and being well acquainted with the secret avenues of a woody and mountainous country, skilled in forming ambuscades and concealing themselves from pursuit, shifted their ravages and depredations from place to place, as circumstances required, and became so formidable at last, that the alarm was given that Roseau itself was an object of their attack…after a very active warfare in the various quarters of the island, in which Governor Ainslie took great responsibility upon himself, ..the rebellion was squashed.[1]

By early 1817, the fear of the Maroons had not completely subsided notwithstanding their ordeal suffered during the governorship of Ainslie. On 4 January 1817, Governor Charles William Maxwell pushed through the Legislature an Act to '*Establish a Company of Rangers for the Apprehending and Suppressing of Runaway Slaves*.' Although deprived of their many leaders, the Maroon community continued to thrive and proved to be an ongoing option for those not wishing to remain enslaved on the slave plantations. The act read in part:

An act to establish a company of rangers, for the apprehending and suppressing of runaway slaves, for regulating their pay, clothing and discipline, for purchasing eighteen slaves to serve as privates in the said company, for employing them in tracing and keeping in repair roads across the country, and for granting encouragement for the apprehending or suppressing of any of the runaways, and to empower magistrates, or captains commandants of parishes or districts, on the requisition of the commanding officer of the said company of Rangers, to issue warrants to call to the assistance of the said company of Rangers, a certain number of slaves from the neigbouring plantations in cases of emergency, and to prevent the importation of slaves convicted, or known to have been guilty of murder, insurrection, or other capital offenses, and to prevent the sale of gunpowder, firearms or other offensive weapons to runaways.[2]

Clause 6 of the act, for instance, provided for cash payments to the rangers for the capture of runaways accordingly: 'for every slave who shall have absented him, or herself from his, or her proprietor or employer, above the space of six months…the said company shall be entitled to receive the sum of three pounds six shillings, and for every less number of days sixteen shillings and six pence.'[3] Not only were the rangers empowered to hunt down the Maroons, but whites and free people of colour with the permission of a magistrate were allowed under Clause 9 of the act to 'attack runaways…to form parties to attack any camp or body of runaway slaves, and for apprehending or destroying any of them.'[4] Such white persons or free persons of colour would be paid similarly to the rangers.

In addition, the act allowed for the governor to use Maroons who surrendered as guides in the woods for the company of rangers, 'without any pay or pecuniary reward whatever to the owner or owners of such runaway slave or slaves.'[5] The act also placed a premium on 'the best possible intelligence respecting the runaway slaves, their haunts, force and motions…,' that could then be given to the Governor or the rangers who were in pursuit of the Maroons. To further entice persons in the search for the Maroons, the slaves were promised their complete freedom and manumission by the Legislature. Other persons would be renumerated in cash.

Proof that the Maroons still posed a clear and present danger to the plantations was seen in Clause 15 of the act, which gave the authorities permission 'to call into action, at least 50 male slaves from any plantation, to help suppress any major revolt on the estate or attack by the Maroons. Those who would otherwise assist and abet the Maroons in escaping or evading capture would be found guilty of a felony and 'suffer death' without the benefit of Clergy.'[6]

No one would be spared the punishment for assisting the Maroons in their rebellion. Clause 21 summed it up as such: 'and it is hereby enacted and ordained by the authority aforesaid, that no white person, or free person of colour, or slave, from and after the publication of this Act, shall give, sell, or barter any fire-arms, gun-powder, or other offensive weapons, salt, salt provisions, clothes, or other necessaries whatever, or hold any intercourse or correspondence directly or indirectly to, or with any runaway slave or slaves, knowing them to be such, under penalty on conviction of suffering death as a felon, or such other punishment as may be awarded by the court.'[7]

Finally, in an effort to strike fear in the hearts of the slave population, and to curb the numbers leaving the estates, Clause 24 of the act noted: 'and it is hereby further enacted and ordained by the authority aforesaid, that if any slaves, being of the age of sixteen years and upwards, shall after the publication of this Act, absent themselves in any number or gang amounting to ten in number or upwards, from any one plantation, to which such slaves shall belong, and shall continue runaway or absent from the service as afore said, then one or more of the said slaves, such as the Justices shall think the greatest offender or offenders, shall be put on, and if the said slave or slaves shall be found guilty, the Justices composing the said court shall pass sentence of death, banishment, or such other punishment as they in their discretion, shall think fit.'[8]

Then on 10 September 1817 the Legislature passed: 'an act to establish courts of Petty Sessions at stated times, for the trial by Jury of runaway, or other slaves in custody of the Provost Marshal, for crimes under any of the laws of this island now existing, or hereafter to exist, for regulating and in some instances varying their punishment as established by laws now in force…'[9] This was the third such court set up to try the Maroons after the Court of Special Sessions and the Courts Martial set up by Governor Ainslie.

> *An ACT to establish courts of Petty Sessions at stated times, for the trial by jury of runaway or other slaves in custody of the Provost Marshall, for crimes under any of the laws of this island now existing, or hereafter to exist.*

On Wednesday 22 April 1818, as the debate for the abolition of slavery heated up in the House of Commons in London, Sir Samuel Romilly, rose to submit a motion, regarding the state and condition of slaves in the island of Dominica. Just three years earlier, on 8 June 1815, Romilly had backed MP Gordon, who before that same House, had called for a Committee of enquiry into the conduct of Governor Ainslie, both in Dominica and Grenada.[10] Romilly had also requested that Ainslie provide the House of Commons complete information on his treatment of the 613 black Maroons who were captured during his declared war on them.[11]

Needless to say, the inhumane and cruel treatment to which the runaways were put in Dominica was foremost on Romilly's mind, with new reports out of the colony suggesting the continued flogging and generally inhumane treatment meted out to them. This included those who were captured after being runaways from the plantation. Romilly bitterly complained that as punishment the slaves received 100 lashes compared to the 39 lashes allowed in other territories, and were subjected to even more barbaric treatment. 'In every case those responsible were never charged or prosecuted,' [12] Romilly observed.

On this occasion before Parliament in 1817, Romilly pointed to the 'several cases that had come before a Grand Jury [in Dominica], and some of them showed that the greatest cruelty had been exercised against the slaves.'[13] The cruel punishment was not however limited to the slaves on the plantations, but was particularly severe on those Maroons who continued to take refuge in the forests of Dominica.

One such case of cruel punishment meted out by the whites relates to John Mc Corry, a slave master who had, with chords, whips, sticks, and rods, scourged and flogged his slave who was guilty of been absent from the plantation. Another was that of Jeanton, a female slave who had been assaulted by her master, and afterward he confined her in an iron chain, by fastening the chain to her neck, arms and legs, with padlocks. She was further maimed, defaced, mutilated, and cruelly tortured, and her arms fractured. Both cases were brought before a grand jury, presided over by WW Granville, who by now was the Attorney General of Dominica, after serving as the judge advocate during the courts martial of the Maroons. Romilly maintained that "neither the slave, nor his family, nor friends could obtain any redress against the cruelties of his master. The slave was cruelly treated, and the public sympathized with the master.'[14]

Clearly, the information coming out of Dominica was shocking and proving very significant in bolstering the argument of the abolitionists for doing away with slavery all together. Earlier, in 1791, the Maroon insurrection in Dominica had featured prominently in the debate to end the slave trade, after the Bill was introduced by William Wilberforce.[15] Visual images of the horrific treatment of the Maroons, helped to cement his case for the abolition of the slave trade, with the Slave Trade Act signed into law on 25 March 1807. Twenty-seven years after drawing the attention of the British to the treatment of Maroons in Dominica, Wilberforce, now a veteran of the abolitionist campaign saw merit in again pointing to the treatment of runaways and slaves in Dominica, to argue for the eventual abolition of slavery.

The Leeds Mercury provides an enlightened account of the debate that took place on 22 April 1818 as follows. 'In the House of Commons on Wednesday [22 April], Mr. Wilberforce and Sir Samuel Romilly brought forward motions, which elicited a good deal of information respecting the present condition of Negro Slaves in the West Indies; and more particularly in the island of Dominica. It appear from the speech of Sir S. Romilly that the conduct of the Grand Jury in that island had been most reprehensible, and that they had most grossly abused the high trust reposed in them, for the purpose of screening the most abominable cruelties committed upon a number of slaves. The severe conditions imposed on the manumission of slaves, in this island, was also adverted to and deservedly reprobated, and *the oppressive nature of other laws respecting people of colour* was strongly pointed out; one of which is so enormously unjust that we cannot refrain from mentioning it.

'The law to which we refer, declares that all men of colour found in the island shall be taken up as runaways and if they are not claimed by their masters (which if free they could not be) shall be sold for the benefit of the public – One single instance of cruelty out of a thousand will shew the tender mercies of these slave holders. Two negro boys had been cruelly flogged for a petty theft; there were present at the infliction of this punishment two female slaves, one was the sister of one of the boys and the other a relation, who overpowered by the dreadful spectacle burst into tears; this commiseration was so grievous an offense to these worse than savages, that the females were sentenced to be flogged and the sentence was immediately executed.

'We consider this act of cruelty as equal in atrocity to any that has ever been committed by any NERO either of ancient or modern times. But we have not yet finished; the wretch who inflicted this outrage was indeed tried, but though these facts were clearly established against him he was acquitted! *Negro slavery as it exists in the West Indies is more cruel, more degrading, more alien from humanity than any such event, which ever before disgraced the history of mankind.* The slavery of the ancient world was in a considerable degree softened by sympathy, it was a state into which any man might by accident be thrown, the slaves were still considered as men, and entitled to some degree of regard. But in the estimation of the great body of the planters, a negro, though he has the form of a man, is considered as if he had none of the feelings of human nature, and is treated with a degree of rigour, which few, even hard-hearted men, exercise towards their cattle.

'We trust that this subject will be thoroughly debated in Parliament, and that some effectual means will be adopted to ameliorate the condition of this large and neglected portion of the family of man; which though long treated as unworthy either of justice or compassion, has at length awakened that sympathy in the Christian world, which will, we trust, ultimately reinstate them in those rights from which they have been so long and so wrongfully ejected.'[16]

At that same debate, Wilberforce, cognizant of the ongoing treatment of the Maroons in Dominica, 'moved for copies of all laws passed in or for the British colonies and not yet presented, respecting the condition and treatment of the slaves, the prevention of illicit importation, and the state of the free coloured population.'[17] Some of these laws, included two passed during the time Ainslie was governor of Dominica, an Act to alter punishment of burning in the hand and an Act to punish receivers of stolen goods, both passed on 16 November 1814. In addition, there was an Act to establish the company of Rangers for the pursuit of runaway slaves of 4 January 1817, an Act to provide for the maintenance of the Ranger Corps on 7 August 1817; and an Act to establish a court of Petty Sessions;

10 September 1817.

Romilly for his part, noted the rather oppressive Act passed in Dominica respecting manumission, which became law on 15 June 1810.[18] No man of colour on the island was at liberty without paying a tax of 16*l* 10*s*; others not born on the island were not at liberty without paying a sum of 35*l*. This particular act, sought to clarify the one of 7 September 1784, which was of even greater concern, and Clause 7 of the act read: 'and be it and it is hereby further enacted, that if any free negro, mulatto or mustee, shall harbour, conceal, or employ, any runaway slave, knowing her, or him to be a slave, and thereof be convicted before any two justices of the Peace for this island by the oath of one or more credible witness, or witnesses, the person so convicted, shall forfeit to his Majesty, his heirs and successors the sum of one hundred pounds current money, to be paid into the public Treasury of this island for the public uses thereof, or shall suffer three months imprisonment in the common goal, without bail, or mainprize, or be punished by whipping with any number of lashes, not exceeding fifty, at the discretion, and by order of the said justices.[19]

Importantly, Romilly stressed that the object of his motion was to 'confine the inquiry to the island of Dominica.' He noted that 'there was in Dominica a species of punishment called '*The Public Chain*' and if any master thought that his slave had offended, he had a right to send him to that punishment. During Ainslie's courts martial many of the Maroons who were tried and found guilty, if not sentenced to death were condemned to work in the chains until their banishment from Dominica. This 'torture' was applied to men and boys and even girls of tender age; and worse the Governor found that he could not intervene in either preventing or limiting the punishment. He was informed by Attorney General WW Granville that he had no right to remit the punishment awarded by the master.

'*The Public Chain* was described as follows: 'the slave who has been found guilty of any misdemeanor shall be put into the workhouse, where his labours are much harder than in the usual course of employment; he is employed to dig and to perform other difficult duties, with a chain fixed about his body, and attached to other culprits, leaving him merely room to walk, while he is driven on to work by cattle whips and other modes of castigation.'[20] Romilly lamented the fact that in any other colony the King [and by extension the Governor] had the power of mitigating all sentences; except those on impeachment from the House; yet, in Dominica, the prerogative is limited by the powers of the masters. 'If the evils that existed in the administration of the laws in the colonies could be remedied, it was right that should be done as soon as possible,'[21] Romilly argued.

Romilly went on to note that 'if it were possible that there could be any check given to grand juries and to petty juries in Dominica, it was proper that that should be given.'[22] He confessed that while he could not offer a remedy, he accepted the opinion shared by two other House members Burke and Dundas, which was to constitute the Attorney Generals guardians of the slaves, to make it an essential part of their duty to interpose between the master and the slave when there should be a necessity. 'By such a regulation it would become their duty to ensure that the slaves were properly treated.'[23]

Perhaps the most articulate rendering of Romilly's impassioned plea on behalf of the Maroons, slaves and other free people of colour came with his comments on manumission, which allowed for slaves to either purchase their freedom or to be set free. 'The constitution (British) should be taken in every part; it should be taken as a whole. It held that all men stood in a state of equality; that all men stood equal by the law; and that was talked of where it could not possibly exist. The moment an individual should set his foot upon the British shore, he became as free as any other individual. But what could be more inconsistent than those who talked of establishing that principle in the West Indian islands? The constitution would then be reversed and destroyed.

'What was recommended would be under the auspices of British liberty rendering slavery worse than under the most arbitrary government. Arbitrary governments indeed did make laws for their colonies. But the principle that no man could be bound by laws to which he had not consented, could be applied to islands so situated, no man could imagine anything more absurd. He meant the laws that had been passed on the subject of manumission, some of which were most extraordinary on the island of Dominica. It seem that in the island of Dominica a freeman of colour by law became a slave, till he had paid a certain tax.

'There was another law, by which all men of colour found on the island were liable to be taken up as runaways, and if not claimed by their masters, sold for the benefit of the public. If a man was not claimed, it was nevertheless taken for granted he was a slave, and he was sold. These laws were certainly made upon an oppressive principle. Since the abolition there ought rather to be some measure in favour of manumission than a restraint upon it.

'There was no man who did not entertain hopes that the time might come when there would be no slavery in any part of the world; but slavery could not be destroyed instantaneously; it could only be done by gradual manumission, by religious instruction, by alterations in the state of marriages, by improving the conditions of the slaves. The abolition, he was sorry to say had not had all the effect that had been anticipated. It was by laws to be made, and by laws to be enforced as well as made that that object was to be obtained. There was very high authority to show that, with respect to many laws that had passed, it had never been intended that they be executed.' [24]

Romilly begged to call the attention of the House to what had been stated by General Prevost on that island, in answer to a circular letter. 'In a letter to Lord Camden, in 1805, he said that the act for encouraging and bettering the condition of the slaves appeared to have been considered as a political measure, to avert the interference of the mother country in the management of the slaves. He might ask whether there remained a doubt that such had been the intention of those laws? It was a duty that that country owed to that part of her dominions; it was duty of government to take the affairs of Dominica seriously into consideration. It should be recollected that the slaves were servants to the King; they owed him allegiance, and would be as severely punished, as any other men, nay, more so, if they were to violate that allegiance. The King was bound to afford protection to them as well as to any one; they were as much subjects as Englishmen were.'[25]

On the same day that the British House of Commons was debating the cruel treatment of slaves and Maroons on Dominica, the local Legislative Assembly passed '*an act for regulating the government and conduct of slaves, and for their more effectual protection, encouragement, and the general amelioration of their condition*.' However, although the Act suggested better treatment for the slaves, it nonetheless significantly increased the penalties for slaves supporting runaways, proving further that the Maroons war of resistance was anything but over. Clause 20 of the act specifically noted that 'if any slave or slaves shall be guilty and convicted of rebellion, conspiracy, or of robbery, …burning or destroying of any cane piece, house or houses, or negro houses, …shall suffer death.'

Clause 21 continued: 'that any slaves who shall be found assembled for any mutinous or other dangerous purposes, and who shall refuse to go home to their different houses and plantations when ordered so to do, by any white or free persons whatsoever, …the ringleader or principal offender shall suffer death.' More compelling was Clause 22 of the same act which went further to state that 'any slave or slaves who shall be convicted, of giving selling or battering, gunpowder, firearms, or other offensive weapons, salt, salt provisions, clothes or other necessaries, lead or shot, whatsoever with runaways, or having intercourse, or correspondence with runaways, directly or indirectly, shall (according to the degree of the delinquency of such slave or slaves), suffer death.' [26]

The Maroons would continue to operate in the mountains of Dominica for many more years to come. In November 1818, Chief Tamba who had replaced Jacko was captured by the colonial rangers along with Hector his second in command, and seven other Maroons. Hector had faithfully served as the second in command for Chief Jacko.[27]

It would take a further fifteen years before the eventual abolition of slavery in the British West Indies through the Slavery Abolition Act of 1833. In the interim, countless more slaves and Maroons were brutalized, killed or otherwise suffered at the hands of the white planter class. For abolitionists like Wilberforce, Clarkson and Sharpe it was indeed a life's journey. On 26 July 1833, Wilberforce heard of government concessions that guaranteed the passing of the Bill for the Abolition of Slavery, three days later on 29 July 1833, he died.

Laws to Govern Suppress and Punish Maroons

Date	Laws via Various Administrations
	Administration of Governor Robert Melville
28 Jan. 1765	For the regulation and trial of the slaves in all criminal matters in the islands of Grenada, the Grenadines, Dominica, St Vincent and Tobago.
23 Apr.1765	For the more effectual suppression of the runaway slaves.
28 July 1769	To prevent the importation of slaves who have been convicted, or known to have been guilty of murder, or attempt to murder, or poison, insurrections, or other capital offences.
26 Mar.1770	An act to suppress runaways and for the better government of slaves, to prevent slaves being fraudulently carried off and to enable the commander in chief to send out detachments of free persons in pursuit of runaways
13 Mar.1771	To form a militia.' who were issued caps fronted with silver, on which his Majesty's arms were set, and underneath was the label, '*Dominica Light Dragoons*
	Administration of Governor William Young
24 Mar.1772	An act to continue the Militia Act of 1771.
	Lieutenant Governor Stuart
23 Aug.1773	An Act for suppressing runaways and for their better government. Same title as the one passed on 26 March 1770.
	Governor Shirley 12 November
23Dec. 1775	An Act to establish a Militia.
15 Sept.1777 No. 61.	An Act to establish a Militia, and repealing former Act.
15 May 1778 No. 67	An act to appoint a company of Rangers, for the suppression of runaway slaves
	French Rule 1778 – 1784.
20 Mar.1782 No. 100	An act to aid the Act entitled 'an act for suppressing runaways called a Slave Act, and to alter and amend the same, and to provide a fund to defray expenses, and for encouraging a party of rangers for suppressing runaways, and to oblige the Planters to make returns of runaways,

Date	**Laws via Various Administrations**
	and for transportation of those taken or surrendered, and dangerous to the community.
	Governor John Orde (April 1784 -
17 Dec. 1784 No. 117	An Act to regulate the sale of gunpowder and firearms, or provisions, salt, or other necessaries with runaway slaves, or having intercourse with them, directly or indirectly, and to authorize the governor, to issue proclamations and to grant more powers to magistrates, than heretofore, with respect to vessels at anchor, or hovering about the coast having arms or ammunition, or from onboard of which, slaves may have been landed
15 Mar.1785	An act to establish and form a militia
26 Mar.1785	An act to make the testimony of negroes and persons of colour admissible in certain cases and under certain restrictions for a limited time, to forfeit runaway slaves who have been absent a certain time from their masters, and to oblige the inhabitants knowing situations of runaway slaves to communicate the same in manner described
31 Mar.1785	An act to encourage persons to go as commanders in the woods as leaders of parties or detachments in pursuit of runaways.
23 Nov.1785	An act to suppress runaways by obliging proprietors of slaves to furnish, a proportion of their slaves, to be sent into the woods. To provide officers by engaging white and free people, and granting encouragement to apprehend and destroy runaway slaves; and to empower magistrates to search and examine vessels, suspected of holding correspondence with them
26 Aug.1786	An act to establish corps of Rangers to act against runaway slaves
23 Dec. 1788	An act to establish a militia
23 Dec. 1788	An act for the encouragement, protection, and better government of slaves
31 Oct. 1793	An act to form militia, and ascertaining what persons are to compose councils of war, and other purposes respecting militia.
June 1794	An act to alter militia act

LAWS TO GOVERN SUPRESS AND PUNISH MAROONS

Date	**Laws via Various Administrations**
16 Oct. 1794	An act to authorize the Commander in Chief to employ armed parties of white persons, free persons of colour, and slaves with proper officers, to discover and apprehend runaways, and suspected white and coloured persons, and for the purpose of payment of such parties
	Governor Henry Hamilton
6 Dec. 1794	An act to procure guides to discover runaway camps and places of resort in the woods
3 Dec. 1795	An act to raise a corps of healthy male slaves, to act as soldiers in defence of the colony, for a limited time, appraising, regulating their hire, and for other purposes
16 Jun.1797	An act to declare the law concerning the cognizance trial and punishment of spies, and to enable the governor to issue warrants to hold court martial for their trial, to prevent foreigners from landing or remaining in the island without licence, and to punish inhabitants receiving or concealing such foreigners
	Governor Johnstone
7 Nov. 1797	An act to declare when martial law is in force, to provide refreshments for militia on march, and slaves and mules to carry provisions and other necessaries, to have weekly meetings of militia, during war, to prevent, in martial law debtors leaving the island without payment or security, and to enable the judges and others to exercise their offices during martial law, and for other purposes.
15 Dec. 1797	An act to provide carriers of ammunition and provisions for parties sent out by the Governor against runaways, to fix their pay or hire, and mode of payments
30 Apr. 1798	An act to make testimony of slaves admissible in certain cases, and under certain restrictions, for a limited time, to forfeit runaway slaves who have been absent from the service of their masters a certain time; and to oblige the inhabitants of this Island having intelligence of the situation, or

Date	**Laws via Various Administrations**
	motions of the runaway slaves to communicate the same to the persons and in the manner prescribed by this act; and to prevent persons from harbouring or employing slaves on their plantations without a written permission from the owner or person having charge of such slaves; and for other purposes;
30 Apr. 1798	An act for apprehending of runaways and to oblige the Provost Marshall to receive and advertise them, and if unclaimed within limited time, to oblige him to sell them for the public benefit; for appointing a committee of the council and assembly to inspect the common goal from time to time, and for other purposes in this act mentioned
4 Sep. 1800	An act to provide carriers of ammunition for parties sent into the woods, against the runaway slaves, to enforce affidavits from proprietors of the numbers of slaves runaway and to oblige magistrates to return such affidavits to the Legislature
16 Oct. 1800	An act for the trial and effectual punishment of such runaway slaves as may hereafter be taken, and be known to be chiefs, or leaders of camps, or bands of runaway slaves in the woods,
19 Dec. 1800	An act for the banishing of sundry runaway slaves, now in confinement and also for the banishment of such runaways of certain descriptions as shall hereafter be taken or surrender themselves and for other purposes
	Governor George Prevost
11 Feb. 1803	An act to prevent the return to this island of persons who were banished therefrom by sentences of general courts martial held in the year one thousand seven hundred and ninety-five for the trial of sundry persons charged with high treason, and to prevent aliens, as well whites as free persons of colour possessing sentiments inimical to His Majesty's government, from introducing and establishing themselves in this colony, and for other purposes

LAWS TO GOVERN SUPRESS AND PUNISH MAROONS

Date	**Laws via Various Administrations**
14 July 1803	An act to amend act to regulate militia
	Governor Lucas(President)
16 Nov.1816	An act to repeal all former militia acts and forming militia
4 Jan. 1817	An act to establish a company of Rangers, for the apprehending and suppressing of runaway slaves, for regulating their pay, clothing and discipline, for purchasing eighteen slaves to serve as privates in the said company, for employing them in tracing and keeping in repair roads across the country, and for granting encouragement for the apprehending or suppressing of any of the runaways, and to empower magistrates or Captains Commandants of parishes of districts, on the requisition of the commanding officer of the said company of Rangers, to issue warrants to call to the assistance of the said company of Rangers, a certain number of slaves from the neighbouring plantations in cases of emergency, and to prevent the importation of slaves convicted or known to have been guilty of murder, insurrection, or other capital offenses, and to prevent the sale of gunpowder, fire arms, or other offensive weapons to runaways
21 Jun. 1817	An act to provide for maintenance of ranger corps
10 Sep. 1817	An act to establish courts of Petty Sessions at stated times, for the trial by Jury of runaway, or other slaves in custody of the Provost Marshal, for crimes under any of the laws of this island now existing, or hereafter to exist, for regulating and in some instances varying their punishment as established by laws now in force; for the more speedy trial of slaves committed for misdemeanours or petty offences by Justices of the said court without a trial by Jury; and to enable the Justices of the courts of King's Bench and Grand Sessions of the Peace immediately on the termination of their Sessions, to hold courts

Date	**Laws via Various Administrations**
	of Petty Sessions for the trial, or gaol delivery of slaves then in custody of the said Marshal, and for other purposes connected there with.

A CUDGELLING MATCH BETWEEN ENGLISH AND FRENCH NEGROES IN THE ISLAND OF DOMINICA

by BRUNIAS (1728-1796)

Dominica: The Period 1764 – 1818

Date	Activity
18 Oct 1748	Signing of the Treaty of Aix La Chapelle by Britain, France and the Dutch Republic, in which the neutrality of the islands of Dominica and St Vincent was reaffirmed.
6 June 1761	Dominica captured by a British amphibious force commanded by Lord Andrew Rollo.
10 Feb 1763	Signing of the Treaty of Paris in which France formally ceded possession of Dominica to Great Britain.
1766	Passage of the Freeport Act of Jamaica and Dominica
July 1767	Balla arrives in Dominica
April 1771	William Young Bart becomes Governor of Dominica
10 June 1777	British diplomat Stephen Sayre proposes to Prussian King, Frederick the Great that Dominica become a protectorate of Prussia.
7 Sept 1778	The French under the command of The Marquis de Bouillé successfully capture Dominica from the British.
Sept 1778	The Marquis Duchilleau appointed governor of Dominica.
29 August 1779	A massive hurricane wreaks havoc on Dominica completely wiping out the country's cane plantations, coffee trees and other provisions.
15 April 1781	Fire completely destroys the town of Roseau.
1781	Robert Grahame a planter murdered by the Maroons in a first attack of its kind.
9-12 April 1782	Admiral Rodney defeats French forces just outside of Dominica during the Battle of the Saints or to the French the *Bataille de la Dominique* (Battle of Dominica).
October 1783	Governor John Orde arrives in Dominica.
7 Sept 1784	British rule restored to Dominica, after the signing of the 1783 Treaty of Paris.

Date	Activity
6 Dec 1785	Balla successfully attacks the Rosalie Estate.
18 Mar 1786	Balla is killed by a party of Rangers led by Lieutenant John Egan.
1784 - 1786	Period of the First Maroon war.
Feb 1787	Prince William Henry, younger brother of King George II visits Dominica
1789 -1790	Thomas Bruce serves as acting Governor
1790 - 1792	Governor John Orde returns as Governor
I Jan 1791	Pharcelle unveils a plan to take over several estates on the Windward Coast.
1 Feb 1791	Polinaire taken prisoner for his role in the January 1791 uprising.
1 March 1791	Polinaire executed for his role in the January uprising.
18 April 1791	William Wilberforce introduces the first Parliamentary Bill in the British House of Commons, to abolish the slave trade.
1792 - 1794	Thomas Bruce serves as acting Governor
21 May 1794	Victor Hugues lands on Guadeloupe.
15 Oct 1794	The Legislature proposes a full pardon to Pharcelle in exchange for him helping with capturing of the Maroons.
1794 - 1796	Henry Hamilton serves as Governor.
4 June 1795	Victor Hugues launches unsuccessful invasion of Dominica.
15 Sept 1795	Formation of the 8th West India Regiment, an all-black militia, under the command of Lieutenant Colonel John Skerrit.
1796 - 1797	John Matson acts as Governor.
16 June 1797	Dominica authorities discover another plan by Victor Hugues to take over Dominica.
1797 - 1802	Andrew James Cochrane Johnstone serves as Governor of Dominica.
19 April 1802	Members of the 8th and 9th West India Regiment stage an open mutiny at Prince Rupert Bay in Portsmouth.
Dec 1802	Governor George Prevost arrives in Dominica.

Date	Activity
19 Feb 1805	The French launch an unsuccessful invasion of Dominica.
21 Feb 1805	The town of Roseau set on fire.
1805 - 1808	George Metcalfe serves as Acting Governor of Dominica.
6 February 1807	Act to abolish the Slave Trade passed in the British Parliament.
Dec 1805	George Metcalf replaces Governor Prevost as Acting Governor
1808	Edward Barnes briefly takes over as Governor.
1808 - 1809	James Montgomerie serves as Governor
1809 -1812	Edward Barnes serves as Governor
1812 - 1813	John Corlet acts as Governor.
1812 - 1814	Period of the Second Maroon War
17 April 1813	Governor Ainslie arrives in Dominica.
17 July 1813	Trials begin for Maroons captured soon after the arrival of Ainslie.
16 Jan 1814	Ainslie declares Martial Law in Dominica.
19 Jan 1814	Maroon trials under martial law commences.

1793 Guadeloupe: Liberty Egality Brotherhood or Death.

Governor George Prevost in 1802.

Summary of Maroon Trials in 1814

Date	Names	Charges	Punishment
15-16 January	Jean Pierre	--Providing provisions to the Maroons	Death by hanging
	Peter	-- Starting a mutiny of 20 slaves and providing Maroons with provisions	Death by hanging
	Hector	-- Being a runaway	Flogged with 100 lashes of the whip
	Rachel (F)	-- Being a runaway	Flogged with 50 lashes of the whip
	Sarah (F)	--Part of the Mutiny of 20 slaves	Flogged with 50 lashes of the whip
	Hetty (F)	D°	D°
	Placet (f)	D°	Flogged with 100 lashes of the whip
	Daniel	D°	D°
	Dick	D°	D°
28 January	Joseph	-- Supplying the runaways	Not guilty
	Pierre	-- Encouraging the runaways	Flogged with 100 lashes of the whip
	Charles	-- Runaway for 17 months	Flogged with 100 lashes of the whip
	Augustin	-- Runaway for 3 months	Discharged, deemed an 'idiot'
26 February	Victor	--Providing gunpowder and provisions to the Maroons	Death by hanging
6 March	Joe	-- Harbouring and supplying the runaways	Death by hanging

Date	Names	Charges	Punishment
	Gabriel	-- Robbing the Negro grounds	Flogged with 100 lashes of the whip
13 March	Jenny (F) Betty (F) Perine (F) Francois (F) Registe (F) Hester (F)	--Being a runaway D° D° D° D° D°	Set free (poor health) Set free (poor health) Flogged with 50 L Death by hanging Set free Death by hanging
27 March	Flora Adelaide (F) Caroline (F)	-- Being a runaway D° D°	Chain gang and banishment Death by hanging Chain gang and banishment
3 April	Zabet (F) Ebo(Vielle) Rebecca (F)	-- Being a runaway --Practicising witchcraft and being a runaway -- Being a runaway	Death by hanging Death by hanging Death by hanging
9 April	Andrew Julian Jane (F) Selimane (F)	-- Intercourse with the runaways -- Being a runaway -- Being a runaway -- Being a runaway	Chain gang and banishment Flogged with 39 L Flogged with 39 L Flogged with 39 L
3 May	Michel Louisonne F) Eugenie (F) Flora (F) Angelique F)	-- Being a runaway D° D° D° D° D°	Death by hanging Chain gang and banishment D° D° D° D°

Date	Names	Charges	Punishment
	Sandrine (F) Lisette (F) Madge (F)	D° D°	D° Flogged with 39 lashes of the whip
	Quashie Mills Beauty (F) Eualie (F)	-- Intercourse with the runaways D° D° --Being a runaway	Death by hanging Flogged with 100L D° Flogged with 39 Lashes

LIBERTÉ  ÉGALITÉ

PROCLAMATION.

VICTOR HUGUES, commissaire délégué par la convention nationale aux iles du vent :

CITOYENS,

VIVE LA RÉPUBLIQUE!

VICTOR HUGUES.

Victor Hugues proclamation of the abolition of slavery in 1794.

Dominica: An Account of Runaway Slaves Killed Taken and Surrendered, between the 10th Day of May 1813 the date of Governor Ainslie's Proclamation and the 22nd day of November 1814 the day of his departure from Dominica; -- Distinguishing the sexes and the children; with the manner with which they have been disposed of

Date	Names of Slaves Killed	Men	Women	Names of Owners	By whom, or how killed	
1814 February	Elephant or Policy	1	- -	Geo Anderson	Manger of Edenbro Estate	A chief
Unknown	Unknown	1		Unknown	D° and Negroes of D°	
March 10	John	1		Mr. Hunt	Loyal Dominican Rangers	
28	Pope	1		B. Marceau		
April 2	Desiré		1	F. Trocard		
20	Moco George	1		----Blondel		A Chief
	Andrew	1		Mr. Dubin		
	Francois	1		G. Metcalfe		
	Unknown	1		Unknown	Fell down a precipice	
30	Gabriel	1		D°	Loyal Dominica Rangers	
	Unknown	1		D°	Fell down a precipice	
May 22	Alexander	1		Lapichawdeere	Loyal Dominican Rangers	
28	Montagne	1		Mr. Arnaud	- - - ---- D°	
31	Frejus	1		Mr. Courché	- - - ---- D°	
	Aliba	1		Clark Hall Estate	- - - ---- D°	
	Geneviève		1	York Valley Estate	- - - ---- D°	
June 29	Celemone		1	Mr. Bentier	- - - ---- D°	
July 12	Old Jacko	1		Mr. Beaubois	- - - ---- D°	The oldest Chief
	Total	15	3			

No 2. Runaway slaves taken by the Loyal Dominican Rangers, by the Militia or Volunteers sent against the Runaways, or by Soldiers at Signal Posts, or sent to Jail as Runaways, having been in camps or Parties of Runaways in the Woods

Names of Slaves	**Men**	**Wome**	**Childr**	**Names of Owners**	**By Whom taken, or committed**	**When taken, or committed**	**When released**	**How disposed of**
John	1			Mrs. Nibbs	Manager at Mr George	1813 14 July	1813	Sold
Billy	1			Mr. Larogne	His Owner	21		
Sampson	1			Mr. Laronde		26 Aug	22 Nov	Banished
Hypolite	1			Mr. Lockhart	Mr. Fraser	27	20 Oct.	D^o^
Charles	1			Mr. Marceau	His Owner	9 Sept	3 Jan 1814	D^o^
Germain	1			Mr. McCorry		13	10 Nov 1813	D^o^
Harry	1			Mr. Courché	Dr Clarke at Clarke Hall	10 Oct	15 Oct	D^o^
Johnstone	1			Canefield Estate		13	3 Jan 1814	D^o^
Jem		1		Mr Lionné	Mr. Watson at G.Bay	20	13 Nov 1813	Sold by Provost Marshal
Jack, Germaine and Marie Saintes	2	1		D^o^	Governor Ainslie	24	27 Oct	To Owner
Madelaine		1		Dr. Spencer	Dr. Laidlaw at Prince Rupert	9 Nov	12 Dec	Banished
Marceline		1		A. Aubert Guad	D^o^		11 Feb 1814	To Owners Agent
Mingo				Mad Scipio	Dr. Garraway Mt Prosper	22	30 Nov 1813	Banished

Names of Slaves	Men	Wome	Childr	Names of Owners	By Whom taken, or committed	When taken, or committed	When released	How disposed of
Robert	1			Mr. Marrack Trinidad	Governor Ainslie	25 Nov	18 Dec	To Owners Agent
Joseph	1			Mr. Pene Guad	D°	3 Dec	22	D°
Rachel		1		Mr. Grand	Militia	14 Jan 1814	19 Apr 1814	D°
and her Children			2				22 Jan	D°
Jean Pierre	1			D°	D°		16	Executed
Hector	1			J. Lionné	D°		21	D°
David Stewart Hill & Ambrose	4			Goodwill Estate	Lt. Mc Donald of L.D. Rangers	15	17	To Owners att.
Sarah		1		E. Wallis	Governor Ainslie	22	21 Feb	D°
Tom	1			J. Corlet	D°		1 March	D°
Oaspard, Manuel, Lindor, Gagnia & Anowoi	5			Mr. Letang	D°	23	3 Feb	D°
Charles	1			Mrs. Bourgain	Court Martial	24	16 April	D°
Watty and Toby	2			Hampstead Estates	Volunteer Party		3 Feb	D°
Toney	1			Mr. Ryris	D°		17 March	D°
Cutty and Child		1	1	D°	D°		18	To Owner
Bella		1		G. Titre	Firmin, at Prince Rupert	25	18 July	D°
Francoise		1		J. Nugent	Militia	11 Feb	30 Feb.	D°
Louisonne		1		C. Jolly	D°		10 March	D°
David and Daniel	2			Mr. Powell	D°	5 Mar	8 March	D°

DOMINICA: AN ACCOUNT OF RUNAWAY SLAVES

Names of Slaves	Men	Wome	Childr	Names of Owners	By Whom taken, or committed	When taken, or committed	When released	How disposed of
Strano	1				L. D. Rangers	10 Mar		In the Ranger corps
Registe	1				D°		17	To owner
Francoise		1		D°	D°		13	Executed
Margarite al'Perine		1		Mrs. Powell	D°	11	30 June	To Owners att.
Betty		1		Mrs. Warner	D°		15 March	D°
Hester		1		Mr. Menier	D°	12		Condemned 13 March died 24 in jail
And her Children			2					Sold by Provost Marshal
Jenny		1		Hillbro Estate	D°			To owners att.
Brandy		1		Miss Foye	Militia guard		13 March	D°
Nelson	1			Mr. Jolly	D°		23	D°
Margaret		1		Mr. Lionné	D°		17	D°
& her Child			1	Miss Foye	L.D Rangers	19		D°
Benjamin	1			Mr. Consel	Manager at Hertfd Estate	24	29 Aug.	Sold by Provost Marshal
Flore (Mulatto)		1		Mr. Roger	L.D Rangers	25	16 April	Sold by D°and banished to owner
And her child		1	1		D°			
John Philip	1			Mr. Roger Beliar	D°		1	D°

Names of Slaves	Men	Wome	Childr	Names of Owners	By Whom taken, or committed	When taken, or committed	When released	How disposed of
Supby and Child		1	1	Unknown	D°		16	To the Gov and by him given to his Sec who sent them off the island
Adelaide		1		Miss Foye	D°		27 March	Executed
Caroline		1		D°	D°		22 April	Sold and banished
Tomby			1	Mr. Marceau	D°			To Owner
Anne Marie		1		D°	Militia Guard		19 April	D°
Marie Jeanne		1		Mr. Desmariniere	D°	26	22	D°
Marie Jeanne		1		Mad. Picklin	L.D Rangers	27		D°
Kelle Ebe, alias Marie Claire		1		Mr. Marceau	D°	1 April	3	Executed
Rebecca		1		D°	D°			Condemned but pardoned to owner
And her Children			3	D°	D°			D°
Bassigo	1			D°	D°		22	D°
Zabeth		1		D°	D°		17	Executed
Lucile & Florentine		2		Mr. Lockhart	D°		15 Nov	To Owner
Simon alias Julien	1			Mr. Dubue	D°		16 April	Sold and banished
Greg	1			Mrs. Grey	Governor Ainslie		11 June	To Owner's attn.
Jenny		1		Dr. Greenway	L.D Rangers		16 April	Sold and banished to owner

Names of Slaves	**Men**	**Wome**	**Childr**	**Names of Owners**	**By Whom taken, or committed**	**When taken, or committed**	**When released**	**How disposed of**
And her Child			1	D°	D°			
Clementine, alias Celectine		1		Gonne	D°		16 April	Sold and banished
and her Child			2		D°		13	Died in jail
Moco	1			Mr. Roger	D°		16	sold
Joseph	1			Mr. Roger	Governor Ainslie	1814 19 April	1814 27 April	To Owners agent
Virginie		1		Mr. Charrurier	L.D Rangers	21	11 June	To be banished
Michel	1			D°	D°		1 May	Executed
Louisonne		1		D°	D°		18 June	To Owner
Francoise				D°	D°			D°
Madge (a Mulatto)		1		Mrs. Nibbs	D°			Banished
her Children			6	D°	D°			Delivered to owners att.
Flore		1		Mr. Marceau	D°		21	Banished
Her Children			2	D°	D°		2 May	To Owner
Angelique		1		Mr. Daroux	D°		6 June	Banished
Lisette, alias Betsey		1		Mr. Hurtault	D°		10	D°
Louisenne alias Alexandrine		1		Marseille	D°		10	D°
Dorinda, alias Belinda		1		Permansio Estate	D°		3 June	Pardoned for killing a runaway and

Names of Slaves	Men	Wome	Childr	Names of Owners	By Whom taken, or committed	When taken, or commi tted	When released	How disposed of
								delivered to owner
Her Children			2	D°	D°		23 April	
Sally		1		E Wallis	Governor 's Secretary	4 May	6 May	D° Agent
Children			2	Miss Foye	L.D Rangers			D°
Child			1	Mr. Beauclair	D°			D°
D°			1	Mr. Laing	D°			To owners' att.
William	1			Estate of Beaumon t	D°	5	19	D°
Pierre	1			Mad. Toussaint	D°	1 8	13 June	D° Agent
Eulalie		1		Mr. Belair	D°		30 May	D°
Clarissa & Children		1	3	Mr. Marceau	D°	2 3	25	To Owner
Madelaine		1		Mad. Toussaint	D°		13 June	D°
Rachel		1		Laville	D°		29	D°
Zabeth		1		C. Giroux	D°		30 May	Died in jail
Lucy & Children		1	2	Mr. Moore	D°		13 June	To Owner
Margaret		1		Mad. Fidelin	D°			D°
Zabeth		1		E. Petit	D°			D°
Marie Ursula		1		Unknown	D°		6 July	Died in jail
Etienne alia Adder	1			D°			29 August	Sold
Robert Browne	1			Mr. Turner	Governor Ainslie		14 June	To owners agent

Names of Slaves	Men	Wome	Childr	Names of Owners	By Whom taken, or committed	When taken, or committed	When released	How disposed of
Prince Buckley	1			D°	Governor Ainslie	23		
Toussaint	1			Mad, Brumant	Cap. Savarin's Negroes	30 May	1 July	To owners agent
Issac	1			Mr. Metcalfe	L.D Rangers	31	31 May	In the Rangers Corps
Jem		1		G. Anderson	D°		16 June	To Owner
Paul	1			Carelle	D°		13	D°
Maximom	1			Mr. Lavadie	D°		14	D°
Felix	1			Anselme	D°		11	D°
Lazar	1			Mr. Molinie	D°		10	D°
Margaret & Justine		1	1	D°	D°		13	D°
Cecile		1		Mad. Sicard	D°		18	D°
Scolastique & Child		1	1	Mr. Bowles	D°		11	D°
Marie Noel		1		Aubin	D°		18	D°
Sandrine		1		Mr. Jaquin	D°		14	D°
Madelaine		1		Girandel	D°		30	D°
Honorine & Child		1	1	Gir ault	D°		22	D°
Mary		1		Me tcalfe	D°	1 June	10	D°
Celia, Cumba & Child		2	1	Mr. Aberdein	D°		21	D°
Jane		1		Curry's Rest Estate	D°		10	D°
Beatrice & Zabeth		2		Mr. Henderso n	D°		13 July	D°

Names of Slaves	Men	Wome	Childr	Names of Owners	By Whom taken, or committed	When taken, or committed	When released	How disposed of
Zabeth's Child			1	D°	D°		11 June	D°
Betsey		1		Darrom	D°		14	D°
Clarissa alias		1		Darsom	L.D Rangers	1814 1 June	1814 14 June	To owners agent
Heliofa & Child		1	1	Mr. Langlais	D°		18	D°
Jenny & Child		1	1	Mad. Toussaint	D°		23	D°
Leonora & Children		1		Mr. Blane	D°		11	D°
John	1			Bayonne	Gov. Ainslie	9	14	D°
Angelique & Child		1	1	Laville	D°		18	D°
Casimir	1			Mr. Aberdeen	L.D Rangers	13	21 Aug.	D° Att
Renette	1			Dr. Parsons	Dr. Hortle	18	29 Sep.	Sold
Jenny & child		1	1	Mr. Courche	L.D Rangers			Died before they could be conveyed to Roseau
Azare	1			Lamure	D°		24 Jan. 1815	To owner
Jeanne		1		Est. of P Leblanc	D°	29	8 Aug. 1814	To D° Creditors
Lundy, a Boy	1			Mr. Le Villouse	D°		4 July	D°
Priscilia alias Nancy		1		Mr. Aberdeen	D°		7	D°
Celests, and Child		1	1	Miss Foye	D°		5	D°
Fanny		1		Mrs Warner	D°		4	D°
Joseph	1			Mr. Courche	D°		24 Jan. 1815	D°

Names of Slaves	Men	Wome	Childr	Names of Owners	By Whom taken, or committed	When taken, or committed	When released	How disposed of
Cola	1			D°	D°		D°	D°
Samber	1			Mad. Toussaint	D°			D°
Bertine, & Child		1	1	Mr. Marceau	D°		20 & 29 July 1814	D°
Isidore	1			Mr. Roger	D°	10	16 Nov	Sold & Banished
Mary & Eliza, Pelagu and Adrien		2	2	D°	D°		19	To owner
Martin or Maton	1			Mad. Toussaint	D°	10 July	24 Sep.	Died in jail
Condo	1			Dr. Greenway	D°		30 Jan. 1815	To Owners
Laurencine		1		Mr. Deshauteurs	D°		20 Jul 1814	D° Agent
Kate		1		Moore	D°			D°
Adelaide & Guay		1	1	S. Grey	D°			D°
Mary & Angelle		1	1	Mr. Fournette	D°		25	D°
Marthe & Children		1	3	Mr Dubue	D°		30	D°
Anne & Children		1	2	Miss Foye	D°		25	D°
Children			2	Mr. Marceau	D°		26	D°
Mondesir			1	Unknown	D°		28 Oct	Sold
Bastienne & Children		1	2	Miss Foye	D°		25 July	To Owners Agent
Lafleur	1			T. Vidal	D°	25 July	11 Oct	D° To be banished
Josephine		1		A Stewart	D°		3 Nov	D°

Names of Slaves	Men	Wome	Childr	Names of Owners	By Whom taken, or committed	When taken, or committed	When released	How disposed of
Margaret		1		Mr. Metcalfe	D°		16 Aug.	D°
Victoire		1		Gourd	D°		3	D°
Mary & Child		1	1	Miss Foye	D°		5	D°
Betty		1		Mrs. Powell	D°		2	D°
Fortune	1			Mr. Metcalfe	Gov's Secretary	1 Aug	17	D°
Cuffy	1			Estate of Cap. Hall	D°	3	30 Sep	D°
Gravesend	1			Permasis Estate	D°	5	9 Aug.	D°
Venus		1		D°	L.D Rangers			D°
Catilio	1			D°	D°		14 Sep	
Bazile	1			T. Henderson	By the Owner	6	3 August	D°
Lubin	1			Mr. Courche	L.D Rangers	A Guide	24 Jan 1815	D°
Thermedor	1			Currys Rest	D°	D°	D°	D°
Abraham	1			Mr. Renault	A Ranger	8 Aug	5 Sep 1815	D°
Boatswain	1			Mrs Monigne	Gov's Secretary	10	15 Aug	D°
Zephyr	1			E Petit	L.D Rangers	Guide	14 Jan 1815	D°
Castalio	1			A Daniel	D°			D°
Paddy				Hillsbro Estate	D°			D°
Quashy	1			Mr Pagan	D°			Old Chief banished
Julie		1		Roger	D°			To owner without being sent to jail

DOMINICA: AN ACCOUNT OF RUNAWAY SLAVES

Names of Slaves	Men	Wome	Childr	Names of Owners	By Whom taken, or committed	When taken, or committed	When released	How disposed of
Celotte		1		Marceau	D°			D°
Rosette & Children		1	2	Mrs. Nibbs	D°	5 Aug.	24 Aug 1814	To owners Att.
Penny		1		Cubbin	L.D Rangers	1814 15 Aug	1814 19 Aug	D°
Seven Slaves	6	1		Mr. Marceau	Surrendered to owner	16	22	D°
Jacob, and Jem	2			Londonderry Estate	A party of volunteers		24	D°
Joseph	1			Mr. Moore	D°		1 Sept	D°
John Louis	1			Belaire	D°		12 Aug	D°
Zephyr	1			Mad. Desire	D°		18	D°
Joseph, and Celeste	1	1		Th. Marie	D°		24	D°
John				Mr. Corlet	D°		27	D°
Sophie, and Daphne		2		Mrs. Charrurier	D°		29	D°
Michel	1			Bastian	Governor's Secretary	19	3 Oct	Died in Jail
Jack	1			Mad. Voisel	Corp at Layou Post	21	22 Sep	To Owners Agent
John	1			Dr. Garraway	Serj at Pte Crabier		1 Dec	D°
Judah (a boy)			1	Rose Hill Estates	Gov's Secretary	16	6	D°
Daniel	1			Doctor Clarke	One of the Rangers	30 Aug	3 Oct	Died in Jail
Adelaide		1		Mr. Hurtault	L.D Rangers		4 Dec	To Owner
Joe	1			Dubocq	D°	3 Sep	19 Sep	D°

Names of Slaves	Men	Wome	Childr	Names of Owners	By Whom taken, or committed	When taken, or committed	When released	How disposed of
Pitchum	1			De Beltgens	A soldier at Layou	7	14	D°
Nelly, and Nanagal, Nicole		3		Mr Syers	L. D Rangers	14	16 Nov	D°
Tom	1			Pointe Pound Estate	Gov's Secretary	17	4 Oct	D° Att
Emma		1		Mr Read	A Soldier		20	D°
Modeste		1		Plissoneau	Gov's Secretary	5 Oct	8	D° Agent
Dominique		1		Petit	L. D Rangers	Guide	29 Nov	D°
Tom, and Aberdeen	2			Moore	D°	18 Sept	25 Sept	D°
Felix	1			Birmingham	D°	Guide	26 Sept	D°
Leandre		1		Lamothe	D°	D°	3 Jan 1815	D°
Adelaide		1		Metcalfe	Soldiers at Layou Post	24 Oct	14 Nov 1814	D° Att
Jeannette		1		Mad. Maton	L.D Rangers	6 Nov	13	D°
Neptune, Venus & Child		2	1	Mr. Jolly	D°		11	D°
Petronille		1		Larouve	D°		15	D°
Clarissa		1		Mrs. Addison	D°		11	D°
Eliza		1		Mr. Giraudel	D°		10	D°
Melissa		1		Molinte	D°		12	D°
Jeannot		1		Mr. Letang	D°	6 Nov	14 Nov	To Owners
Francois		1		Destache	Cprl at Pte Crabier	8	28 Feb 1815	D°

Names of Slaves	Men	Wome	Childr	Names of Owners	By Whom taken, or committed	When taken, or committed	When released	How disposed of
Saba		1		Citra	Soldier at Layou Post	9	15	D°
Lawrencine		1		Duett	D°		18	To Owners Agent
Jem		1		Mad. Joseph	Mil at Blenheim	12	18	Sold
Emma		1		Canefield Estates	One of the Rangers	13	15 Nov 1814	To Owners Agent
Peggy		1		El. Dodds	Srg at Crabier Post	17	25	D°
TOTAL	109	111	68					

N0.3 RUNAWAY SLAVES Surrendered to the Loyal Dominican Rangers

Date	Name of Slaves	Men	Wom	Child	Name of Owners	When Released	To Whom Released
1814 March 27	Marie Sainte		1		Capt. Savarin	1814 April 23	To Owner
	John Louis	1			Hillsbro Estate		D°
	Modeste	1			Mad. Toussaint		D°
	Francois	1			Roger	Sep 25	D°
	Joe	1			Estate of Gibson		In the Ranger Corps
	Jean Charles	1			Curry's Rest Estate		
	Annenville	1			Mr. Laroque		
	Total	6	1				

No. 4 Slaves taken up by Managers of Plantations by Constables etc in Towns loitering about off the Plantations to which they belong without passes, caught breaking canes, or pilfering in the neighbouring provision grounds, but who do not appear to have been in any camp or to have joined any party of RUNAWAYS

Names of Slaves	**Men**	**Wome**	**Childr**	**Names of Owners**	**By Whom taken or committed**	**When taken or reunited**	**When released**	**How disposed of**
Joseph	1			Lacorne's estate	Manager at Castle Bruce	1813 17 May	1813 17 June	To owners Agent
Adelaide		1		Aubries	D° Rosalie	20 ---	14 Oct	Died in jail
Robin and Will	2			Mr Sandford	D° Bath Estate	21 ---	22 May	To Owners Agent
Joseph	1			Defraviniere	Mr. Bertrand	22 ---	17 ---	D°
Isaac	1			Mad. Toussaint		24 ---	17 Sep	D°
Lancaster	1				Mr. Al Robinson	10 June	10 June	D° being diseased
Noel	1			Lacorne's Estate	On Morne Bruce	15 ---	4 Dec	To Owners Agent
Middleton	1			Canefield Estate	Constable in Roseau	16	20 July	D°
Jean Pierre	1			Goadwell	Manager at Elmshall estate	7July	12 ---	D°
Rose		1		Mad. Pagurd	In road near Roseau	13	6 Aug	D°
Landrick	1			J.B Raby		16 ---	16 July	D°

DOMINICA: AN ACCOUNT OF RUNAWAY SLAVES

Names of Slaves	Men	Women	Children	Names of Owners	By Whom taken or committed	When taken or reunited	When released	How disposed of
William	1			Mr. Metcalse	Mr. Labadie	17 ---	14 Oct	D°
Celestine		1		Fraser	Owners Attorney	25 ---	20	Died in jail
Adam	1			Daniel		27 ---	4 Sep	To owners Agent
Jem	1			Dusasey	Mr Court	14 Aug	17 Aug	D°
Noel	1			Fournier	Near Roseau	19 ---	21 ---	D°
Gabriel	1			Sorhaindo	Manager at River Estate	20---	---	D°
George	1			---Mc Corny		24 ---	3 Nov	D°
Zabeth		1		Dr, Clark	Manager at Canefield Estate	---	16 Aug	D°
Francois	1			Mr. Noble	Mr. Danglobermes	3 Sep	10 Oct	D°
Francios	1			Mad. Bourgan	Manager at Canefield Estate	7 ---	9 Sep	D°
Isaac	1			Mr Ried	At Grand Savanne	18 ---	28 Oct	D°
Jean Baptiste				---Lafond	At Grand Bay	---	20 Sep	D°
Linder	1			--- Martin	Manager at Canefield Estate	23 ---	24 Nov	D°
Parceline		1		--- Latouche	D° of Bath D°	29 ---	25 Oct	D°
Solomon	1			--- Lockhart	D° of Grand Bay D°	30 ---	14 ---	D°
Joseph	1			--- Cenicour	D°	---	2 ---	D°

Names of Slaves	Men	Women	Children	Names of Owners	By Whom taken or committed	When taken or reunited	When released	How disposed of
John and Harris	2			--- Whitaker	Mr Morillon	3 Oct	3 ---	D°
Lindor and Michel	2			--- Morillon	D° their owner	---	--	D°
Jean and Cameron	2			--- Ried	Man of Check Hall Estate and Mr Henderson	4 ---	28 ---	D°
Marceline		1		Miss Ribet	At St Davids	5 ---	7 ---	D°
Betsey		1		Mr. Fournier	D°	---	14 ---	D°
Charles	1			--- Metcalfe	Manager of Bath Estate	6 ---	27 Dec	Escaped retaken and returned to owner
Maximin	1			--- Jacquia	D°	8 ---	11 Oct	To Owner
Jack	1			Mad. Michaud	Manager of Goodwill Estate	---	13 ---	D°
Rose		1		Mr David	D° Canefield	---	10 ---	D°
Caliste		1		--- Renault	D° Goodwill	---	16 Jun 1814	D°
Joacinthe				--- Sablon	Dr Clark at Clarkhall Estate	10 ---	3 Oct 1813	D°
Jack				--- Curry	Dr Genet	11 ---	0 Nov	D°

Names of Slaves	**Men**	**Wome**	**Childr**	**Names of Owners**	**By Whom taken or committed**	**When taken or reunited**	**When released**	**How disposed of**
Remahn				--- Gerard	Manager at Roschill Estate	13 ---	---	Do Agent
Victor				--- Lockhart	D° of Unign	17 ---	3 Oct	Died in Jail
Gabriel	1			--- Giraudel	D° of Canefield	5 Nov	7 Nov	To Owner
Marie Louise		1		C Johnstone	Mr. Laidlow, F Ruperts	9 ---	14 Sept 1814	D°
Jean	1			--- Delmaire	Manager of Clarkhall Estate	16 ---	20 Dec	D°
Hilliare	1			R. Rightson		18 ---	14 Jan 1814	Banished
Louis	1			Mr. Richardson	Mr Robinson Rosalie	22 ---	---	Died in jail
Flamm	1			T. Reeves	Mr. Deschamps	24---	10 Nov 1813	To Owner
Charles	1			Mr. Franchon	Manager of Tarreau Estate	25 ---	27 Nov 1813	D°
Lisette		1		--- Lafond	On Morne Bruce	10 Dec	20 Dec	D°
Appas	1			--- Dubisson	On Morne Daniel	11 ---	18 ---	D°
Cola	1			Mc Corry	Manager of Canefield estate	22 ---	24 ---	D°

Names of Slaves	**Men**	**Wome**	**Childr**	**Names of Owners**	**By Whom taken or committed**	**When taken or reunited**	**When released**	**How disposed of**
Sopby	1			--- Secher	Constable in Roseau	24 ---	1 Apr 1814	D°
Toussaint	1			Duboisson	D°	27 ---	18 Dec 1813	D°
Jean Pierre				Canefield Estate	D°	28 ---	17 Jan 1814	D°
Isaac				Mr Metcalfe	Manager at Elmshall estate	1813 21 Dec	1814 25 March	To Owners attn.
Charles				--- Lionne	Checkhall estate	4 Jan 1814	13 Jan	D°
Ambrose	1			--- Giraudel	Constable in Roseau	13 ---	---	D°
Catherine		1		--- Metcalfe	D°	15 ---	22 June	D°
Modeste		1		Descaviniere	Manager of Goodwill estate	17 ---	29 Jan	D°
Victor	1			Dom 9th Legion	D°	---	24 ---	D°
Bastian	1			Mr. Jacquin	Constable in Roseau	---	30 ---	D°
Jeanpierre	1			Letany	By owner	19 ---	3 Feb	D°
Marianne		1		Petit	------	21 ---	22 Jan	D°
Parfaite	1			Fournier	At Morne Daniel	23 ---	8 Feb	D°

DOMINICA: AN ACCOUNT OF RUNAWAY SLAVES

Names of Slaves	Men	Wome	Childr	Names of Owners	By Whom taken or committed	When taken or reunited	When released	How disposed of
Joe	1			Dr. Garraway	Mr Welsh in Roseau	--- ---	8 May	Died in jail
Matthew	1			Dº	Manager at Bath Estate	14 Feb	4 ---	
Alexis	1			Mr Lowndes	Constable in Roseau	28 ---	16 April	To owner
Kingway	1			Bellot	Manager of Canefield estate	---	7 March	Dº
Marseille	1			Deschamps	On Morne Daniel	5th March	6 ---	Dº
Felegie		1		Metcalfe	Manager of Checkhall Estate	9 ---	5 May	Dº
Marceline		1		Mrs Boland	Mr Beech J. P	14 ---	14 March	Dº
Pierre				Mr. Grand	---Lionne	---	8 ---	Dº
Jean Pierre				---Letany	Dº	---	8 Sep	Dº
Charles	1			Maria Antoinette		17 ---	April	Dº
Charles (Modeste)	1			Mary Chick	At Boery	18 ---	---	Dº
Rose				D.Constance		19 ---	27 March	Dº
Casimir	1			Mr. Serrant		20 ---	---	Dº
Louis	1			C,Barron	Mr Gueft	1 ---	---	Dº
Alphonse	1			Mr. Canonier	His Owner	28 ---	21 June	Dº

Names of Slaves	Men	Women	Children	Names of Owners	By Whom taken or committed	When taken or reunited	When released	How disposed of
Joseph	1			--- Larieux	Mr Charruriar	8April	14 April	D°
Charles	1			Dr. Garraway	Manager Canefield Estate	12 ---	13 May	D°
Bontier	1			Mr. Giroux	D° Macoucherie	13 ---	22 April	D°
Solaffique	1			--- Grand	D° Wallhouse	14 ---	25 ---	D° Agent
Robinson	1			--- Curry	D° At Mad. Rolle's	---	7 May	Died in jail
Jack	1			--- Hayes	His Owner	18 ---	5 ---	To owner
Pompey	1			--- Lockhart	Manager of Bericou Estate	---	20 April	D°
Timothy	1			Dr Genet	--- at Layou	4 May	6 May	D°
Joseph	1			Mr Girault		16 ---	17 ---	D°
Joseph	1			Ai Charles	Manager at Hartford Estate	23 ---	24 ---	D° Agent
Sarah		1		Mad. Ceseir	Constable in Roseau	29 ---	31 ---	D°
Uno		1		Mr. Grand	C Kings Pte Michel	31 ---	20 June	Died in jail
Margaret		1		Liniere	Miss Audien's Manager	1 June	9 ---	To owner
Temalin		1		--- Grand	Mr Corlet Pte Michel	5 ---	3 July	D°
Zemir		1		P Phillips Bellevice	P Phillips at Bellevrice	9 ---	16 ---	D°

DOMINICA: AN ACCOUNT OF RUNAWAY SLAVES

Names of Slaves	Men	Wome	Childr	Names of Owners	By Whom taken or committed	When taken or reunited	When released	How disposed of
Charles	1			Mr Blanc	Manager at Woodforhill	13 ---	16 June	D°
Ceasar	1			---Joly	Elmshall	---	---	D° Agent
Ermine		1		Dr Clark	Woodfordhill	---	20 ---	D°
Eustache	1			MrPlissoneau	Constable in Roseau	16 ---	5 July	D°
Celestine		1		Unknown	Mr. Beech J.P Morne Bruce	19 ---	22 June	To Mr Beech
Jeanvieve		1		Mr Letany	Manager at Bell Hill	30 ---	5 July	To owner
Joseph	1			Mr AC Johnstone	Constable in Roseau	30 July	18 ---	To owners att
Judy		1		--- Richardson	D°	---	11 ---	D° Agent
Philip	1			Dr Brenner	D°	---	12 ---	D°
Simeon	1			Mr. Gerard	Mrs Audien's manager	14 ---	14 ---	D°
Joseph	1			--- Laing	Mr Sutherland Rosalie	---	27 Sep	D°
Adelaide		1		--- Metcalfe	Manager of Bericoo	20 ---	16 Aug	D°
Sally		1		Jordan	On Morne Bruce	22---	2 ---	D° Agent
Henry	1			Richardson	Constable in Roseau	26 ---	19 ---	D°
Belinda		1		J Henderson	Manager at Hillsbro	---	8 Oct	D°
Jacquin		1		J Taylor	D° At Clark Hill	31 ---	27 Aug	D°
Sabine		1		R Dyer	Mr Glanville stealing canes	3 Aug	---	Died in jail

Names of Slaves	Men	Women	Children	Names of Owners	By Whom taken or committed	When taken or reunited	When released	How disposed of
Matilda		1		Dr. Garraway	Mr Sutherland, Rosalie	1814 6 Aug	1814 13 Aug	To Owner
Dedine		1		J Marie	Manager at Grand Bay	---	8 --	D°
Alexis	1			Mr. Boland	--At Bath Estate	10 ---	6 Oct	D°
George	1			Desraviniere	--At Massacre	---	19 Aug	D°
Sabine and Mary		2		---Jacquia	--At Elmshall Estate	11 --	12--	D°
Francoise		1		---Isaac	Mr Corlet Bagatelle Estate	12 --	15--	D°
Mary		1		---Metcalfe	Manager at Mrs, Chopin's	14 --	9 Sept	D°
Toussaint	1			--Latouche	Mr Courche on his estate	15--	21--	Died in jail
Alick	1			Dr. Johnstone	Mr Lionne	18 --	19 Aug	To owner
Zabeth		1		Mr. Atkinson	Manager of Belfast Estate	--	22 Sept	D° Agent
Boyer		1		---Blancard	--River Estate	19 --	20 Aug	D°
Maria		1		C Hobson	Goodwill Estate	22 --	16 Sep	D°
Jaze	1			D. Long	D°	--	23 Aug	Owner
Jean Baptiste	1			Unknown	Bath Estate	26 --	1 Oct	--
Chevalier	1			P Dource	D°	--	1 Sep	To owner

DOMINICA: AN ACCOUNT OF RUNAWAY SLAVES

Names of Slaves	Men	Wome	Childr	Names of Owners	By Whom taken or committed	When taken or reunited	When released	How disposed of
Matthew	1			Mad. Chopin	Hertford Estate	2 Sept	5 --	D°
Jack	1			Unknown	Mr Labadie	3 --	20 --	Died in jail
Bella		1		Dr Garraway	Manager of Hillsbro Estate	6 --	9 --	To owner
Mary		1		Mr Robinson	Hillsboro	7 --	19 --	D° Agent
Sophy		1		Plissonneau	Mr Beltgens, on his estate	8 --	--	D°
Jean		1		Delamere	Mad. Deschamps manager	---	9--	D° Agent
Jeannette		1		Defraviniere	Mad. Sicard's --	12 --	13 --	D°
Nicolas	1			F Dubue	Mr Matthews Rosalie	--	14 --	D°
Townsend	1			Plissonneau	Constable in Roseau	15 --	21 --	D° Agent
Jem		1		G Anderson	On Morne Bruce	17 --	22 --	D°
Maximin	1			Holmes	D°	--	--	D°
Sabine		1		Labadie	Manager of Elmshall Estate	18 --	19 --	D°
George	1			Dr Foreman	Constable in Roseau	24 --	10 Oct	D° Agent
Eliza and child		1	1	Point Round Estate	Mr Malagamba,on his estate	13 Oct	19 Nov	D°
Christmas				Mr Atkinson	Constable in Roseau	--	6 Oct	To owners clerk
Hector				--AC Johnstone	Mr Malagamba,on his estate	--	6 --	To owners att

Names of Slaves	Men	Wome	Childr	Names of Owners	By Whom taken or committed	When taken or reunited	When released	How disposed of
Leece				Bermingham	Mr Corlet --	20--	Nov	D°
Mondesir				--Petit	Constable in Roseau	22--	4 Oct	D°
Elize				-- Court	D°	--	-	D°
John Baptiste				-- Watson	Manager of Richmond Estate	31 --	16 Dec	D°
Charlotte				-- Boland	A soldier in Roseau	8 Nov --	9 Nov	D°
Total	100	48	5					

No. 5 Slaves stated by Mr. Bruce, the Governor's Secretary, to have surrendered to the Governor, and pardoned by him; and restored to their Owners

Names of Slaves	Men	Wom	Chil	Names of Owners	Names of Slaves	Men	Wom	Chil	Names of Owners
					Brought Forward	47	16	4	
Adelaide		1		Mr. Bertier	Joseph Watson				Mr. Watson
Toussaint	1			Anderson	William				--- Moran
Garvey	1			Dr. Garraway	Jack	1			G. Anderson
John Francis	1			Mr Douglas	Celestine		1		Marceau
Trim	1			D°	Ana Marie		1		Long

Names of Slaves	**Men**	**Wom**	**Chil**	**Names of Owners**	**Names of Slaves**	**Men**	**Wom**	**Chil**	**Names of Owners**
John Philip	1			D°	Achille	1			Ruse
Masse	1			Mr. Chopin	Andrew	1			Edwards
Larion	1			D°	Rosalie		1		Marceau
Noel	1			D°	Adelaide		1		Roger
Olive		1		D°	Martha & Child		1	1	Marceau
Guillame	1			Mr. Trocard	Pascal	1			Mr Brumant
Felix	1			Mernia	Azur	1			Lamare
Duncan	1			Godfrey	Adelaide		1		Lionne
Joseph	1			Arnaud	Eve		1		Mad. Simon
Campbell	1			Laidlaw	Sukey	1			Chaset
Clarisa		1		Powers	Marianne		1		Michelle
Names not taken		1		Wid. Bermingham	Names Unknown		1	1	Modeste
D°		1		S. Mattee	Pierre	1			Fournette
D°		1	1	M. Trocard	Jean	1			Mr. Bayomne
D°		1	1	M. Welsh	Nancy		1		Lockhart
D°	1			Mr. Aberdein	Franchine		1		Mr Trochard
D°	2			Ann Fournette	Sarah		1		D°

Na mes of Slaves	Men	Wom	Chil	Names of Owners	Names of Slaves	Men	Wom	Chil	Names of Owners
D°		1		Mrs. Goldsmith	Bill	1			Mr Marceau
George Charrurier	1			Mr Charrurier	Cuceau	1			D°
Leger				Dom 9th Leg	Gabriel	1			D°
Names not taken	2			Mr Lionne	Francois	1			D°
D°	2			Surrendered and pardoned	Francois	1			D°
D°	2			D° Moran	Azor	1			D°
D°	3			D°	Nicholas	1			D°
D°	1			D°	Blaize	1			D°
D°	1			Mr. Keay	Edward	1			D°
D°	1			Mrs J Liang	Adela		1		Miss Foye
Bruno	1			Miss Foye	William	1			Dr Clark
Justina		1		Mr Chauvel	Felicite		1		Mr Roger
Noel	1			Gosling	Charlotte		1		Mr Beliar
Names not known	2			Labadie	Charlotte		1		D°
D°	2			--Righton	Alexander				D°
Breechy				--Molinie	Nicholas				--Rodet
Breechy				--G Fraser	Pierre. Christopher ,Harry, Danot				--Marceau

Names of Slaves	Men	Wom	Chil	Names of Owners	Names of Slaves	Men	Wom	Chil	Names of Owners
John Philip				--Moran	Philip, Andre, Capidon, Charles and Pulidore				D°
Joseph				--Arnold	Peter				Mr Lamothe
Nicolas				--Blake	Julie				Mad Roger
Noel				-Fontaine	Alexander				D°
Paul				--Pagan	Constance				S Laroque
Francois				--Roger	John Lewis				Mr Belair
George				--Reid					
Carried up	47	16	4		**TOTAL**	**75**	**31**	**5**	

No. 1	Slaves killed	15	3	
.2	Runaway slaves taken by the Loyal Dominican Rangers, by the Militia or Volunteers sent against the Runaways, or by Soldiers at Signal Posts, or sent to Jail as Runaways, having been in camps or Parties of Runaways in the Woods	109	111	68
.3	RUNAWAY SLAVES Surrendered to the Loyal Dominican Rangers	6	1	
.4	Slaves taken up by Managers of Plantations by Constables etc in Towns loitering about off the Plantations to which they belong without passes, caught breaking canes, or pilfering in the neighbouring provision grounds, but who do not appear to have been in any camp or to	100	48	5

	have joined any party of RUNAWAYS			
.5	Slaves stated by Mr. Bruce, the Governor's Secretary, to have surrendered to the Governor, and pardoned by him; and restored to their Owners	75	31	5
	TOTAL	**305**	**194**	**78**

Some slaves from time to time surrendered to their Owners, who have not reported them; and as neither the names of the Slaves, nor of their Owners, are known, they are not included in this account. Capt. Sevarin believes
they may account to one hundred.
Total Number of Men ------ 305
Total Number Women ------194
Children --------------------- 78

Total number of Slaves 577

Dominica (Signed) B. LUCAS 28th August 1815

Notes

PREFACE: THE PRINCES OF CALABAR

[1] A bight is a large bay or inlet formed by a curve in the continental shoreline. The Bight of Biafra, also called the Bight of Bonny, on the Atlantic Ocean on the western coast of Africa, extends east, then south, for 370 miles (600 km) from the Nun outlet of the Niger River (Southern Nigeria) to Cape Lopez (Northern Gabon). It is bounded by South Eastern Nigeria, Cameroon, Equatorial Guinea, and North Western Gabon.

[2] Randy J Sparks (2002) *The Two Princes of Calabar: An Eighteenth-century Atlantic Odyssey*, p. 557.

[3] The vast majority of the slaves coming through the Bight of Biafra and landing on the shores of Dominica would have come from the ethnic group known as the Igbo.

[4] Randy J Sparks (2002) *The Two Princes of Calabar: An Eighteenth-century Atlantic Odyssey*, p. 562.

[5] The Derby Mercury 27 October 1791, p.3. https://www.newspapers.com/image/394417442/.

[6] From the content of a letter dated 20 August 1771 and reprinted in *The Derby Mercury*, Friday 4 October 1771, p. 4. https://www.newspapers.com/image/394522106/.

[7] Julius S. Scot *Crisscrossing Empires: Ships, Sailors, and Resistance in the Lesser Antilles in the Eighteenth Century*, p.152.

[8] Paul Gilroy (1993), *The Black Atlantic: Modernity and Double Consciousness*, p. 16.

[9] The term "*Neg Mawon*" is the French Creole derivative of the word Maroons, and is literally translated as 'Escaped Negro'.

1. ARRIVAL OF THE EUROPEANS AND EARLY SETTLEMENT

[1] For hundreds of years the name given to the native islanders by Columbus would prevail, with the spelling moving from Caraibes to Caribs, from which the word Caribbean is derived. In 2017, the government of Dominica, in whose country the last remnants of the indigenous people remain, renamed the Carib as Kalinago, which was the name by which they referred to themselves before the arrival of Columbus.

[2] Coma's letter to the Duke of Milan, written in 1494, may be found in the volume of '*Journals and other Documents on the Life and Voyages of Christopher Columbus*.' Translated and Edited by Samuel Eliot Morison (1963).

[3] Diego Alvarez Chanca was a native from Seville and doctor to the royal family who was appointed surgeon during the second voyage of Columbus. Reprinted from a translation in Peter Hulme and Niel L Whitehead (1992) *Wild Majesty: Encounters with Caribs from Columbus to the Present Day*, p. 30.

[4] George Clifford Earl was considered one of the most prolific of British privateers. He organized twelve visits to the Caribbean between 1587 and 1598, each time stopping in Dominica. He would go on to capture Puerto Rico in 1598, a feat which eluded John Hawkins. Francis Drake accompanied Hawkins on his third voyage and was with him when he died late in 1595. Drake himself died a few months later. Drake's journals revealed a clear endearment to Dominica.

[5] This is taken from an extensive description of Clifford's last voyage, when his fleet stopped on Dominica to refresh themselves before the assault on Puerto Rico. The letter is reproduced in Peter Hulme and Niel L. Whitehead (1992) '*Wild Majesty: Encounters with Caribs from Columbus to the Present Day,*' pp. 58 – 61.

[6] Taken from an account of Dominica, written by Laudonnière and translated by Hakluyt and reprinted in Peter

Hulme and Niel L Whitehead, (1992) '*Wild Majesty: Encounters with Caribs from Columbus to the Present Day*, p. 51.

[7] This is an extract taken by from Hakluyt's Principal Navigations and reprinted in Peter Hulme and Niel L Whitehead, (1992) '*Wild Majesty: Encounters with Caribs from Columbus to the Present Day*, p.53.

2. SLAVE TRADE BEGINS

[1] The Seven Years War has often been referred to as 'a struggle for global primacy between Britain and France', which also impacted the Spanish Empire.

[2] Sir James Douglass was a Scottish naval officer and Commodore of Newfoundland at the time he led the Royal Navy attack on Dominica.

[3] During the period where he served as Commander-in-Chief of Dominica, Lord Rollo took a prominent part in the British capture of Martinique and in the British expedition against Cuba in 1762.

[4] Thomas Coke (1810) *History of the West Indies*, Vol II. p. 335.

[5] William F. Stewart (1818) *The Laws of the Colony of Dominica Commencing from its Earliest Establishment to the Close of the Year 1818*, pp. llxii - llxiii.

[6] Ibid., p. lxxvii. The nineteen member lower House of Assembly , or house of Representatives, was made up of elected representatives as follows: the town of Roseau (3 representatives), town of Portsmouth in Prince Rupert's Bay (2 representatives); the parishes of St. John, St. George, St. Andrew, St. Patrick(2 representatives each); and the parishes of St. Peter, St. Paul, St. Mark, St. Luke, St. David and St. Joseph (one representative each). The eligible candidates were expected to own at least 50 acres of land, Protestant, and be at least 21 years of age. Persons eligible to vote were expected to be above the age of 21, subjects of Great Britain and own at least 10 acres of land or twenty pounds per annum.

[7] Following the emancipation proclamation, the 1027 acres estate which still bears his name in Dominica, Melville Hall was valued at £33,190 16s 0d (currency).

[8] John Greg (1716-1795), the son of a Scot settled in Belfast in 1715, went to the West Indies in 1765, married there and became the first Government Commissioner for the sale of land. Greg had two estates (50% in Hertford, later sold, and Hilsborough) in Dominica, and his wife Catharine (née Henderson) in 1773 inherited Cane Garden in St Vincent. https://www.open.uwi.edu/sites/default/files/bnccde/dominica/conference/papers/Honychurch.html.

[9] Thomas Atwood (1791) *The History of the Island of Dominica,* p.2.

[10] The Maryland Gazette (Annapolis), Thursday 20 February 1766, p.4. https://www.newspapers.com/image/590941110.

[11] Thomas Coke made three voyages to Dominica. The first in 1787, the second in 1788 and the third in 1793 as he attempted to set up a religious mission in Dominica.

[12] Thomas Coke (1810) *History of the West Indies*, Vol II, p. 335.

[13] Extracted from a letter out of Dominica and reprinted in The Caledonian Mercury 18 January 1772, p.2. https://www.newspapers.com/image/395704015/.

[14] The Leeds Intelligencer and Yorkshire General Advertiser 10 September 1765, p.2. https://www.newspapers.com/image/404057885.

[15] Ibid.

[16] From 1763 to 1768 Dominica was a constituted part of the government of the Ceded Islands, under the administration of the first representative of the King, Robert Melville Esq. and a General Council, selected from all the ceded islands of Grenada, the Grenadines, Dominica, St Vincent and Tobago. It was this General Council that was responsible for passing legislation that would be applicable to all the Ceded Islands.

[17] William F. Stewart (1818) *The Laws of the Colony of Dominica Commencing from its Earliest Establishment to the Close of the Year 1818,* p.vii.

[18] The opening of free ports in Dominica and Jamaica continued a trend in the eighteenth century, where free ports were established in several Caribbean colonies. In 1675, the Dutch

West India Company granted Willemstad, Curaçao a free port, which status allowed Dutch merchants to engage in a contraband trade with nearby Spanish colonies. The Danish colonies, of Saint Thomas and Saint John opened free ports in 1763, and in the French Caribbean, Martinique and Guadeloupe opened free ports in 1763 and Saint Lucia and Saint-Domingue in 1767.

[19] Data on slaves arriving in Dominica is taken from: The Trans-Atlantic Slave Trade: A Database on CD-ROM compiled by David Eltis et al., and produced in 1999 by Cambridge University Press.

[20] Atwood would go on to serve in the Bahamas before returning to England where he was imprisoned for none payment of taxes. He died in prison a broken man on 27 May 1793.

[21] Thomas Atwood (1791) *The History of the Island of Dominica* p.2.

[22] Ibid.

[23] The Derby Mercury 18 January 1771, p.2. https://www.newspapers.com/image/394498446.

[24] The Pennsylvania Gazette 21 February 1771, p.1. https://www.newspapers.com/image/39403761.

[25] The Pennsylvania Packet, 7 August 1775, p.5. https://www.newspapers.com/image/39419497.

[26] Ibid.

[27] Ibid.

[28] The American War of Independence also known as the American Revolutionary War, started on 19 April 1775 and lasted until 3 September 1783. During that time, America declared its independence from Great Britain on 4 July 1776.

[29] Alexander von Hase, "*Eine amerikanische Kritik am spatfriederizianischen System. Zum Tagebuch von Colonel William Stephens Smith, George Washington* (7 8 5)," Archiv fir Kulturgeschichte, LIV (1974), p.376. This is translated in Walter Holzinger, "*Stephen Sayre and Frederick the Great: A Proposal for a Prussian Protectorate for Dominica (1777*)", p.304.

[30] Ibid., p.305.

[31] Ibid.

[32] Ibid.

[33] Ibid.

[34] Ibid.

[35] The Jackson's Oxford Journal, 3 January 1778, p.1. https://www.newspapers.com/image/396508480/.

3. FRENCH CONQUEST OF DOMINICA

[1] Duchilleau, *Memoire sur les Antilles*, IS Mar. 1765, Archives Nationales, Section Outre-Mer, Paris, Memoires Generaux, Amerique Meridionale et Antilles, Carton I, no. 44.

[2] CO 711/7, Germain to Shirley, 2 September I778.

[3] E. Chevalier (1877*), Histoire de la marine Franfaise pendant la guerre de l'independance ameri- caine* (Paris), p. 123 (History of the French Navy during the American War of Independence).

[4]The Newcastle Weekly Courant, 18 December 1784, p.2. https://www.newspapers.com/image/404022161/

[5] Gabrouse would later become harbour master of the Port of Roseau.

[6] The Derby Mercury Friday 6 November 1778 p. 2. https://www.newspapers.com/image/394239830.

[7] The Public Advertiser 3 December 1778. p. 3. https://www.newspapers.com/image/34413125

[8] The Marquis de Bouillé's pleasantries toward the defeated English appears to be to return the favour extended to the French after the British capture of Dominica seventeen years earlier in 1761.

[9] De Bouille, Instructions pour le Mis Duchilleau, I5 Sept. Carton II, no. I38. Reprinted from Jerome Barome, *Dominica During French Occupation*, 1778 – 1784.

[10] From the British Annual Register of 1779 republished in The Hartford Courant, 2 July 1787, p.1. https://www.newspapers.com/image/233791196/.

[11]Thomas Atwood (1791) *The History of the Island of Dominica,* pp. 5-6 and pp. 147 – 48.

[12] Thomas Cooke (1810), *History of the West Indies*, Vol II, p.339.

[13] Ibid.

[14] Taken from the memoires of de Bouille and recounted in Jerome Barome,*Dominica During French Occupation*, 1778 – 1784, p. 41.

[15] That same hurricane also wreaked havoc on Barbados and St Vincent, leaving scores dead in Barbados.

[16] In Britain an appeal was made for donations to the island in the wake of the hurricane. Five years later the monies collected was given to Thomas Rainy Esq. by the British authorities 'to be distributed among the sufferers by the hurricane and inundation by the sea, and to build a public goal.

[17] The Edinburgh Advertiser, 10 April 1781, p. 3. https://www.newspapers.com/image/601820766.

[18] Thomas Cooke (1810), *History of the West Indies*, Vol II, p. 342.

[19] Of the Kalinago families, Thomas Coke would note that "they live retired from the European settlers, speak a language of their own, intermixed with a little French, and retain those modes of domestic life which they have derived from their progenitors.'

[20] Thomas Cooke (1810), *History of the West Indies*, Vol II, p.341.

[21] Thomas Atwood (1791) *The History of the Island of Dominica*, p.151, places the blame squarely on Duchillean.

[22] The Edinburgh Advertiser, 3 July 1781, p.5. https://www.newspapers.com/image/601821623.

[23] Thomas Cooke (1810), *History of the West Indies*, Vol II, p.342.

[24] Ibid.

4. REVOLTS AND THE FIRST MAROON WAR

[1] Thomas Atwood (1791) *The History of the Island of Dominica*, p.226.

[2] Ibid., p.227.

[3] Lennox Honychurch (2019), *In the Forests of Freedom* (Caribbean Studies Series), p. 55. University Press of Mississippi.

[4] Ibid.

[5] The Caledonian Mercury 4 November 1816, p. 4. https://www.newspapers.com/image/393209740/.

[6] Ibid.

[7] William F. Stewart (1818) *The Laws of the Colony of Dominica Commencing from its Earliest Establishment to the Close of the Year 1818,* p.lxxvi.

[8] Ibid.

[9] Ibid., p. 1.

[10] Ibid., p.2.

[11] Ibid.

[12] Ibid.

[13] See, '*Message of the Governor to the Legislature*', September 10, 1799, in Official Communications.

[14] An Act passed on 30 March 1774 made it punishable by death for any slave who should willfully and maliciously set fire to any cane, pasture, cocoa or other provisions.

[15] Rev. Fr. Prosemans. *Trials of Runaway Slaves, 1786-87,* The Proseman's Collection.

[16] Ibid.

[17] Ibid.

[18] William F. Stewart (1818) *The Laws of the Colony of Dominica Commencing from its Earliest Establishment to the Close of the Year 1818,* p.xi. This bill was given the same title as the one of 26 March 1770, which had since expired.

[19] Thomas Atwood (1791) *The History of the Island of Dominica*, p.151.

[20] The Pennsylvania Packet 16 May 1786, p. 2. https://www.newspapers.com/image/39535844.

[21] Thomas Atwood (1791) *The History of the Island of Dominica* pp. 145, 228.

[22] The Edinburgh Advertiser, 10 April 1781, p. 6. https://www.newspapers.com/image/601820766.

[23] Thomas Atwood (1791) *The History of the Island of Dominica* p.230.

[24] Thomas Atwood (1791) *The History of the Island of Dominica*, p. 229; Atkinson to London, 9 Feb. I782, British

Museum], Egerton MSS. 26I2; Dominica, P.C.M., I June I78I.

[25] The Edinburgh Advertiser, 9 February p. 5. https://www.newspapers.com/image/601820086.

[26] The Hartford Courant, 16 March 1784. p. 3. https://www.newspapers.com/image/233567286/. A detailed account of the incident surrounding this daring attack and escape of the two Maroons seeking freedom in the hills of Dominica was printed in the Connecticut US newspaper.

[27] The Public Advertiser, 6 February 1786, p.2. https://www.newspapers.com/image/34418100. The report noted that up to September 1784, the Maroons appeared content to limit their raids to petty theft focused on getting supplies of provisions. This however, changed for the worse with the attack of Eden Estate.

[28] The Public Advertiser, 6 February 1786, p. 2. https://www.newspapers.com/image/34418100.

[29] The Independent Gazetteer, 11 December 1784, p. 3. https://www.newspapers.com/image/39983844.

[30] William F. Stewart (1818) *The Laws of the Colony of Dominica Commencing from its Earliest Establishment to the Close of the Year 1818,* p xix.

[31] Thomas Atwood (1791) *The History of the Island of Dominica* p. 237.

[32] Ibid.

[33] William F. Stewart (1818) *The Laws of the Colony of Dominica Commencing from its Earliest Establishment to the Close of the Year 1818,* p xix.

[34]. Ibid.

[35] The Pennsylvania Gazette, 19 October 1785, p.2. https://www.newspapers.com/image/41023443.

The eyewitness account is part of an extract of a letter written by a gentlemen from Layou. As was customary during that time, names were never appended to the letter. It does, however appear that the letter was written by a Planter.

[36] The Public Advertiser, February 1786, p. 2. https://www.newspapers.com/image/34418100.

[37] The Freeman's Journal, 21 February 1786, p.2. https://www.newspapers.com/image/59331883/. This was one of the several papers to reprint eyewitness accounts of the attack on the Tarreau estate.

[38] The Public Advertiser, 6 February 1786, p.2. https://www.newspapers.com/image/34418100.

[39] Thomas Atwood (1791) *The History of the Island of Dominica* p.230.

[40]The Public Advertiser, 6 February 1786, p.2. https://www.newspapers.com/image/34418100.

[41] William F. Stewart (1818) *The Laws of the Colony of Dominica Commencing from its Earliest Establishment to the Close of the Year 1818,* p. XX.

[42] The Public Advertiser, 6 February 1786, p. 2. https://www.newspapers.com/image/34418100.

[43] Pennsylvania Packet, 23 March 1786, p. 2. https://www.newspapers.com/image/39535276.

[44] There is every reason to believe that Balla aided in those attacks on the West Coast. When he was captured in March 1786, he revealed that he had last fought alongside Pharcelle in November.

5. BALLA AND THE ROYAL RANGERS

[1] The Public Advertiser, 21 February *1786*, p.3. https://www.newspapers.com/image/34418695/. An extract of a letter published in this paper from an unknown writer reveals that Balla was a Prince from Guiney when he arrived in Dominica more than twenty years earlier.

[2] Ibid.

[3] The Hampshire Telegraph and Naval Chronicle Gazette, 22 February 1819, p.1. https://www.newspapers.com/image/390126000/. Quoted a Dominica Newspaper that commented on the capture in November 1818 of the maroon chief who had replaced Jacko; noted that Jacko "was one of those concerned with the Chief Balla in the murder of Mr. Gamble the manager of Rosalie, an amiable young man together with three other white people.

[4] The Pennsylvania Packet, 17 June 1786, p. 2. https://www.newspapers.com/image/39536188. In a letter Dated March 21 from an unknown person in Dominica writing to a friend in the United States.

[5] The Public Advertiser, 6 February 1786, p.2. https://www.newspapers.com/image/34418100/. A report in the paper argued that the estate was so well defended and that "if watched, could have avoided surprise and even if when surprised, if well arranged, might have been defended against 500 men, or indeed any number without canon."

[6] Several local Dominica newspapers of the day also carried detailed accounts of the destruction of the Rosalie estate based upon eyewitness accounts of the devastation.

[7] One such account is in the Freeman's Journal of Tuesday 21 February 1786, p. 2. Others contained in The Leeds Intelligencer and Yorkshire General Advertiser, Tuesday 7 February 1786, p. 2; The Vermont Gazette p.3; The Times of London, Thursday 02 February 1786, p.4; Hartford Courant Monday 13 March 1786, p.3. The Public Advertiser, Friday 3

February 1786, p.3; The Caledonia Mercury Wednesday 8 February 1786, p.3.

[8] The Public Advertiser, 6 February 1786, p. 2. https://www.newspapers.com/image/34418100.

[9] The Freemans Journal or the North American Intelligencer, 15 March 1786, p. 3 https://www.newspapers.com/image/39957680.

[10] The Pennsylvania Packet, 19 June 1786, p. 2. https://www.newspapers.com/image/39536199.

[11] The Pennsylvania Packet, 17 February, 1786, p. 2. https://www.newspapers.com/image/39534998. Reference to the soldiers most likely referred to the time when the Marquis du Chilleau ordered troops in search of the Maroons.

[12] The Edinburgh Advertiser, 7 February 1786, p. 5. https://www.newspapers.com/image/601804997.

[13] The Edinburg Advertiser, 17 February 1786, p. 4. https://www.newspapers.com/image/601805444. , reports that when the alarm was raised "it threw the whole town of Roseau into confusion."

[14]The Pennsylvania Packet – Wednesday 15 February, 1786, p. 3. https://www.newspapers.com/image/39534984. An account

of the fear and dread that spread around Roseau after the historic attack was conveyed by an individual who himself left the island, for Antigua, just days after the event unfolded. Subsequently, his account was printed in the Antigua Gazette of 14 December 1785 and republished.

[15] The Public Advertiser, 7 February 1786, p. 2. https://www.newspapers.com/image/34418142 . Although published in February of 1786, the information was actually collected in Dominica on 13 December 1785.

[16] The Derby Mercury, 2 June 1785, p.3. https://www.newspapers.com/image/394266733. An account of the arrival of the distressed loyalists to Dominica.

[17] The Pennsylvania Packet, 23 March 1786, p.2. https://www.newspapers.com/image/39535276. Referred to the rangers as chiefly American woodsmen refugees.

[18] The Public Advertiser, 7 February 1786, p.3. https://www.newspapers.com/image/34418142, provides a detailed breakdown of the composition of the various ranger detachments as they existed on 13 December 1775.

[19]The Pennsylvania Packet, 17 June 1786, p.2. https://www.newspapers.com/image/39536188.

[20]Ibid.

[21] The Pennsylvania Packet, 14 March 1786, p.2. https://www.newspapers.com/image/39535175. This partial portion of the letter written by Captain Marshall just two days after the historic destruction of the Rosalie estate was later reprinted in several newspapers in the United Kingdom and the United States, as the enormity of the attack on Rosalie gained the public spotlight.

[22] The Independent Gazetteer, 4 March, 1786, p.2; https://www.newspapers.com/image/39984100. Republished article taken from what it referred to as a Dominica Paper Extraordinary of Roseau, 24th December 1785. "A letter is just received by his Excellency Governor John Orde from Captain Marshall, commanding the center legion of Rangers, dated from Balla's Camp, from whence he has drawn the runaways, of whom he was then in pursuit, giving an account of the force at present collected under the gentleman's command. N.B the heads mentioned in this letter are this moment arrived in town."

[23] The Pennsylvania Packet, 18 March, 1786, p.2. https://www.newspapers.com/image/39535227.

[24] Other reports at the time also indicated that in addition to the five children several women were also captured and taken to Roseau for trial, including Calypso, Charlotte, Marie-Rose, Angelique, Tranquille, Rosay, and Victorie, believed to be among the wives of Balla, Sandy, and Goree Greg.

[25] There appears to be some confusion on whether it was the son of Mubayah or that of Balla. Thomas Atwood in his account states that it was the son of Balla, but Frank who was eventually captured by Captain John Marshall revealed that it really was the son of Mubayah.

[26] The Pennsylvania Packet, 28 April, 1786, p. 2. https://www.newspapers.com/image/39535659.

6. THE DEATH OF BALLA

[1] The Edinburgh Advertiser, 7 February 1786, p. 5. https://www.newspapers.com/image/601804997. Extract of a letter from a gentleman in Dominica dated 8 December 1785.

[2] The Times of London, 10 April 1786, p. 3. https://www.newspapers.com/image/32595197.

[3] Ibid.

[4] The Times of London , 8 April 1786, p. 3. https://www.newspapers.com/image/32595053.

[5] The Pennsylvania Packet, 13 April, 1786 p. 2. https://www.newspapers.com/image/39535505.

[6] The Belfast Mercury or Freeman's Chronicle, 10 April 1786, p. 1. https://www.newspapers.com/image/61261585

[7] Ibid.

[8] The Times of London, 3 April 1786, p. 3. http://www.newspapers.com/image/32594569.

[9] According to Honychurch, Loftus A. Roberts used notes from the research of Fr. Proesman to detail this account of the capture and sentencing of Cicero.

[10] The Hartford Courant, 15 May 1786, p. 2. https://www.newspapers.com/image/233731595. A detailed account of the events, which took place in St. Kitts was recounted by an eyewitness, who wrote about it to his friend in Charlestown, South Carolina.

[11] Ibid.

[12] Ibid.

[13] The fact that there were only around ten Maroons in Balla's camp when he was caught showed the success of the new strategy the Maroons employed to avoid capture. Rather than stay together in large camps numbering over one hundred, they successfully dispersed all over the island's interior in smaller more mobile camps.

[14] The Pennsylvania Packet, 30 June 1786, p. 2. https://www.newspapers.com/image/39536318.

[15] Ibid.

[16] Ibid.

[17] Ibid.

[18] The Pennsylvania Packet, 17 June 1786. https://www.newspapers.com/image/39536188.

[19] Ibid.

[20] CO 71/10. Letter from Governor John Orde to Lord Greenville.

[21] The Pennsylvania Packet, 13 May 1786, p .2. https://www.newspapers.com/image/39535820.

[22] The Edinburgh Advertiser, 7 November 1786, p. 4. https://www.newspapers.com/image/601816899.

7. THE 1791 NEW YEAR'S DAY REBELLION

[1] The Pennsylvania Packet, April 28, 1786, p. 2. https://www.newspapers.com/image/39535659.

[2] The Edinburgh Advertiser, 5 December 1786, p.5; https://www.newspapers.com/image/601818165. Extract of a letter from an officer of the 30th Regiment; 29th September 1786.

[3] Ibid.

[4] The Times of London, 10 April 1787, p. 3. https://www.newspapers.com/image/32818679.

[5] "Minutes of the House of Assembly", Official Gazette, op. cit., September 14, 1787.

[6] CO 71/15. Minutes at a Privy Council Meeting in Roseau, Dominica on February 22, 1788.

[7] CO 71/15. Minutes at a Privy Council Meeting in Roseau on February 29, 1788.

[8] The Pennsylvania Packet, 10 April 1788, p. 3. https://www.newspapers.com/image/39722393.

[9] The Times (London), 13 October 1789, p. 3. https://www.newspapers.com/image/32771119. Reprint of a full copy of the letter from James Bruce, President of the Dominica Council.

[10] The Edinburg Advertiser, 5 February 1790, p.4. https://www.newspapers.com/image/601805174. Extracts of the Assembly's letter to King George III.

[11] The Public Advertiser, 28 July 1790, p. 2. https://www.newspapers.com/image/34416570

[12] CO 71/19. Examination of Charles the Driver, Jack Sailor, New Tim, John Baptiste…Rosaly Estate by Alex.

January 18, 1791.

[13] Mulattoes were generally considered to be persons born out of a relationship between the white population and those of African descent on the plantations. They were often distinguished by their fairer skin colour to that of the African slaves.

[14] The Maryland Gazette, 15 July 1790, p.2. https://www.newspapers.com/image/590974996.

[15] CO 71/17. Copy of a Letter from the Viscount de Damas to Lt. Governor Bruce. June 15, 1790 and the response letter from Bruce to the Viscount de Damas, June 16, 1790.

[16] CO 71/21. Letter from Governor John Orde to Grenville, 3 March 1791,

[17] CO 71/19. Letter from Alex Ross to John Orde. January 18, 1791.

[18] Jean Baptiste Polinaire, The Examination of Polinaire, February 7 – 11, 1791, The Gilder Lehman Institute of American History GLCO2542.32.15.

[19] CO 71/9. "Examination of Charles the Driver", January 18, 1791.

[20] CO 71/19. Examination of Primus taken on January 15, 1791.

[21] CO 71/19. "Examination of New Tim, January 18, 1791.

[22] CO 71/19. Examination of New Tim. January 18, 1791.

[23] CO 71/19. Government House to Governor John Orde. January 13, 1791.

[24] CO 71/19. Letter from Thomas Jemmith from the Hartford Estate to Governor John Orde. January 17, 1791.

[25] The presence of a mulatto among the Maroons was certainly an indication that they were part of the larger conspiracy being hatched out by Pharcelle. However, the fact that they reported to the slave that they were not about to rob or kill could very well be their way of protecting their plans.

[26] Jean Baptiste Polinaire, The Examination of Polinaire, February 7 – 11, 1791, The Gilder Lehman Institute of American History GLCO2542.32.15.

[27] Ibid.

[28]Ibid.

[29] CO 71/19. Letter from Charles Bertrand to Alex Ross. January 18, 1791.

[30] Jean Baptiste Polinaire, The Examination of Polinaire, February 7 – 11, 1791, The Gilder Lehman Institute of American History GLCO2542.32.15.

[31] CO 71/19. Examination of Primus taken on January 15, 1791.

[32] CO 71/19. Examination of Nedd a Negro of Mr. Charles Bertrand at Sabiry. January 17th, 1791 at 8:00am.

[33] CO 71/19. Examination of Charles the Driver, Jack Sailor, New Tim and John Baptiste, January 18, 1791. It is conceivable that the Rosalie slaves were unaware of the mulatto involvement since Polinaire was only introduced into the plan the Sunday before at the dance, where they were not present.

[34] CO 71/19. Copy of a letter from Charles Bertrand. January 18, 1791.

[35] Jean Baptiste Polinaire, The Examination of Polinaire, February 7 – 11, 1791, The Gilder Lehman Institute of American History GLCO2542.32.15.

[36] Ibid.

[37] CO 71/19. Letter from Henry Constable to Governor John Orde. January 21, 1791.

[38] CO 71/19. Letter from Captain John Marshall to Governor John Orde from the Hirriart Plantation January 23, 1791.

[39] Ibid.

[40] CO 71/19. Letter from Alex Ross to Governor John Orde. January 22, 1791.

[41] The Jackson's Oxford Journal, 5 March 1791, p. 2. https://www.newspapers.com/image/396542530. *Extract of a Letter from Barbados* dated 18th January 1791.

[42] CO 71/19. Letter from Alex Ross to Governor John Orde. January 22, 1791.

[43] CO 71/19. Letter from William Oliver to Governor John Orde. January 20, 1791.

[44] CO 71/19. Minutes of the Council Chamber Meeting. January 25, 1791.

[45] The Jackson's Oxford Journal, 8 June 1793, Page 1. https://www.newspapers.com/image/396532183. Based largely on his exploits in quelling the insurrection, Colonel Myers was rewarded with a promotion to Quarter Master of the Royal Navy by Henry Dundas, Secretary of State for War, less than two years later. In making the appointment, he wrote. I had sent for Colonel Myers, of the 15th regiment from Dominica, as been an officer of known abilities, and had chosen him to be a proper person to be at the head of the Quarter Master General's Department in this country to which I have appointed him Deputy until His majesty's pleasure be known.

[46] CO 71/20 Combe to Orde, 3 February 1791.

[47] Jean Baptiste Polinaire, The Examination of Polinaire, February 7 – 11, 1791, The Gilder Lehman Institute of American History GLCO2542.32.15.

[48] CO 71/19. Letter from Alex Ross to Governor John Orde. January 22, 1791.

[49] Ibid.

[50] By this time it was clear that Pharcelle was no longer involved in the plot but that it was driven and commanded by Jean Baptiste Polinaire.

[51] CO 71/19. House of Assembly. Thomas Rainy, Speaker Pro Tempore. January 21, 1791.

[52] The Caledonian Mercury, 14 March 1791 p.2. https://www.newspapers.com/image/395703748.

[53] Ibid.

[54] The Hartford Courant – 4 July 1791, p. 3. https://www.newspapers.com/image/233777904. Extract of a letter from the Committee of Correspondence in Dominica to the Agent W Knox in London dated Feb 15 1791.

[55] This was an organisation established in London in the 1735 to represent the views of the British West Indian planters. The organisation originally consisted of West Indian planters and London sugar merchants, and was a key player in resisting and opposing the abolition of the slave trade and that of slavery. It eventually morphed into the West India Committee.

[56] The Times (London), 16 March 1791,p.2. https://www.newspapers.com/image/32802729/.

[57] The Times (London), 7 April 1791, p. 1. https://www.newspapers.com/image/32803572/.

[58] The Independent Gazetteer, 14 May 1791, p.3. https://www.newspapers.com/image/39937554/.

[59] Jean Baptiste Polinaire, The Examination of Polinaire, February 7 – 11, 1791, The Gilder Lehman Institute of American History GLCO2542.32.15.

[60] The Caledonian Mercury, 14 March 1791 p.2. https://www.newspapers.com/image/395703748.

[61] Two years earlier Governor John Orde had been conferred with the title of Bart.

[62] The Independent Gazetteer, 14 May 1791, p.3. https://www.newspapers.com/image/39937554/.

[63] The Waterford Herald, 23 June 1792, p.2. https://www.newspapers.com/image/59332950/.

[64] William F. Stewart (1818) *The Laws of the Colony of Dominica Commencing from its Earliest Establishment to the Close of the Year 1818,* p. lv.

8. STRUGGLE TO END THE BRITISH SLAVE TRADE

[1] At the start of the debate Newspapers in London stated that the present value of the slaves in the British Islands in the West Indies was equivalent to 18, 491, 955 pounds with slaves

estimated to be worth 40 pounds each except in Bermuda where they were estimated at 45 pounds each. The present value of the British sugar colonies was estimated at 70 000 000 pounds.

[2] The Independent Gazetteer, 9 July 1791, p.1. https://www.newspapers.com/image/39937584/.

[3] The Pennsylvania Gazette, 6 July, 1791, p.2. https://www.newspapers.com/image/41023357/.

[4] The Derby Mercury, 21 April 1791, p.2. https://www.newspapers.com/image/394401300/.

[5] This was in reference to the 15th and 30th regiments which fought for more than a week to suppress the uprising in the French Quarter, led by Martinique revolutionary Jean Baptiste Polinaire.

[6] W. Woodfall (1791): From The Debate on a Motion for the Abolition of the Slave-trade, in the House of Commons on April 18 and 19, 1791, London, available in http://www.books.google.co.uk.

[7] The Times (London), 20 April 1791, p. 2, https://www.newspapers.com/image/32804033/

[8] The Independent Gazetteer, 9 July 1791, p.1, https://www.newspapers.com/image/39937584/.

[9] For the purposes of the debate, Governor John Orde was requested to furnish additional information to the House of Commons.

[10] The Newcastle Weekly Courant, 16 April 1781, p.2. https://www.newspapers.com/image/404068951/

[11] The Derby Mercury, 14 April 1781, p.2. https://www.newspapers.com/image/394399123/. Provides a detailed account of the proceedings of 9 April 1781 on the debate surrounding the slave trade and the insurrection in Dominica.

[12] The Aurora General Advertiser, 10 June 1791, p. 2. https://www.newspapers.com/image/584922095/.

[13] The Freeman's Journal or the North American Intelligencer, 13 July 1791, p.1. https://www.newspapers.com/image/39958896/.

[14] The Hartford Courant (Connecticut), 4 July 1791, p.2, https://www.newspapers.com/image/233777904/.

[15] The Independent Gazetteer, 16 July 1791, p.2, https://www.newspapers.com/image/39937589/.

[16] The Derby Mercury, 27 October 1791, p.3. https://www.newspapers.com/image/394417442/.

[17] The Evening Mail, 4 April 1792, p.2 https://www.newspapers.com/image/35635376/.

[18] Ibid.

[19] The Observer, 29 April 1792, p.4. https://www.newspapers.com/image/258402637/.

[20] The Evening Mail, 25 February 1793, p.1, https://www.newspapers.com/image/35637357/.

[21] Ibid.

[22] The Ipswich Journal, 29 June 1793, p.4. https://www.newspapers.com/image/396394774/.

[23] The French Revolutionary Wars were a series of military battles stemming out of the French Revolution, which pitied French forces against the British, Roman Empire, Prussia and Russia, among other monarchies.

[24] The Derby Mercury, 25 February 1796, p. 2, https://www.newspapers.com/image/394338896/.

[25] The Evening Mail, 01 March 1799, p.1. https://www.newspapers.com/image/35638792/.

[26] Reverend Charles Peters, *Two Sermons Preached at Dominica.* The three cases presented to Wilberforce are found in the appendix.

[27] Ibid., p.36.

[28] Ibid., p. 42.

[29] Ibid.

[30] Ibid.

[31] *The Barbados Glove* was said to be made of thin pieces of wood, fitted for insertion between the fingers, which by means of a screw, or something similar, the tormentor is enabled to constrict as forcibly as he pleases.

[32] Reverend Charles Peters, *Two Sermons Preached at Dominica*, pp.53-66.

[33] The Morning Chronicle, 22 May 1804, p.2. https://www.newspapers.com/image/394020588/.

[34] Ibid.

[35] The Morning Post, 31 May 1804, p.1. https://www.newspapers.com/image/396822307/.

[36] The Caledonian Mercury, 28 February, 1807, p.2. https://www.newspapers.com/image/393023874/.

9. MAROONS AND FRENCH REPUBLICANS COLLUDE

[1] CO 71/21. Letter from Governor John Orde, May 6, 1791.

[2] CO 71/21. Letter from Governor John Orde to Henry Dundas. November 7, 1791.

[3] CO 71/22. Correspondence from Governor John Orde to the Government House. December 21, 1791.

[4] The Caledonian Mercury, 11 April 1793, p.3. https://www.newspapers.com/image/395721329/.

[5] The Aurora General Advertiser, 3 April 1793, p.3. https://www.newspapers.com/image/584908065/. From a report out of Roseau, Dominica dated 5 March 1793.

[6] William F. Stewart (1818) *The Laws of the Colony of Dominica Commencing from its Earliest Establishment to the Close of the Year 1818,* p. xxiv.

[7] CO 71/24. Minutes at a Meeting of His Majesty's Privy Council, March 27, 1793.

[8] This particular act previously passed through the House but was repealed in November 1785.

[9] British House of Commons Miscellaneous Papers, viz Private Bills, Agriculture, Finance, Vaccine With a General Index to the Whole, Session 1 February to 16 July 1816. Vol XIX.

[10] The Jackson's Oxford Journal, 1 June 1793, p.3. https://www.newspapers.com/image/396531863/.

[11] CO 71/25. Letter from James Bruce to Henry Dundas, September 2, 1793.

[12] CO 71/26. A letter from John Trotter to Lieutenant Governor Bruce. May 27, 1794.

[13] CO 71/27. Minutes from the House of Assembly Meeting. October 15, 1794.

[14]British House of Commons Miscellaneous Papers, viz Private Bills, Agriculture, Finance, Vaccine With a General Index to the Whole, Session 1 February to 16 July 1816. Vol XIX, p.3.

[15] The six men named Jaime, Guillaume, Andre, Valentine, Lunb, and Francois together with their wives named Justine, Creole Agatha, Betsey, Fitiate, Scholas Reque and Justin Ebbo.

[16] William F. Stewart (1818) *The Laws of the Colony of Dominica Commencing from its Earliest Establishment to the Close of the Year 1818,* p. 129.

[17] Laurent Dubois, Citizenship Through Assimilation and Citizenship Through Autonomy: Guadeloupe, 1792-1802, p. 93.

[18] Ibid.

[19] The Philadelphia Inquirer, 22 May 1794, p. 3. https://www.newspapers.com/image/466483691

[20] George Craik and Mcfarlane (1843), *The Pictorial History of England During the Reign of George the Third: Being a History of the People, as well as a History of the Kingdom.*

[21] Victor Henri Georges Collot (1750 -1805) was Governor of Guadeloupe from 1793 until his defeat in April 1794. He was sent by the British to New York to face charges, but was acquitted of wrongdoing. Later he was commissioned by the French to complete a detailed clandestine reconnaissance of military preparedness in Ohio and Mississippi river valleys in anticipation of a French invasion of Spanish Louisiana.

[22] The North Carolina Journal, 8 December 1794, p.2. https://www.newspapers.com/image/66179085/.

[23] Ibid. An extract of a letter from Victor Hugues, the Commissary from the National Convention in the Leeward islands.

[24] Hartford Courant, Monday 13 April 1795, p. 3. https://www.newspapers.com/image/233745237.

[25] William F. Stewart (1818) *The Laws of the Colony of Dominica Commencing from its Earliest Establishment to the Close of the Year 1818,* p. lvi.

[26] Hartford Courant, Monday 13 April 1795, p. 3. https://www.newspapers.com/image/233745237.

[27] The Derby Mercury, 30 April 1795, p.2. https://www.newspapers.com/image/394506414/. Extract from *The Scorpion at Sea,* 28 March 1795.

[28] The Black Caribs came about when a slave ship bound for the

Caribbean was shipwrecked on one of the Grenadine islands, late in the seventeenth century. The escapees from the boat ended up in St Vincent and intermarried with the indigenous Caribs on the island to form the unique mix of African and Carib culture.

[29] The Northern Star, 5 October 1795, p.3. https://www.newspapers.com/image/61264351/.

[30] The Northern Star, 2 July 1795 p.3. https://www.newspapers.com/image/61263861.

[31] Lennox Honychurch (2019), *In the Forests of Freedom*, p. 120.

[32] Ibid.

[33] The Pennsylvania Packet, 15 July 1795, p. 3. https://www.newspapers.com/image/466130245

[34] The Gentleman's Magazine and Historical Chronicle, 1765, Vol 65, Part 2.

[35] The Northern Star, 5 October 1795, p.3. https://www.newspapers.com/image/61264351/.

[36] The Laws of the Colony of Dominica Commencing from its earliest Establishment to the Close of the Year 1818, p. LVI.

[37] William F. Stewart (1818) *The Laws of the Colony of Dominica Commencing from its Earliest Establishment to the Close of the Year 1818,* pp. 171- 73.

[38] Ibid.

[39] The Edinburg Advertiser, 9 February 1796, p.5. https://www.newspapers.com/image/601804815/.

[40] Some newspaper reports at the time note his name as La Coste, while others referred to him as La Course.

[41] William F. Stewart (1818) *The Laws of the Colony of Dominica Commencing from its Earliest Establishment to the Close of the Year 1818,* p. xxvii.

[42] The Edinburg Advertiser, 22 August 1797, p.5. https://www.newspapers.com/image/601895743/.

[43] The Evening Mail, 27 September 1797, p.4. https://www.newspapers.com/image/35635607/.

[44] Earl Stanhope (1867*), Life of the Late William Pitt*, p. 331.

[45] The Morning Chronicle (London), Monday 19 April 1802, p. 3 https://www.newspapers.com/image/394012815.

[46] The Edinburgh Advertiser, Friday 21 September 1810. P.3 https://www.newspapers.com/image/601814647.

[47] One newspaper account of his death said simply: 'The notorious Victor Hugues who has been called the Robespierre of the Colonies, died lately at Bordeaux.' The National Gazette (Philadelphia), Thurs 18 January 1827, p.2. https://www.newspapers.com/image/346704968.

10. THE WEST INDIA REGIMENT

[1] There were large scale rebellions in Grenada and St Vincent in early 1795, influenced largely by the activities of Victor Hugues who was sent out as a Commissioner to Guadeloupe. There he helped in expelling the British and fomented rebellion in other Caribbean islands.

[2] Roger Buckley (1979) *Slaves in Red Coats: The British West India Regiment, 1795-1815,* New Haven: Yale University Press.

[3] William F. Stewart (1818) *The Laws of the Colony of Dominica Commencing from its Earliest Establishment to the Close of the Year 1818,* p.xxv.

[4] Ibid.

[5] Ibid.

[6] The Leeds Intelligencer and Yorkshire General Advertiser, 21 September 1795, p.1. https://www.newspapers.com/image/404099562/.

[7] William F. Stewart (1818) *The Laws of the Colony of Dominica Commencing from its Earliest Establishment to the Close of the Year 1818*, p. xxvi.

[8] Ibid.

[9] Slave numbers in the other islands during that time were estimated in Jamaica 174 000, Barbados 81 000, Antigua 36 500, Grenada 31 000, St Kitts 27 000, St Vincent 14 000, Nevis 10 000, Montserrat 9 000, Anguilla, Tortola etc. 14 000 as reported in *The Observer (London)*, 29 May 1796, p. 2.

[10] Extract of a Letter from Lt. Colonel Johnstone to Secretary Dundas. January 23, 1796.

[11] Extracts from the minutes of the General Assembly of Barbados, from *The Barbados Mercury* 3 June 1797 in which the letter from Abercrombie was ordered to be read. Reprinted in *The Observer (London),* 20 August 1797, p.4. https://www.newspapers.com/image/263026933/.

[12] William F. Stewart (1818) *The Laws of the Colony of Dominica Commencing from its Earliest Establishment to the Close of the Year 1818*, p. xxvi.

[13] Ibid., p. xxvii.

[14] The Times (London) 10 March 1798, p. 3. https://www.newspapers.com/image/32755465/.

[15] The Act was previously brought to the House in March 1785 but had since expired.

[16] William F. Stewart (1818) *The Laws of the Colony of Dominica Commencing from its Earliest Establishment to the Close of the Year 1818*, p.142.

[17] Ibid., p. 152.

[18] Ibid., p.xxviii.

[19] CO 71/31 An Act of the Legislature of the Island of Dominica Intitled 'An Act for the Encouragement, Protection, and better Government of Slaves 1799.

[20] CO 71/32. House of Assembly 6 September 1799.

[21] CO 71/32. Letter from Portland to Governor Cochrane Johnstone November 25, 1799.

[22] CO 71/32. Minutes at a Meeting of His Majesty's Privy Council February 22, 1800.

[23] Letter from Andrew Cochrane Johnstone to The Duke of Portland. September 4, 1800.

[24] William F. Stewart (1818) *The Laws of the Colony of Dominica Commencing from its Earliest Establishment to the Close of the Year 1818*, p.xxix.

[25] Ibid., p.162.

[26] CO 71/32. Correspondence between Andrew Cochrane Johnstone and The Duke of Portland, October 7, 1800.

[27] CO 71/38. A list of all convictions ……… 31 December 1803

[28] CO 71/33. Minutes read and approved at the House of Assembly Meeting on December 16, 1800.

[29]William F. Stewart (1818) *The Laws of the Colony of Dominica Commencing from its Earliest Establishment to the Close of the Year 1818*, p.143.

[30] An extract of Clause 2 of An act for the banishing of sundry runaway slaves, now in confinement and also for the banishment of such runaways of certain descriptions as shall hereafter be taken or surrender themselves and for other purposes; from William F. Stewart (1818) *The Laws of the Colony of Dominica Commencing from its Earliest Establishment to the Close of the Year 1818*, p.143.

[31] Ibid., p.166.

[32] Ibid..

[33] The Dominica Journal, or Weekly Intelligencer, 26 April 1800, reprinted in Rev. C Peters (1802) *Two Sermons Preached at Dominica on the 11th and 18th of April 1800,* p.6.

[34] Rev. C Peters (1802) *Two Sermons Preached at Dominica on the 11th and 18th of April 1800,* p.8.

[35] Ibid., p.8.

[36] Ibid., p. 15.

[37] In 1793, the British captured two French slave vessels the *Louis Marie* from St. Mallo and the *Bon Menage* from Marseilles, which were headed for Guadeloupe and rerouted them with their cargo of enslaved persons to Dominica.

[38] Figures on the number of slaves imported into Dominica during that period are taken from 'The Trans-Atlantic Slave Trade: A Database on CD-ROM' compiled by David Eltis et al., and produced in 1999 by Cambridge University Press.'

[39] Much later, it was determined that the swamp was a breeding place for mosquitoes, which were responsible for spreading the dreaded yellow fever and resulted in scores of deaths. The local population had far better immunity than the whites to the disease. However, at the time, it was not known that mosquitoes was the cause of the spread of yellow fever. Portsmouth was originally the capital of Dominica but the conditions led to the town being abandoned around 1765 in favour of Roseau.

[40] CO 71/34. A letter from Governor Cochrane to Lord Hobart on April 4, 1802.

[41] The Edinburgh Weekly Journal, 16 June 1802, p.4. https://www.newspapers.com/image/601815016/.

[42] The Caledonian Mercury 17 June 1802, p.3. https://www.newspapers.com/image/393030154/.

[43] The Times of London 10 June 1802, p.3. https://www.newspapers.com/image/32879269/.

[44] The Caledonian Mercury 10 June 1802, p.3. https://www.newspapers.com/image/393029947/.

[45]Cobbetts Weekly Political Register 5 June 1802, p.12. https://www.newspapers.com/image/387834831/.

[46] CO 71/34. General Court Martial held at Prince Ruperts Dominica….April 26, 1802.

[47] The Observer (London), Sunday 19 February 1804, p. 3. https://www.newspapers.com/image/258852027/.

[48] William F. Stewart (1818) *The Laws of the Colony of Dominica Commencing from its Earliest Establishment to the Close of the Year 1818,* p.169.

[49] Ibid.

[50] CO 71/35. Report of Detachment, by George Provost on April 19, 1803.

[51] The Tennessee Gazette and Metro District Advertiser (Nashville Tennessee) 01 May 1805. https://www.newspapers.com/image/586270957/.

[52] The Lancaster Gazette 11 May 1805, p.4. https://www.newspapers.com/image/404043607/.

[53] Ibid., p.2.

[54] The Caledonian Mercury 11 May 1805, p.2. https://www.newspapers.com/image/393041263/.

[55] The Times of London 24 May 1805, p.2. https://www.newspapers.com/image/32766893/.

[56] Governor Prevost eventually went to Nova Scotia in 1808 as lieutenant governor. Four years later he was transferred to Quebec, where he was administrator of Lower Canada, then governor in chief of both Canadas. He died in London in 1816 at the age of 48.

[57] CO 71/40. Letter from George Metcalfe to the Government House on February 16, 1806.

[58] Ibid.

[59] The Observer (London) 9 November 1806, p.4. https://www.newspapers.com/image/258009718/.

[60] CO 71/46. Letter from George Beckwith to Governor Barnes on September 5, 1810.

[61] CO 71/46. Letter from Governor Barnes to Lord Bathurst on February 5, 1811.

[62] CO 71/46. Letter from Governor Barnes to the President and Board of Council on January 2, 1811.

11. MAROON TRIALS OF 1813 AND 1814

[1] The Examiner (London) 3 April 1814, p.2. https://www.newspapers.com/image/387859424/.

[2] CO 71/49. Proclamation by Governor Ainslie on 10 May 1813.

[3] The Examiner (London) 13 October 1816, p.2. https://www.newspapers.com/image/387767799/.

[4] Polly Pattullo (2015), *Your Time is Done Now: Slavery, Resistance and Defeat: the Maroon Trials of Dominica (1813-1814)*. London: Papillote Press.

[5] CO 71/51. The Trials of Caliste, Angelle, Guillaume, Dundas and Toussaint.

[6] He would later serve as Chief Justice in Dominica and editor of the Dominica Gazette.

[7] Polly Pattullo (2015), *Your Time is Done Now: Slavery, Resistance and Defeat: the Maroon Trials of Dominica (1813-1814)*. London: Papillote Press.

[8] CO 71/49 Letter from Governor George Ainslie to Lord Bathurst, 16 January 1814.

[9] CO 71/51 The Courts Martial 15 January to 22 May 1814.

[10] Ibid.

[11] Ibid.

[12] Ibid.

[13] The Liverpool Mercury 15 April 1814, p.7. https://www.newspapers.com/image/390628421/.

[14] CO 71/49. Letter from Governor George Ainslie to Lord Bathurst, 26 February 1814.

[15] A collection of plain and authentic documents in Justification of the Conduct of Governor Ainslie , London 1815, p.18.

[16] The Caledonian Mercury 26 May 1814, p.3. https://www.newspapers.com/image/393207375/.

[17] The Caledonian Mercury, 26 May 1814, quoting from a 12 March extract from Dominica. This most likely originated from the account in the Dominica Journal. https://www.newspapers.com/image/393207375/.

[18] The Observer (London) 10 July 1814, p. 2. https://www.newspapers.com/image/258950201/.

[19]The Morning Post July 11 1814, p.2. https://www.newspapers.com/image/396808293/.

[20] Hester and Francois were the same two women referred to in the account of the Caledonian Mercury of 26 May 1814.

[21] CO 71/51 The Courts Martial 15 January to 22 May 1814.

[22] Polly Pattullo (2015), *Your Time is Done Now: Slavery, Resistance and Defeat: the Maroon Trials of Dominica (1813-1814)*. London: Papillote Press.

[23] CO 71/51. Letter from Lucas to Bathurst, 24 August 1815.

[24] This was in reference to the 24 February 1814 proclamation by Ainslie in which he ordered the Rangers to take no prisoners, but to "put to death men, women and children."

[25] The Observer 10 July 1814, p.2. https://www.newspapers.com/image/258950201/

[26] Ibid.

[27] The Caledonian Mercury 13 October 1814, p.3. https://www.newspapers.com/image/393221196/.

[28] The Morning Post (London)22 October 1812, p.3. https://www.newspapers.com/image/396815588/.

[29] The governors were: Marie-Charles, Marquis du Chilleau (1778–1781), Comte de Bourgon (1781–1782), M. de Beaupré (1782–1784), Sir John Orde (1784–1792), Thomas Bruce (acting) (1789–1790), Thomas Bruce (acting) (1792–1794), Henry Hamilton (1794–1796), John Matson (acting) (1796–1797), Andrew James Cochrane Johnstone (1797–1802), George Prévost (1802–1805), George Metcalfe (acting) (1805–1808), Edward Barnes (1808), James Montgomerie (1808–1809), Edward Barnes (1809–1812), John Corlet (acting) (1812–1813).

[30] CO 71/49. Letter from Governor Ainslie to Earl Bathurst on August 4, 1814.

[31] Ibid.

[32] William F. Stewart (1818) *The Laws of the Colony of Dominica Commencing from its Earliest Establishment to the Close of the Year 1818* p.lviii.

[33] As late as October that year, the rangers were still in pursuit of the Maroons. The Caledonian Mercury of 12 January 1815 reports that a melancholy accident occurred on the 14th of October to the Windward of Dominica near Morne Paix Bouche. A party of the rangers going out to join the detachment, Sergeant

Allan of that corps and Alexander McGinnis of Roseau stopped to take shelter, from the rain, under a cliff, when an immense mass of earth fell down and smothered them both. Their bodies were dug out the next day.

[34] The Morning Post 14 November 1814 p.2. https://www.newspapers.com/image/396817267/.

[35] Polly Pattullo (2015), *Your Time is Done Now: Slavery, Resistance and Defeat: the Maroon Trials of Dominica (1813-1814)*. London: Papillote Press.

[36] Jackson's Oxford Journal, 8 January 1814, p.4; The Royal Cornwall Gazette, Falmouth Packet and General Advertiser, 8 January 1814, p.2; The Examiner (London), 16 January 1814,p.8; Hampshire Telegraph and Naval Chronicle, 10 January 1814 p.1; and The Liverpool Mercury, 4 February 1814, p.8.

[37] CO 72/10. Letter of Henry Goulburn to George Ainslie, 10 February 1814.

[38] Further Papers Relating to Governor Ainslie, Ordered by the House of Commons to be Printed 15 June 1815.

[39] CO 71/49. Letter from Governor Ainslie to Lord Bathurst, March 10 1814.

[40] CO 72/10.Letter from Lord Bathurst to Governor Ainslie, March 29 1814.

[41] This is in obvious reference to the letter written by his Undersecretary Henry Goulburn to Ainslie dated 10 February in which he revealed that he had received newspaper accounts of Ainslie's proclamations.

[42] CO 72/10 Letter from Lord Bathurst to Governor Ainslie April 23 1814.

[43] Liverpool Mercury (Liverpool) 6 May 1814, p.2. https://www.newspapers.com/image/390628576/.

[44] Ibid.

[45] The Morning Chronicle (London) 14 November 1814 p.2. https://www.newspapers.com/image/392089759/

[46] CO 72/10. Letter from Lord Bathurst to Governor Ainslie, September 8 1814.

[47] The Morning Chronicle (London) 9 January 1815 p.3. https://www.newspapers.com/image/392078554/.

[48] The Caledonian Mercury 13 October 1814 p.3. https://www.newspapers.com/image/393221196/.

[49] Extract of an address to the House of Assembly by Governor Ainslie in: "A collection of Plain Authentic Documents in Justification of the Conduct of Governor Ainslie: In the reduction of a Most Formidable Rebellion among the Negro

Slaves in the Island of Dominica, at a Crisis of the Most Imminent Danger to the lives and Properties of the Inhabitants." C. Lowndes, London, p.39.

[50] CO 71/49. Letter from Governor Ainslie to Lord Bathurst September 8 1814.

[51] CO 71/49. Letter from Captain Savarin September 14 1814.

[52] Letter from the proprietors of estates and merchants to Lord Bathurst in: "A collection of Plain Authentic Documents in Justification of the Conduct of Governor Ainslie: In the reduction of a Most Formidable Rebellion among the Negro Slaves in the Island of Dominica, at a Crisis of the Most Imminent Danger to the lives and Properties of the Inhabitants." C. Lowndes, London 1815, p.39.

[53] The Derby Mercury 8 June 1815 p.4 https://www.newspapers.com/image/390591368/.

[54] The Morning Chronicle 3 June 1815 p.2. https://www.newspapers.com/image/392090575/.

[55] It would appear that Governor Ainslie deliberately misled the British Parliament concerning the number of maroons who were killed as later accounts would prove including.

[56] The Examiner 4 June 1815 p.9. https://www.newspapers.com/image/388190334/.

[57]Ibid.

[58] Ibid.

[59] House of Commons Debate 2 June 1815 vol 31 pp. 596-606.

[60] Extract of an address to the British Parliament by Robert Heron in: "A collection of Plain Authentic Documents in Justification of the Conduct of Governor Ainslie: In the reduction of a Most Formidable Rebellion among the Negro Slaves in the Island of Dominica, at a Crisis of the Most Imminent Danger to the lives and Properties of the Inhabitants." C. Lowndes, London, pp. 41 – 47.

[61] The Morning Post, London 8 June 1815, p.2. https://www.newspapers.com/image/396813892/.

[62] CO 72/11. Letter from Lord Bathurst to Governor Ainslie December 21 1814.

[63] CO 71/50. Letter from Ainslie to Lord Bathurst December 22

1814. Ainslie set out in this letter a detailed explanation of what he considered his justification for opting for the courts martial rather than the civil sessions.

[64] Ibid.

12. MAROONS AND THE SLAVE ABOLITION DEBATE

[1] William F. Stewart (1818) *The Laws of the Colony of Dominica Commencing from its Earliest Establishment to the Close of the Year 1818,* p.lvii.

[2] William F. Stewart (1818) *The Laws of the Colony of Dominica Commencing from its Earliest Establishment to the Close of the Year 1818*, p.487.

[3] Ibid., p. 492.

[44] Ibid., p. 495.

[5] Ibid., p. 495, Clause 10 of the act.

[6] Ibid.; p. 498.

[7] Ibid., p. 503.

[8] Ibid., p. 505.

[9] Ibid., p.527.

[10] The Morning Chronicle 3 June 1815 p.2. https://www.newspapers.com/image/392090575/. The Committee was eventually disallowed but it permitted the House to focus on the cruel and unjust treatment meted out to the Maroons on Dominica.

[11] The Caledonia Mercury 10 June 1815 p.3. https://www.newspapers.com/image/393171839/.

[12] Ibid.

[13] The Times (London) 23 April 1818, p.2. https://www.newspapers.com/image/32796582/.

[14] Ibid.

[15] Those opposed to the ending of the slave trade blamed Wilberforce for the insurrections of the maroons across Dominica. They falsely claimed that it was on hearing of the possible abolition of the slave trade that they revolted. Wilberforce would declare that his resolutions should not be calculated to promote insurrections, but rather to quell them, and if it was imagined that such motion was to go to the emancipation of the blacks, now on the island that such opinion was mistaken. His only intention was to put an end to the slave trade.

[16] The Leeds Mercury 25 April 1818 p.3. https://www.newspapers.com/image/389068927/.

[17] The Derby Mercury 30 April 1818 p.3. https://www.newspapers.com/image/390591054/.

[18] This particular Act to regulate the manumitting of slaves, sought to clarify or pose added restrictions on the original Act respecting manumission, which was passed on 7 September 1774.

[19] William F. Stewart (1818) *The Laws of the Colony of Dominica Commencing from its Earliest Establishment to the Close of the Year 1818,* p.43.

[20] The Times (London) 23 April 1818, p.2. https://www.newspapers.com/image/32796582/.

[21] Ibid.

[22] Ibid.

[23] Ibid.

[24] Ibid.

[25] Ibid.

[26] William F. Stewart (1818) *The Laws of the Colony of Dominica Commencing from its Earliest Establishment to the Close of the Year 1818,* p.570.

[27] The Hampshire Telegraph and Naval Chronicle Gazette, 22 February 1819, p.1.
https://www.newspapers.com/image/390126000/.

References

Armytage, Frances. *The Free Port System in the British West Indies: A Study in Commercial Policy*, 1766 - 1822 , London: Longmans, Green, Imperial Studies, Vol. XX, 1953.

Atwood, Thomas. *The History of the Island of Dominica,* London 1791.

Boromé, Joseph. Dominica During French Occupation, 1778–1784. *The English Historical Review*, Vol. 84, No. 330 (Jan., 1969), pp. 36-58. JSTOR 562321.

Bernard, Marshall. Maroonage in Slave Plantation Societies: A Case Study of Dominica, 1785 – 1815: *Caribbean Quarterly*, University of the West Indies, Mona Vol. 22 Nos 2 & 3 June to September 1976.

Boucher, Philip. *Cannibal Encounters: Europeans and Island Caribs, 1492–1763,* John Hopkins University Press, 2009.

Buckley Roger. *Slaves in Red Coats: The British West India Regiment, 1795-1815.* New Haven: Yale University Press, 1979.

Burke, Wayne. *Shaping the Edge of Empire: Dominica and the Antillean Colonial Experience, 1493 – 1686*, Queens University, Kingston, Ontario, Canada, January 1998.

Campbell, Susan., Africans to Dominica: 100, 000 Middle Passages from Guinea to the Eastern Caribbean, 1764 – 1808, 2007

Chanca, Dr., [1494] 1847. *Letter* to *the City* of Seville. In RH. *Major* (trans. *and* ed.) *Select Letters of Christopher Columbus. With Other Original Documents Relating to his Four Voyages to the New World.* London:Hakluyt Society.

REFERENCES

Coma, G., [1494] 1963. Letter to the Duke of Milan, In *S.E.*Morïson (trans. and *ed.) Journals and Other Documents on the Life and Voyages of Christopher Columbus.* New York: The Heritage Press.

Cooke, Thomas. *A History of the West Indies, Containing the Natural, Civil and Ecclesiastical History of Each Island,* London 1810.

Craik, George Lillie. and MacFarlane, Charles., The Pictorial History of England, 1843, London. https://books.google.com/books?id=J_0vAAAAYAAJ

Dubois, Laurent. *Citizenship Through Assimilation and Citizenship Through Autonomy: Guadeloupe, 1792-1802,* Revista Mexicana del Caribe, vol. V, núm. 10, 2000, p. 91 – 106, Universidad de Quintana Roo, Chetumal, México.

Edward, Cox. *Free Coloureds in the Slave Societies of St. Kitts and Grenada, 1763-1833.* Knoxville: University of Tennessee, 1984.

Eltis, David S.D. Behrendt, D. Richardson, and H.S. Klein: The Trans-Atlantic Slave Trade: A Database on CD-ROM. Cambridge: Cambridge University Press, 1999.

George, L. Craik and Charles, MacFarlane. *The Pictorial History of England During the Reign of George the Third: Being a History of the People, as well as a History of the Kingdom,* 1843.

Gilroy, Paul. *The Black Atlantic: Modernity and Double Consciousness*, Harvard University Press, 1993.

Gott, Richard. *Britain's Empire: Resistance, Repression and Revolt.* New York: Verso, 2012.

REFERENCES

Grell, Francis. *Politics of Survival and Change in Dominica, 1763 – 1973: An Interpretation of the Political Life Experience of Dominicans in the Colonial and Post-Colonial Situation*, McMaster University, 1976.

Holzinger Walter, "Stephen Sayre and Frederick the Great: A Proposal for a Prussian Protectorate for Dominica (1777), The William and Mary Quarterly, Vol. 37, No. 2 (Apr., 1980), pp. 302-311.

Honychurch, Lennox. In the Forests of Freedom (Caribbean Studies Series). University Press of Mississippi.

Hulme. P.. and Whitehead, N.. 1992. (Eds.). *Wild Majesty: Encounters with Caribs from Columbus to the Present Day. Oxford*: Clarendon Press.

Hunt, Nadine. *Contraband, Free Ports, and British Merchants in the Caribbean World, 1739-1772. Diacronie* [Online], N° 13, 1 | 2013, document 2, Online since 01 April 2013, connection on 19 April 2019. URL http://journals.openedition.org/diacronie/672.

Lowell. J Ragatz. The Fall of the Planter Class in the British Caribbean, 1763–1833. *The American Historical Review*, Volume 35, Issue 1, October 1929, p.131–133.

Lowndes C. A collection of Plain Authentic Documents in Justification of the Conduct of Governor Ainslie: In the reduction of a Most Formidable Rebellion Among the Negro Slaves in the Island of Dominica, London, 1815.

Morison, E. Samuel. *Journals and other Documents on the Life and Voyages of Christopher Columbus*, 1963.

Nichols, John. *The Gentleman's Magazine and Historical Chronicle, 1765*, Vol 65.

REFERENCES

Peters, Charles Reverend (1802), *Two Sermons Preached at Dominica on the 11th and 18th of April 1800; and Officially Noticed by His Majesty's Privy Council in that Island*, Printed for John Hatchard, London.

Pattullo, Polly. *Your Time is Done Now: Slavery, Resistance and Defeat: the Maroon Trials of Dominica (1813-1814),* London: Papillote Press, 2015

Prosemans, Rev. Trials of Runaway Slaves, 1786 -1787 and Official Communications in Connection with Runaway Slaves, 1787 -1803, Pointe Michel: The Proseman's Collection.

Scott, S. Julius. *Crisscrossing Empires: Ships, Sailors, and Resistance in the Lesser Antilles in the Eighteenth Century*, in Robert L. Paquette and Stanley L. Engerman, eds., *The Lesser Antilles in the Age of European Expansion,* Gainesville, Fla., 1996, pp. 138-41.

Sparks Randy J. Two Princes of Calabar: An Atlantic Odyssey from Slavery to Freedom: The William and Mary Quarterly, Vol. 59, No. 3, Slaveries in the Atlantic World(Jul., 2002), pp. 555-584.

Stanhope, E.Phillip Henry. *The Life of the Right Honourable William Pitt, London 1867* Vol 3, 1861-62.

Stewart, F. William. *The Laws of the Colony of Dominica Commencing from its earliest Establishment to the Close of the Year 1818; and Tables of the Several Acts with Preface and Index*, Printer to the Legislature, Roseau, 1818.

Vaz, Niel C. Maroon Emancipationists: Dominica's Africans and Igbos in the Age of Revolution, 1763–1814, *Journal of Caribbean History, Volume 53, Number 1*, 2019, pp. 27-59 (Article).

Index

A

B

C

D

E

F

G

N

O

P

Q

R

S

www.ingramcontent.com/pod-product-compliance
Lightning Source LLC
LaVergne TN
LVHW020533100826
845148LV00010B/1439

9781737008101